# THE BOOK OF ENOCH

## VOLUME 1 IN THE NEPHILIM SERIES

COMMENTARY & CONCEPT ART ON
### THE BOOK OF THE WATCHERS

INTRODUCTION BY TIMOTHY ALBERINO

RELICPRESS

The Book of Enoch
Volume 1 in the Nephilim Series

Relic Press
First Paperback Edition, 2024

Cover design: Timothy Alberino, Nathan Henry
Interior design: Andy Meaden, Timothy Alberino, Luke Rodgers
Concept art: Nathan Henry

ISBN 9798328526920

# CONTENTS

VOLUME 1
IN THE NEPHILIM SERIES

The Nephilim Series by Relic Press is devoted to the reproduction of critical ancient texts corresponding to the biblical narrative, especially as they pertain to the subject of Nephilim.

To purchase the other volumes in the series, or for more information, visit **NephilimSeries.com**

This edition of the Book of Enoch was inspired by:

## BLURRY CREATURES
### PODCAST

Blurry Creatures is a US Top 200 podcast hosted by Nate Henry and Luke Rodgers. The show delves into the enigmatic realm of creatures on the fringe, exploring Bigfoot, Ancient Giants, the Nephilim, and more, all while providing a unique biblical perspective. With expert interviews and meticulous editing, Blurry Creatures seeks better answers to age-old questions and to uncover the secrets of mysterious and elusive beings.

## BIRTHRIGHT
### BY TIMOTHY ALBERINO

In this revolutionary book, Timothy Alberino retraces the pages and reveals the secrets of the greatest story ever told, the one in which we are all inescapably embroiled. From the galactic rebellion in the pre-Adamic past to the creation of mankind on Planet Earth; the fall of the Watchers in the pre-Flood world to the machinations of Luciferian forces in modern times; the unveiling of the alien presence to the final battle at Armageddon; Alberino unpacks the synchronicity of these events with scholarly precision and leaves you breathless on the brink of a posthuman apocalypse.

We would like to acknowledge the Blurry Creatures Podcast audience for inspiring the publication of this book. Special thanks to Dave Chesson for his encouragement and guidance along the way.

# Introduction to the Book of Enoch

## by Timothy Alberino

In 1773, the famous Scottish explorer James Bruce of Kinnaird had finally arrived in France after a long and arduous expedition in North Africa, where he was searching for the source of the Blue Nile, a tributary to the Nile proper. During the course of his daring enterprise, which led him along the perilous Barbary Coast, Bruce did eventually find the source of the Nile at Lake Tana, deep in the heart of Ethiopia. This, however, would turn out to be the least of his discoveries. He was returning home to England, but before departing France he visited the city of Paris to deliver a truly remarkable gift into the hands of King Louis XV. Bruce, an accomplished linguist fluent in Arabic, Spanish, Portuguese, and most fortuitously, Ge'ez, the liturgical language of Ethiopia, had managed to procure in that country three copies of a sacred manuscript that was once widely circulated in the ancient world but subsequently lost to history—the Book of Enoch.

The first copy, he gave to the king of France, which still resides to this day in the French National Library. The second he entrusted to the Bodleian Library at Oxford, and the third he retained for his private collection. The unexpected return of the Book of Enoch to the archives of Europe fomented more than a few conspiracy theories and accusations. How had this man, a member of the prestigious Bruce family, no less,[1] come to obtain not one but three copies of the

---

[1] James Bruce was a collateral relative of the illustrious Robert the Bruce, who led the Scots to victory in their war of independence against the English in the early fourteenth century.

lost manuscript? Adding to the mystique of the circumstance was the fact that James Bruce was a Freemason initiated into one of the most influential lodges of the Scottish Rite, Canongate Kilwinning, No. 2, in Edinburgh, which meets (to this day) in the historic Chapel of St. John. Some wondered whether Bruce's expedition to Ethiopia was in reality a clever cover story for a secret Masonic quest to seek out the ancient manuscript (among other lost Hebrew artifacts) and bring it back to the lodge in Edinburgh.[2]

If one *were* to embark on a quest for the Book of Enoch in the eighteenth century, then Ethiopia would have been the only conceivable place to look for it. Due to its controversial exclusion from the Jewish and Christian canons of scripture, Enoch had all but vanished from the world by 500 AD. It seems to have been not only rejected as sacred scripture but deliberately expunged from the libraries of Europe, North Africa, and the Middle East, perhaps in an effort to quell any further conversation regarding its authenticity. So complete was its extirpation that by the sixth century, only fragments of the text remained in Greek (aside from the Aramaic fragments among the Dead Sea Scrolls, which were then still concealed in the caves of Qumran). There was, however, one place where the Book of Enoch was entirely preserved and defiantly reverenced as holy writ by both Jew and Gentile alike—Ethiopia.

The Ethiopian Beta Israel Jews and Orthodox Tewahedo Christians of the fourth century regarded the Book of Enoch as an inspired text and incorporated it into their respective canons of scripture. Copied from an earlier Greek translation, which was itself a translation from the original Hebrew or Aramaic, the Ethiopic Book of Enoch (otherwise known as 1 Enoch), written in Ge'ez, is the only complete version of the manuscript left to us from antiquity.[3] Had

---

[2] The personage of Enoch has always been highly significant to Freemasons, who identify him with Thoth, the Egyptian god of wisdom, and attribute to him the formulation of the rites and secrets central to the practice of Masonry.

[3] A well-preserved Aramaic scroll of the Book of Enoch is purported to exist in an unpublished private collection. The former chief editor of the official Dead Sea Scrolls editorial team, John Strugnell (d. 2007), was allegedly shown the microfilm of the scroll in 1990

the Ethiopians not preserved Enoch as holy writ, then it might have remained lost forever.

As an intriguing aside, there is another legendary Hebrew artifact rumored to be preserved in Ethiopia—the Ark of the Covenant. According to the Ethiopian epic *Kebra Nagast* ("The Glory of Kings"), the Ark was stolen from the temple in Jerusalem during the reign of King Solomon and relocated to Ethiopia, where it still resides to this day.[4] Although scholars dismiss the story, considering that the Ark was clearly still in possession of the Israelites long after the time of Solomon, the Ethiopians maintain that the sacred relic is vigilantly safeguarded by a celibate monk at the Church of St. Mary of Zion in Axum. It is believed that before the Ark reached its final destination in Axum, it was housed for some five hundred years in a replica of the tabernacle on Tana Qirqos, a mysterious island in the midst of Lake Tana, precisely where James Bruce discovered the source of the Nile, and perhaps also the Book of Enoch.

Although the Ethiopic Book of Enoch had been delivered into the hands of European academics by 1773, non-Ge'ez-speaking scholars would not be able to read the text until 1821, when Anglican minister Richard Laurence published an English translation from the copy Bruce had entrusted to the Bodleian Library at Oxford. Laurence's work, though laudable, was unfortunately also rather unreliable, and as a result, various other translations were produced in the nineteenth century. However, it was not until 1906 that an accurate and definitive translation of the Book of Enoch was accomplished by Anglican scholar Robert Henry Charles (R. H. Charles).

---

during the Kuwait crisis. Gerald Lankester Harding, director of Jordan's Department of Antiquities from 1936 to 1956, also testified to having seen the microfilm of the scroll.

[4] The *Kebra Nagast* elaborates on the incident mentioned in 1 Kings 10 and 2 Chronicles 9 in which the queen of Sheba (called Makeda), hearing of King Solomon's great wisdom, decided to embark on a journey to Jerusalem with a splendid retinue of servants and camels bearing gifts of gold, precious stones, and spices. According to the epic, Solomon became enamored of Makeda, who was impregnated by him and bore a son in Ethiopia named Menelik. When Menelik had come of age, he visited his father in Jerusalem, and upon his departure, the sons of the elders of Israel, whom Solomon had commanded to accompany him, stole the Ark from the temple, installed a replica in its place, and secreted the sacred relic away to the land of Abyssinia (Ethiopia).

Charles's translation, from which the present edition is derived, incorporated the Greek fragments of Enoch for comparison with the Ethiopic manuscript and supplemented extensive commentary directed to the scholarly community. After receiving widespread approval from scholars, the work was then republished without commentary in 1912 for the benefit of ordinary readers. Once a reliable English translation of the Book of Enoch was made available to clergy and laity alike, the old, fiery debate regarding its dating and authenticity was reignited.

Modern scholars believe that the Book of Enoch was originally composed in Aramaic or Hebrew (or a combination of both), but a complete manuscript in either language has never been found. Although significant Aramaic fragments of Enoch were discovered among the Dead Sea Scrolls in the caves of Qumran (circa 1946), confirming its considerable antiquity, a decisive dating of the work remains elusive. The difficulty arises from the observation that portions of the text appear to have been produced at various periods of time by different authors. The older sections, namely, the Book of the Watchers (chapters 1–36) and the Book of Parables (chapters 37–71), were undoubtedly compiled long before the birth of Christ, as their content was known to and referenced by the writers of the Old Testament, including the author of Genesis. The later sections, especially those containing astronomical exposition, may have been added between 100 BC and 200 AD. Because the author (or authors) cannot be positively identified, the Book of Enoch is considered pseudepigraphal (a work that falsely claims to be authored by a biblical character); nevertheless, there remains a distinct possibility that the oldest portions of the text were indeed written by the hand of Enoch in the antediluvian age and preserved through the deluge by Noah.

Adding to the confusion concerning authenticity, three separate works bearing the name of Enoch have been circulating since the early eighteen hundreds. As the differences between the texts are too numerous to detail in this modest introduction, the following will suffice as a brief synopsis of their dating and content:

- **1 Enoch**, otherwise known as the "Ethiopic Enoch," is dated from at least 300 BC (the oldest portions) and is the only version found among the Dead Sea Scrolls. The content of 1 Enoch is synchronistic with ancient Hebrew cosmology and seemingly provides the basis for several references in the Bible. It is also distinguished by messianic prophecies pertaining to the Son of Man, which inform the claims of Jesus of Nazareth and the eschatological framework of the New Testament.

- **2 Enoch**, otherwise known as the "Slavonic Enoch" (also called the "Book of the Secrets of Enoch"), is dated to the first century AD, before the destruction of the Temple in Jerusalem (70 AD). The content of 2 Enoch is consistent with early rabbinic Merkabah (Chariot) mysticism and mainly concerns itself with Enoch's journey through the ten heavens.

- **3 Enoch**, otherwise known as the "Hebrew Enoch" (also called the "Revelation of Metatron"), was most likely written in the fifth century AD. The content of 3 Enoch is distinctly Merkabah. It recounts the heavenly visons of Rabbi Ishmael ben Elisha, who is conducted through the mysteries of the cosmos by the angel Metatron (Enoch).

Evidenced by their Merkabah motifs and post–Anno Domini dating, 2 and 3 Enoch are clearly derivatives of the original manuscript; that is to say, they incorporate story and character elements from 1 Enoch without being directly affiliated with it (much like a movie that is loosely based on true events). Apart from its earlier dating, synchronicity with ancient Hebrew cosmology, and Christological content, 1 Enoch is also distinguished by a historical narrative concerning the world before the Flood of Noah, the gravity and consequence of which resonate throughout the Old and New Testaments of the Bible.

Whereas the precise dating of the Book of Enoch remains elusive, there is no question that the story it relates was regarded as veritable history by the ancient Hebrews. Indeed, much of the Tanakh (the Hebrew Bible) assumes a general familiarity with the Enochian tale, without which one is left to grope for meaning when confronted with certain enigmatic passages in the text. Perhaps the most mystifying of these is famously registered in the sixth chapter of Genesis:

> When man began to multiply on the face of the land and daughters were born to them, the sons of God saw that the daughters of man were attractive. And they took as their wives any they chose.... The Nephilim [or *giants*] were on the earth in those days, and also afterward, when the sons of God came in to the daughters of man and they bore children to them. These were the mighty men who were of old, the men of renown.[5]

Notice that no effort is made to further elucidate the details of this peculiar digression in the Genesis narrative. It is evident, therefore, that the author (perhaps Moses) is relying on the reader's presumed knowledge of the infamous affair, which must have been thoroughly chronicled elsewhere in the Hebraic scriptures and widely disseminated as oral tradition. It cannot be coincidental, then, that the first and second verses of Genesis 6 appear to have been directly transcribed from the Book of Enoch (which, curiously, also registers them in the first and second verses of chapter 6):

> And it came to pass when the children of men had multiplied that in those days were born unto them beautiful and comely daughters. And the angels, the children of the heaven, saw and lusted after them, and said to one another: "Come, let us choose us wives from among the children of men and beget us children."[6]

---

[5] Genesis 6:1–2, 4 (English Standard Version).
[6] 1 Enoch 6:1–2 (R. H. Charles).

The story that follows these verses is an amplification of the events intimated in Genesis 6. According to Enoch, a company of renegade angels, called *Watchers*, descended to the earth in defiance of God and chose for themselves wives from the daughters of men. The Watchers copulated with their wives, who conceived and gave birth to hybrid giants (*Nephilim*). Eventually, after all manner of havoc was wrought through their evil deeds, the Watchers were bound in chains and cast into the uttermost depths of the earth until the day of judgment. The Flood of Noah ensued, and the earth was cleansed of their abominable seed (though the accursed spirits of the giants persisted as demons in the post-Flood world).

References to the Enochian tale are not limited to the Old Testament. While writing to persecuted Christians living in the five regions of Asia Minor, the apostle Peter reminds them of the angels who sinned in the days of Noah and who, in consequence of their grave transgression, were cast into the gloomy pits of Tartarus until the day of judgment.[7] There is simply no precedent for this reference within the canon of scripture (the sixty-six books of the Bible). One must look outside the canon to find the source material from whence the incident is derived, namely, to 1 Enoch. That the early church was conversant with Enoch is made abundantly evident by the apostle Jude (the brother of James), who reiterates Peter's admonition regarding those "angels who did not keep their proper domain, but left their own abode, [whom] he has reserved in everlasting chains under darkness for the judgment of the great day."[8] As if intending to establish the source of his reference beyond all doubt, Jude proceeds to quote verbatim from the Book of Enoch:

> It was also about these that Enoch, the seventh from Adam, prophesied, saying, "Behold, the Lord comes with ten thousands of his holy ones, to execute judgment on all and to convict all the ungodly of all their deeds of ungodliness that

---

[7] See 2 Peter 2:4–5.

[8] Jude 1:6 (ESV).

they have committed in such an ungodly way, and of all the harsh things that ungodly sinners have spoken against him."[9]

Concerning Enoch, the seventh from Adam, who was apparently esteemed as a scholar and prophet by the Jews, the Tanakh is oddly mum, offering only this:

> Enoch lived sixty-five years, and begot Methuselah. After he begot Methuselah, Enoch walked with God three hundred years, and had sons and daughters. So all the days of Enoch were three hundred and sixty-five years. And Enoch walked with God; and he was not, for God took him.[10]

Once again, as in Genesis 6, we are confronted with a glaring ambiguity in the narrative. The Hebrew Bible has much to say of Noah, of Abraham, of Moses, of Elijah, and of all its hallowed prophets, so why does it say so little of Enoch, who might be regarded as the greatest of all? The reader has no doubt already discerned the answer: because the story of Enoch was thoroughly chronicled in the scripture attributed to him. It is reasonable to conclude that the Enochian text must have been numbered among the sacred scrolls in the synagogues of Judea and Asia Minor during the first century AD, when Peter and Jude make reference to it.

The question now arises: if Enoch was so highly esteemed as a scribe and prophet by the ancient Hebrews, then why was the Book of Enoch ultimately excluded from the Jewish and Christian canons? The answer to this query may be furnished in two points of contention.

The first point of contention for both Jews and Christians revolved around the dating and authorship of the manuscript. As previously mentioned, 1 Enoch appears to be a compilation of texts written at various periods of time by unknown persons. The latter portions, called the Book of the Course of the Heavenly Luminaries (chapters 72–82) and the Book of Dream Visions (chapters 83–90),

---

[9] Jude 1:14–15 (ESV).
[10] Genesis 5:21–24 (New King James Version).

may have been added in the first or second centuries AD by adherents of the Merkabah tradition. This posed an obvious problem for its induction into the canons. Of course, the predicament could have easily been resolved by incorporating the older portions while excluding the newer. That such a policy was not employed demonstrates that there were other, more serious concerns. The unsubstantiated authorship of Enoch, though often cited as the principal reason for its rejection, is much less of a problem considering that the authorship of several biblical texts (e.g., Genesis, Job, Acts, Hebrews) were also in question at the time of their induction (and are still in question to this day).

The second point of contention revolved around content. Here, we must differentiate between the Jews and Christians. In the decades following the death (and resurrection) of Christ, the Jews adopted a hostile attitude toward Christianity (and vice versa). Rabbinic Judaism emphatically rejects the belief that Jesus of Nazareth was the promised Messiah of biblical prophecy, and this was likely the primary motivation for the exclusion of Enoch in the Jewish canon of scripture. Surprisingly, the Book of Enoch contains some of the most explicit messianic prophecies ever recorded, which, doubtless to the chagrin of first-century Jews, allude to the life and ministry of the man they had crucified. The magnitude of this Christological content should not be lightly considered, as it serves to affirm the veracity of the text through the mechanism of prophecy fulfilled.

Recalling that the oldest portions of 1 Enoch (chapters 1–71) were most certainly written before the birth of Christ, we can examine their content as it relates to the testimony of Jesus.[11] Of all the prophetic epithets pertaining to the Messiah in the scriptures, Jesus oddly preferred to refer to himself as the Son of Man, a title that is not found in the Old Testament. Theologians have attempted to explain his curious preference by citing a passage from Daniel in which the prophet beholds "one like a son of man":

---

[11] The testimony of Jesus, it should be remembered, is the spirit of prophecy (see Revelation 19:10).

> I saw in the night visions, and behold, with the clouds of heaven there came one like a son of man, and he came to the Ancient of Days and was presented before him. And to him was given dominion and glory and a kingdom that all peoples, nations, and languages should serve him; his dominion is an everlasting dominion, which shall not pass away, and his kingdom one that shall not be destroyed.[12]

Apart from the fact that this passage is not employing the term *son of man* as a formal title but a description of one who has the appearance of a human being, what so many theologians fail to realize is that Daniel's vision of the Messiah being presented before the Ancient (or Head) of Days is deliberately synchronistic with Enoch's description of the same event, recorded thusly:

> And at that hour that Son of Man was named in the presence of the Lord of Spirits, and his name before the Head of Days. Yea, before the sun and the signs were created, before the stars of the heaven were made, his name was named before the Lord of Spirits. He shall be a staff to the righteous whereon to stay themselves and not fall, and he shall be the light of the Gentiles [nations], and the hope of those who are troubled of heart. All who dwell on earth shall fall down and worship before him, and will praise and bless and celebrate with song the Lord of Spirits. And for this reason hath he been chosen and hidden before Him, before the creation of the world and for evermore. And the wisdom of the Lord of Spirits hath revealed him to the holy and righteous; for he hath preserved the lot of the righteous; because they have hated and despised this world of unrighteousness, and have hated all its works and ways in the name of the Lord of Spirits: for in his name they are saved, and according to his good pleasure hath it been in regard to their life.[13]

---

[12] Daniel 7:13–14 (ESV).
[13] 1 Enoch 48:2–7 (RHC).

Unlike Daniel, Enoch employs the term *Son of Man* as a formal title ascribed exclusively to the promised Messiah. Long before Jesus was born of Mary in Bethlehem, Enoch foresaw that the Son of Man would be a "staff to the righteous" and the "light of the Gentiles." The very core of Christian doctrine is revealed in the pronouncement "for in his name they are saved." When Jesus referred to himself as the Son of Man, the meaning was crystal clear in the minds of the Jews. The Pharisees and Sadducees understood exactly who he was claiming to be precisely because they were well versed in the oracles of Enoch. Jesus was not merely declaring himself to be *a* son of man, but *the* Son of Man, according to the scriptures. When Caiaphas, the high priest, interrogated him with the question, "Are you the Christ, the Son of the Blessed?" Jesus replied,

> "I am. And you will see the Son of Man sitting at the right hand of the Power, and coming with the clouds of heaven."
>
> Then the high priest tore his clothes and said, "What further need do we have of witnesses? You have heard the blasphemy! What do you think?"
>
> And they all condemned him to be deserving of death. Then some began to spit on him, and to blindfold him, and to beat him, and to say to him, "Prophesy!" And the officers struck him with the palms of their hands."[14]

It has long been taught that the high priest tore his robes because Jesus had committed the ultimate blasphemy by claiming to be God. The blasphemy, however, was much more specific than this. By declaring himself the Son of Man, Jesus was claiming to be the Elect One whom Enoch beheld seated on the throne of his glory and presiding in judgment over the rulers of the earth:

> And thus the Lord commanded the kings and the mighty and the exalted, and those who dwell on the earth, and said:

---

[14] Mark 14:62–65 (NKJV).

"Open your eyes and lift up your horns if ye are able to recognize the Elect One."

And the Lord of the Spirits seated him on the throne of His glory, and the spirit of righteousness was poured out upon him, and the word of his mouth slays all the sinners, and all the unrighteous are destroyed from before his face. And there shall stand up in that day all the kings and the mighty, and the exalted and those who hold the earth, and they shall see and recognize how he sits on the throne of his glory, and righteousness is judged before him, and no lying word is spoken before him.[15]

There must have been at least one cautious member of the Sanhedrin assembled in the home of Caiaphas that fateful night nervously contemplating the words of Enoch as he watched his colleagues spit on Jesus and strike him in the face:

Then shall pain come upon them as on a woman in travail, when her child enters the mouth of the womb, and she has pain in bringing forth. And one portion of them shall look on the other and they shall be terrified, and they shall be downcast of countenance, and pain shall seize them, when they see that Son of Man sitting on the throne of his glory. . . . And all the kings and the mighty and the exalted and those who rule the earth shall fall down before him on their faces, and worship and set their hope upon that Son of Man, and petition him and supplicate for mercy at his hands.[16]

During his apocalyptic discourse on the Mount of Olives, Jesus explicitly identifies himself as the prefigured judge of the nations from the above passage in Enoch, even adopting the peculiar "sit on the throne of his glory" phraseology, which does not appear in the Old Testament:

---

[15] 1 Enoch 62:1–3 (RHC).
[16] 1 Enoch 62:4–5, 9 (RHC).

When the Son of Man comes in his glory, and all the holy angels with him, then he will sit on the throne of his glory. All the nations will be gathered before him, and he will separate them one from another, as a shepherd divides his sheep from the goats.[17]

There are quite a few remarks made by Christ in the gospels that are direct references to eschatological content found exclusively in Enoch. While supping with his disciples on the eve of his crucifixion, for instance, Jesus affirms, "In my Father's house are many mansions; if it were not so, I would have told you."[18] That mansions are prepared for the righteous in heaven must read as a new revelation for those who are versed only in the biblical canon, but for those conversant with the Book of Enoch, the words of Christ ring with a familiar tone:

And after that I saw all the secrets of the heavens, and how the kingdom is divided, and how the actions of men are weighed in the balance. And there I saw the mansions of the elect and the mansions of the holy.[19]

One of the more remarkable allusions to the ministry of Jesus of Nazareth in the Book of Enoch is manifest in the expression "hang upon the Lord of Spirits," which occurs three times in the Parables:

When the congregation of the righteous shall appear, and sinners shall be judged for their sins, and shall be driven from the face of the earth: and when the Righteous One shall appear before the eyes of the righteous, whose elect works hang upon the Lord of Spirits.[20]

And the second voice I heard blessing the Elect One and the elect ones who hang upon the Lord of Spirits.[21]

---

[17] Matthew 25:31–32 (NKJV).
[18] See John 14.
[19] 1 Enoch 4:1–2 (RHC).
[20] 1 Enoch 38:1–2 (RHC).
[21] 1 Enoch 40:5–6 (RHC).

And they persecute the houses of His congregations, and the faithful who hang upon the name of the Lord of Spirits.[22]

In light of the New Testament, these verses inexorably evoke the visage of Jesus hanging on the cross, bearing upon himself the sin of mankind and imputing to those who believe in him the righteousness of God. Here, in the oracles of Enoch, perhaps written at the genesis of human history, we find the doctrine of justification portending to the crucifixion of Christ. It is hard to imagine that Paul was not contemplating how the works of the righteous, and the righteous themselves, hang upon the Lord of Spirits when he wrote to the Galatians:

I have been crucified with Christ; it is no longer I who live, but Christ who lives in me; and the life I now live in the flesh I live by faith in the Son of God, who loved me and gave himself for me.[23]

And to the Corinthians:

For our sake he made him to be sin who knew no sin, so that in him we might become the righteousness of God.[24]

There can be no doubt that the apostles of Christ were distinctly influenced by the Book of Enoch in the formulation of their theology. Indeed, so accordant are the doctrines of the New Testament with 1 Enoch that some scholars, despite concrete evidence, simply cannot accept that the earliest portions of the text, including the Parables, predate the first century AD. When addressing certain eschatological themes (such as the final judgment) in their letters to the various churches, the apostles seem to rely more heavily on the oracles of Enoch than any of the Old Testament prophets. As previously noted, even the gospels exhibit an unmistakable Enochian influence. In volume 12 of his comprehensive tome *The Biblical World*, published

---

[22] 1 Enoch 46:8 (RHC).
[23] Galatians 2:20 (RSV).
[24] 2 Corinthians 5:21 (RSV).

in 1898, Anglican scholar Henry Hayman catalogues some of the most conspicuous parallels between the gospels, the Acts of the Apostles, and Enoch. They are listed as follows:

| MATTHEW. | ENOCH. |
|---|---|
| 5:22, 29, 30; 10:28, where Gehenna is the place of final punishment. | 27:2; 90:26, 27, where Gehenna is similarly mentioned and first definitely so appears. |
| 19:28, when the Son of Man shall sit on the throne of his glory (cf. 25:31), ye also shall sit on twelve thrones. | 62:3, 5, kings and princes ... terrified when they see the Son of Man sitting on the throne of his glory; 108:12, I will seat each on the throne of his honor. |
| 25:41, prepared for the devil and his angels. | 104:5, chains prepared for the hosts of Azazel. |
| 26:24, it had been good for that man if he had not been born. | 38:2, it had been good for them if they had not been born. |

| LUKE. | |
|---|---|
| 1:52, He hath put down the mighty from their seats. | 46:5, will put down kings from their thrones. |
| 16:8, the children of light. | 16:11, the generation of light. |
| 16:9, the mammon of unrighteousness. | 63:10, the mammon of unrighteousness. |
| 18:7, shall not God avenge his own elect, and he is long-suffering over them. | 47:1–2, a prayer of the righteous ... that judgment may be executed ... that He be no more longsuffering over them. |
| 21:26, your redemption draweth nigh. | 51:2, the day of their redemption hath drawn nigh. |
| 23:35, the Christ of God the elect one. | 40:5, the elect one. |

| JOHN. | |
|---|---|
| 5:22, He hath committed all judgment to the Son. | 69:27, the sum of judgment was committed to Him (i.e., the Son of Man). |
| 14:2, many mansions. | 39:4, mansions of the righteous; cf. v. 7; 48:1; etc. |

ACTS.

| | |
|---|---|
| 3:14, the righteous one; cf. 7:52; 22:14. | 38:2, the righteous one (Messiah). |
| 4:12, none other name ... whereby ye must be saved. | 48:7, saved in His (Messiah's) name. |
| 10:4, prayers gone up for a memorial before God. | 99:3, raise your prayers as a memorial before the Most High. |
| 17:31, will judge the world ... by that man whom he hath ordained. | 40:9, will appoint a judge for them all ... judge them all before him.[25] |

In addition to these, Hayman observes that the Pauline epistles contain at least twenty passages that have parallels in Enoch, and that John's Revelation borrows much of its content and phraseology from the same. Considering, then, that Jesus unambiguously identified himself as the Son of Man from the oracles of Enoch and that his apostles professed him as such, synchronizing their Christology with the Elect and Righteous One revealed therein, it is no surprise that the Book of Enoch was rejected by rabbinic Jews living in the early church age.

But what of the Christians? Why would the church fathers be inclined to discard a text from which the apostles clearly derive so much of their theology? Here we may find commonality between the Jews and Christians, whose leading rabbis and bishops objected to the shocking nature of its content.

Although foundational in the cosmology of the ancient Hebrews, Talmudic rabbis of the second century AD were apparently appalled by the Enochian tale, which describes lustful angels having intercourse with human women. They generally refuted the angelic interpretation of Genesis 6, asserting that the sons of God (*b'nei ha'elohim*) were merely the righteous sons of Seth, and repudiated the notion that heavenly beings were capable of such repulsive, carnal sin. Their attitude toward the concept of so-called "fallen angels" may be detected in a famous debate between Trypho the Jew and Justin Martyr, a Christian apologist. In the course of the exchange, Martyr

---

[25] Henry Hayman, "The Book of Enoch in Reference to the New Testament and Early Christian Antiquity," *The Biblical World* 12, no. 1 (July 1898): 37–46.

argued that evil angels are actively influencing the affairs of the world, to which Trypho rejoined, "The utterances of God are holy, but your expositions are mere contrivances, as is plain from what has been explained by you; nay, even blasphemies, for you assert that angels sinned and revolted from God."[26]

In contrast to Jews of the same period, most Christians readily embraced the concept of fallen angels, but even they were scandalized by the sexual escapades of the holy Watchers. Coupled with doubts concerning dating and authorship, as well as the position of the Jews, the unseemly content of Enoch seemingly tipped the scales against its induction into the Christian canon. It might have been convenient for those who simply could not accept that angels were capable of lusting after and copulating with human females to reject the Book of Enoch on grounds of dating and authorship. Whatever the case, the Enochian influence on Christian theology faded into obscurity, and following in the line of Talmudic rabbis, the "sons of Seth" interpretation of Genesis 6 became the dominant view of the Catholic Church by the late fourth century AD (in no small part thanks to Augustine).

Despite the controversy, more than a few prominent church fathers held a favorable view of the Book of Enoch, and some even referenced it as holy scripture.[27] Among these are such luminaries as Clement and Barnabas (the friends of Paul), Irenaeus, Origen, Tertullian, Athenagoras of Athens, and the formerly mentioned Justin Martyr. Tertullian, the famed scholar and defender of the faith in Carthage, was particularly vociferous in support of Enoch, even contending for its inclusion in the canon. In his treatise *On the Apparel of Women*, Tertullian maintains that the Book of Enoch may very well have been passed down to posterity by Enoch himself, either

---

[26] Justin Martyr, "Dialogue 79," *Dialogue with Trypho*, circa AD 155–160.

[27] It is of interest to note that certain church fathers, such as Origen and Athenagoras, quote from passages of Enoch that do not exist in the Ethiopian manuscript, indicating that 1 Enoch is incomplete. There must have been a Greek, Aramaic, or Hebrew manuscript circulating during the first centuries AD that represented a more exhaustive rendition of the text.

in written or oral form, and preserved through the Flood by Noah, his great-grandson. He also intimates the reason for its rejection by the Jews, namely, that it testifies of Jesus Christ. Writes Tertullian,

> I am aware that the Scripture of Enoch, which has assigned this order (of action) to angels [referring to their sexual intercourse with human women], is not received by some, because it is not admitted into the Jewish canon either. I suppose they did not think that, having been published before the deluge, it could have safely survived that worldwide calamity, the abolisher of all things. If that is the reason (for rejecting it), let them recall to their memory that Noah, the survivor of the deluge, was the great-grandson of Enoch himself; and he, of course, had heard and remembered, from domestic renown and hereditary tradition, concerning his own great-grandfather's "grace in the sight of God," and concerning all his preachings; since Enoch had given no other charge to Methuselah than that he should hand on the knowledge of them to his posterity. Noah therefore, no doubt, might have succeeded in the trusteeship of (his) preaching; or, had the case been otherwise, he would not have been silent alike concerning the disposition (of things) made by God, his Preserver, and concerning the particular glory of his own house.
>
> If (Noah) had not had this (conservative power) by so short a route, there would (still) be this (consideration) to warrant our assertion of (the genuineness of) this Scripture: he could equally have *renewed* it, under the Spirit's inspiration, after it *had* been destroyed by the violence of the deluge, as, after the destruction of Jerusalem by the Babylonian storming of it, every document of the Jewish literature is generally agreed to have been restored through Ezra.
>
> But since Enoch in the same Scripture has preached likewise concerning the Lord, nothing at all must be rejected *by*

us which pertains *to* us; and we read that "every Scripture suitable for edification is divinely inspired." By the *Jews* it may now seem to have been rejected for that (very) reason, just like all the other (portions) nearly which tell of Christ. Nor, of course, is this fact wonderful, that they did not receive some Scriptures which spake of him whom even in person, speaking in their presence, they were not to receive. To these considerations is added the fact that Enoch possesses a testimony in the Apostle Jude.[28]

If Tertullian is correct in surmising that the Scripture of Enoch was preserved through the deluge by Noah, then it undoubtedly represents one of the oldest tales ever told in the long and storied saga of the human species on Planet Earth and may be one of the earliest pieces of literature composed by the same. It is important to acknowledge, however, that most modern scholars would eagerly rebuff the proposition that the Book of Enoch originated in the antediluvian world.

Modern scholarship regards the Enochian tale as a theological polemic against the pagan mythologies of Mesopotamia, which are considered to be much more antiquated than the traditions of the Jews. In an article entitled "On the Origin of Watchers: A Comparative Study of the Antediluvian Wisdom in Mesopotamian and Jewish Traditions," Dr. Amar Annus, a distinguished scholar of the Ancient Near East, articulates the prevailing opinion:

> Varying accounts of the antediluvian history in the ancient Mesopotamian and Jewish sources should be regarded as results of ancient debates. Not only direct borrowings took place, but also creative reinterpretations, especially on the Jewish side. Some of these creative reinterpretations must have occurred as deliberate inversions of the Mesopotamian source material. The Jewish authors often inverted the

---

[28] Tertullian, *On the Apparel of Women*, in Phillip Schaff, *Ante-Nicene Fathers*, vol. 4 (Grand Rapids, MI: William B. Eerdmans Publishing Company, 1956).

Mesopotamian intellectual traditions with the intention of showing the superiority of their own cultural foundations.[29]

To summarize the article, Dr. Annus contends that the primary characters in the Enochian tale are mirrored images of their Mesopotamian counterparts. Enoch, for example, is equivalent to Enmeduranki, who registers as the seventh king on the *Sumerian King List* (in juxtaposition to Enoch, the seventh patriarch in the genealogy of Genesis 5), and the Watchers are inversions of the *apkallus*, the divine sages of antediluvian origin. The Book of Enoch essentially flips the script, as it were, and depicts the Mesopotamian heroes—the *apkallus* and their semidivine offspring—as supervillains in the guise of the Watchers and their giant hybrid sons.[30]

The whole premise of the argument is based on a belief that the Mesopotamian account of the antediluvian world is older than that of the Jews'. It is, of course, undeniably true that Mesopotamian civilization predates the inception of the Hebrew nation by thousands of years. Indeed, Abraham was himself a Mesopotamian from the Sumerian city of Ur, which was already ancient in his time. But what if Tertullian was right and modern scholars are wrong? What if the Mesopotamian mythologies are themselves inversions of the original story set forth by Enoch thousands of years before the rise of Sumer between the Tigris and Euphrates? And, to complete the thought experiment, what if the Mesopotamian priesthood deliberately bastardized the traditions conserved by Noah in defiance of God?

According to the Bible, Noah is the father of all peoples in the post-Flood world. It is just as rational to conclude, therefore, that Mesopotamian civilization arose as an outgrowth of the original antediluvian culture propagated through Noah and his sons. Indeed,

---

[29] Amar Annus, "On the Origin of Watchers: A Comparative Study of the Antediluvian Wisdom in Mesopotamian and Jewish Traditions," *Journal for the Study of the Pseudepigrapha* 19, no. 4 (May 2010).

[30] This summary is admittedly an oversimplification of Dr. Annus's position. The reader is encouraged to study the excellent article in its entirety.

we may even attribute the founding of Sumer (or proto-Sumer) to that fabled rebel of biblical infamy Nimrod, who brazenly defied the ordinance of Yahweh by consolidating the people into a city called Babel in the plains of Shinar rather than dispersing to repopulate the earth. Nimrod, whose name literally means "we will rebel," might have deliberately inverted the antediluvian traditions of his antecedents in order to establish a new pagan world order that positioned him above the sons of Noah, who, it should be remembered, were still alive when the Tower of Babel was constructed and might have protested the enterprise. If so, then the opposite of the prevailing opinion is true, namely, that Mesopotamian mythology was conceived as a theological polemic against the God of Noah and is thus an inversion of the Enochian tale, its source material.

In summation, the Book of Enoch may represent a restoration of antediluvian lore preserved through the deluge by Noah in written or oral form. If in the former, then the original manuscript would have been a truly remarkable relic conserved by some means through the rise of Sumer and delivered to the descendants of Abraham. If in the latter, then the Enochian tale, as Tertullian suggests, might have been republished under the inspiration of the Spirit and according to the recollection of the oldest traditions known to man. In either event, the implication is the same: the antediluvian lore of the Hebrews predates that of the Mesopotamians.

Whatever the case may be in regard to its origins, we are deeply indebted to James Bruce, the Anglican academics, and the Ethiopians for reintroducing the Book of Enoch into the corpus of biblical scholarship in the West. Having endured two thousand years of obscurity, nearly expunged forever from the scriptoriums of the Church, Enoch is today enjoying renewed interest among Christians who are rediscovering the ancient Hebraic perception of the pre-Flood world and the extraordinary events that precipitated its cataclysmic destruction.

*– Timothy Alberino*

# I
# ENOCH

Also known as the Ethiopic Enoch
Translation by R. H. Charles, 1917
Commentary by Timothy Alberino

# Abbreviations, Brackets, & Symbols Specially Used in the Translation of 1 Enoch

This translation of the Book of Enoch is based on the translation by R.H. Charles, first published in 1917.

E denotes the Ethiopic Version.

G$^s$ denotes the fragments of the Greek Version preserved in Syncellus: in the case of 8$^b$–9$^b$ there are two forms of the text, G$^{s1}$, G$^{s2}$.

G$^g$ denotes the large fragment of the Greek Version discovered at Akhmîm, and deposited in the Gizeh Museum, Cairo.

The following brackets are used in the translation of 1 Enoch:

{ } The use of these brackets means that the words so enclosed are found in G$^g$ but not in E.

‹ › The use of these brackets means that the words so enclosed are found in E but not in G$^g$ or G$^s$.

< > The use of these brackets means that the words so enclosed are restored.

[ ] The use of these brackets means that the words so enclosed are interpolations.

( ) The use of these brackets means that the words so enclosed are supplied by the editor.

The use of **thick type** denotes that the words so printed are emended.

† † = corruption in the text.

. . . = some words have been lost.

# BOOK OF
# THE WATCHERS

## Chapter 1.

1. The words of the blessing of Enoch, wherewith he blessed the elect <and> righteous, who will be living in the day of tribulation, when all the wicked <and godless> are to be removed.[1] 2. And he took up his parable and said—Enoch a righteous man, whose eyes were opened by God, saw the vision of the Holy One in the heavens, {which} the angels showed me, and from them I heard everything, and from them I understood as I saw, but not for this generation, but for a remote one which is for to come.[2] 3. Concerning the elect I said, and took up my parable concerning them: the Holy Great One will come forth from His dwelling,

4. And the eternal God will tread upon the earth, (even) on Mount Sinai, [and appear from His camp] and appear in the strength of His might from the heaven of {heavens}.[3]

---

[1] There appears to be a duality at work in Enoch's inaugural pronouncements. Evinced in the verses that follow, the day of tribulation is evidently an apocalyptic reference to the return of Christ and final judgment, but it could equally apply to the aqueous cataclysm that would befall the earth in the days of Noah, his great-grandson. The tribulation, then, may simultaneously refer to the impending Flood of Noah *and* the fiery conflagration that will destroy the earth in the last days. Like the quantum entanglement of electrons separated by thousands of miles, these two world-ending cataclysms, separated by thousands of years, are inextricably linked through time.

[2] As will become apparent in the Parables, the vision of the Holy One is a revelation of the Son of Man, Jesus Christ. It is quite intriguing to consider that the Book of Enoch, which may represent the first prophetic text ever composed, is addressed to the last generation that will be living in the day of tribulation when the Son of Man returns with the armies of heaven to vanquish the ungodly and take dominion of the earth.

[3] Enoch's vision of the Holy One treading upon the earth and appearing in the strength of his might is reminiscent of Isaiah's vision of the Lord robed in splendor, striding forward in the greatness of his strength, treading the winepress of God's wrath. (See Isaiah 63.)

5. And all shall be smitten with fear, and the Watchers shall quake, and great fear and trembling shall seize them unto the ends of the earth.

6. And the high mountains shall be shaken, and the high hills shall be made low, and shall melt like wax before the flame

7. And the earth shall be {wholly} rent in sunder, and all that is upon the earth shall perish, and there shall be a judgment upon all (men).

8. But with the righteous He will make peace, and will protect the elect, and mercy shall be upon them. And they shall all belong to God, and they shall be prospered, and they shall {all} be blessed. {And He will help them all,} and light shall appear unto them, {and He will make peace with them.}

9. And behold! He cometh with ten thousands of {His} holy ones to execute judgment upon all, and to destroy {all} the ungodly: and to convict all flesh of all the works {of their ungodliness} which they have ungodly committed, {and of all the hard things which} ungodly sinners {have spoken} against Him.[4]

## Chapter 2.

1. Observe ye everything that takes place in the heaven, how they do not change their orbits, {and} the luminaries which are in the heaven, how they all rise and set in order each in its season, and transgress not against their appointed order.

2. Behold ye the earth, and give heed to the things which take place upon it from first to last, {how **steadfast** they are,} how {none of the things upon earth} change, {but} all the works of God appear {to you.}

3. Behold the summer and the winter, ‹how the whole earth is filled

---

[4] These verses appear verbatim in Jude 1:14-15. The fact that Jude, the brother of James (and thus also the brother of Jesus), attributes this prophecy to, "Enoch, the seventh from Adam," is definitive proof that the apostles and the early church were conversant with the Enochian text (in whatever form it may have had in the first century) and considered it to be divinely inspired scripture.

with water, and clouds and dew and rain lie upon it.›

## Chapter 3.

Observe and see how (in the winter) all the trees ‹seem› as though they had withered and shed all their leaves, except fourteen trees, which do not lose their foliage but retain the old foliage from two to three years till the new comes.

## Chapter 4.

And again, observe ‹ye› the days of summer how the sun is above the earth over against it. And you seek shade and shelter by reason of the heat of the sun, and the earth also burns with growing heat, and so you cannot tread on the earth, or on a rock by reason of its heat.

## Chapter 5.

1. Observe ‹ye› how the trees cover themselves with green leaves and bear fruit: wherefore give ye heed {and know} with regard to all {His works}, and recognize how He that liveth forever hath made them so.

2. And {all} His works go on {thus} from year to year {forever,} and all the tasks which they accomplish for Him, and {their tasks} change not, but according as ‹God› hath ordained so is it done.

3. And behold how the sea and the rivers in like manner accomplish {and change not} their tasks {from His commandments.}

4. But ye—ye have not been steadfast, nor done the commandments of the Lord, but ye have turned away and spoken proud and hard words with your impure mouths against His greatness. Oh, ye hard-hearted, ye shall find no peace.[5]

5. Therefore shall ye execrate your days, and the years of your life shall perish, and {the years of your destruction} shall be multiplied in eternal execration, and ye shall find no mercy.

6a. In those days ye shall make your names an eternal execration unto all the righteous,[6]

---

[5] Enoch is drawing a contrast between the order of nature, which steadfastly obeys the ordinances of God, and the ungodly, who continually defy and revile Him.

[6] These verses are echoed by Solomon: "The Lord's curse is on the house of the wicked, but

*b*. And by you shall {all} who curse, curse.

*c*. {And all} the sinners {and godless} shall imprecate by you,

*7c*. And for you, the godless, there shall be a curse.

*6d*. {And all the . . . shall rejoice,

*e*. And there shall be forgiveness of sins,

*f*. And every mercy and peace and forbearance:

*g*. There shall be salvation unto them, a goodly light.[7]

*i*. And for all of you sinners there shall be no salvation,

*j*. But on you all shall abide a curse.}

*7a*. But for the elect there shall be light and grace and peace,

*b*. And they shall inherit the earth.[8]

8. And then there shall be bestowed upon the elect wisdom, and they shall all live and never again sin, either through ungodliness or through pride; but they who are wise shall be humble.

9. And they shall not again transgress, nor shall they sin all the days of their life, nor shall they die of (the divine) anger or wrath,[9] but they shall complete the number of the days of their life. And their lives shall be increased in peace, and the years of their joy shall be multiplied, in eternal gladness and peace, all the days of their life.

---

he blesses the dwelling of the righteous" (Proverbs 3:33, ESV).

[7] Light is employed throughout the text as a symbol of Christ and a presage of his substitutionary atonement, which imputes to the believer the righteousness of God, resulting in everlasting life. Jesus deliberately associates himself with the light symbolism from Enoch: "I am the light of the world. Whoever follows me will not walk in darkness, but will have the light of life" (John 8:12, NAB).

[8] The elect (*or* righteous) and meek (*or* humble) inheriting the earth is a consistent theme in the scriptures. The psalmist writes, "But the meek shall inherit the land and delight themselves in abundant peace" (Psalm 37:11, ESV), and "The righteous shall inherit the land and dwell upon it forever" (Psalm 37:29, ESV). Jesus reiterates the axiom in the Beatitudes, "Blessed are the meek, for they shall inherit the earth" (Matthew 5:5, ESV).

[9] The divine wrath refers to the day of the Lord when the wicked will be purged from the earth and punished for their sins at the great judgment. The oracles of Enoch reveal that the Son of Man will appear from heaven to preside over the judgment of mankind and will save the righteous from the wrath of God. Paul reiterates this revelation in his commendation to the Thessalonians who, having turned away from their idols to worship God, were now waiting "for his Son from heaven, whom he raised from the dead, Jesus who delivers us from the wrath to come" (1 Thessalonians 1:10, ESV).

## Chapter 6.

1. And it came to pass when the children of men had multiplied that in those days were born unto them beautiful and comely daughters.[10] 2. And the angels, the children of the heaven, saw and lusted after them, and said to one another: 'Come, let us choose us wives from among the children of men and beget us children.'[11] 3. And Semjâzâ,[12] who was their leader, said unto them: 'I fear ye will not indeed agree to do this deed, and I alone shall have to pay the penalty of a great sin.'[13] 4. And they all answered him and said: 'Let us all swear an oath, and all bind ourselves by mutual imprecations not to abandon this plan but to do this thing.' 5. Then sware they all together and bound themselves by mutual imprecations upon it. 6. And they were in all two hundred; who descended {in the days} of **Jared**[14] on the summit of Mount Hermon, and they called it Mount Hermon, because they had sworn and bound themselves by mutual imprecations upon it.[15]

---

[10] This verse, and the next, seem to have been copied nearly word for word in the inaugural verses of Genesis 6, rendered thusly: "When man began to multiply on the face of the land and daughters were born to them, the sons of God saw that the daughters of man were attractive. And they took as their wives any they chose" (Genesis 6:1–2, ESV). As no effort is made to further elucidate the details of this peculiar digression in the Genesis narrative, it is evident that the author (perhaps Moses) is relying on the reader's presumed knowledge of this infamous affair, which must have been thoroughly chronicled elsewhere in the Hebraic scriptures and widely disseminated as oral tradition.

[11] We may distill from this verse three motives for the angel's transgression: 1) they lusted after human women and desired to take them as wives; 2) they intended to procreate with their wives and beget children; 3) they planned to usurp dominion of the earth through the agency of their human-hybrid offspring. The first two motives are apparent in the text, and the third may be inferred by what follows.

[12] The Semitic etymology of the name Semjaza derives either from *shem* ("name," Heb. שם) or *shamaym* ("heavens," Heb. שמים). If from *shem*, then the meaning may be rendered as "he sees the name" which would be indicative of his lofty estate and proximity to the Name in heaven (i.e., the Son of God). If from *shamaym*, then the meaning may be rendered as "gazes from the heavens," which would be indicative of his occupation as a Watcher.

[13] It is important to note that Semjaza and his coconspirators knew full well that what they were about to do amounted to sedition against the King of heaven and were willing to risk the repercussions.

[14] It is perhaps not coincidental that the name Jarod means "to descend," "descent," or "one who descends."

[15] Situated on the border between Syria and Lebanon at an elevation of 9,232 feet above sea level, Mount Hermon is the highest peak in the Anti-Lebanon mountain range. In 1869, Sir Charles Warren discovered a hewn stone structure on the summit of Hermon, which is today recognized by archeologists as the highest temple in the ancient world. Known as

7. And these are the names of their leaders: Sêmîazâz, their leader, Arâkîba, Râmêêl, Kôkabîêl, Tâmîêl, Râmîêl, Dânêl, Êzêqêêl, Barâqî-jâl, Asâêl, Armârôs, Batârêl, Anânêl, Zaqîêl, Samsâpêêl, Satarêl, Tûrêl, Jômjâêl, **Sariêl**. 8. These are their chiefs of tens.

## Chapter 7.

1. And all the others together with them took unto themselves wives, and each chose for himself one, and they began to go in unto them and to defile themselves with them, and they taught them charms and enchantments, and the cutting of roots, and made them acquainted with plants.[16] 2. And they became pregnant, and they bare great giants, whose height was three thousand ells:[17] 3. who consumed all the acquisitions of men. And when men could no longer sustain them, 4. the giants turned against them and devoured mankind. 5. And they began to sin against birds, and beasts, and reptiles, and fish,

---

Qasr Antar, the temple once contained a limestone stele with a Greek inscription that read, "According to the command of the greatest and Holy God, those who take an oath proceed from here." The inscription is believed to commemorate the arrival of the Watchers at Hermon, which has been known since time immemorial as "the mountain of oath."

[16] We should not presume that the Watchers took the women of their choosing by force; rather, as they clearly desired to enter into a covenant of marriage with these maidens, we may surmise that they did so according to the customs of men. In the Ancient Near East, marriage was regarded as a legal contract betwèen the father of the bride and her prospective husband. The contract stipulated a price for the maiden, a dowry of sorts, which was to be paid to her father. Although the text does not specify the details of the transaction, we know that the Watchers taught mankind the secrets they were striving to learn and may therefore infer that this knowledge was given in exchange for the brides. Had the Watchers simply desired to take the woman by force and rape them, which they surely could have done, then there would be no covenant of marriage and no legal contract with the sons of Adam. To understand why such a contract was imperative for the successful execution of the Watcher's plan, see *Birthright: The Coming Posthuman Apocalypse and the Usurpation of Adam's Dominion on Planet Earth* by Timothy Alberino.

[17] The figure given for the giant's height (three thousand ells) may be a corruption from the original manuscript in Aramaic or Hebrew. An ell is equivalent to a cubit, which was roughly the length of one's elbow to the end of the middle finger (approximately 20 inches). By this standard, the height of the giants given in the Ethiopic translation of 1 Enoch would measure some 4,500 feet, which is obviously a gross exaggeration. A creature of such mammoth proportions could not survive in the atmospheric and gravitational conditions of Planet Earth. Some renditions of 1 Enoch register the height of the giants at three hundred cubits, which, although ten times smaller, is still the size of a skyscraper, and much too large to metabolically sustain.

and to devour one another's flesh, and drink the blood.[18] 6. Then the earth laid accusation against the lawless ones.

## Chapter 8.

1. And Azâzêl taught men to make swords, and knives, and shields, and breastplates, and made known to them **the metals** <of the earth> and the art of working them, and bracelets, and ornaments, and the use of antimony, and the beautifying of the eyelids, and all kinds of costly stones, and all coloring tinctures. 2. And there arose much godlessness, and they committed fornication, and they were led astray, and became corrupt in all their ways. 3. Semjâzâ taught enchantments, and root-cuttings, Armârôs the resolving of enchantments, Barâqîjâl (taught) astrology, Kôkabêl the constellations, **Ezêqêêl the knowledge of the clouds**, <Araqiêl the signs of the earth, Shamsiêl the signs of the sun>, and Sariêl the course of the moon.[19] 4. And as men perished, they cried, and their cry went up to heaven ...

## Chapter 9.

1. And then Michael, Uriel, Raphael, and Gabriel looked down from heaven and saw much blood being shed upon the earth, and all lawlessness being wrought upon the earth. 2. And they said one to another: 'The earth, made †without inhabitant, cries the voice of their crying† up to the gates of heaven. 3. <And now to you, the holy ones of heaven>, the souls of men make their suit, saying, "Bring our cause before the Most High."'

4. And they said to the Lord **of the ages**: 'Lord of lords, God of gods,

---

[18] The giants flagrantly transgressed the pre-Flood prohibition against the slaughter and consumption of living creatures. So insatiable were their appetites for flesh and blood that they even resorted to cannibalism.

[19] In many diverse traditions around the world, the origin of civilization is attributed to the gods, or the emissaries of the gods, who instructed mankind in the arts of science and technology. This impartation of divine knowledge is almost universally said to have taken place in the time before the great cataclysm, when the gods dwelt among men in a glorious Golden Age of enlightenment and peace. In stark contrast to the mythologies of the Ancient Near East, and those of nearly all other primeval cultures, the Hebrews depicted the Golden Age as a nightmarish dystopia in which the knowledge of the gods corrupted mankind and wrought chaos on earth.

King of kings <and God of the ages>, the throne of Thy glory (standeth) unto all the generations of the ages, and Thy name holy and glorious and blessed unto all the ages! 5. Thou hast made all things, and power over all things hast Thou: and all things are naked and open in Thy sight, and all things Thou seest, and nothing can hide itself from Thee. 6. Thou seest what Azâzêl hath done, who hath taught all unrighteousness on earth and revealed the eternal secrets which were (preserved) in heaven, which men were striving to **learn**: 7. And Semjâzâ, to whom Thou hast given authority to bear rule over his associates. 8. And they have gone to the daughters of men upon the earth, and have slept with the women, and have defiled themselves, and revealed to them all kinds of sins. 9. And the women have borne giants, and the whole earth has thereby been filled with blood and unrighteousness. 10. And now, behold, the souls of those who have died are crying and making their suit to the gates of heaven, and their lamentations have ascended: and cannot **cease** because of the lawless deeds which are wrought on the earth. 11. And Thou knowest all things before they come to pass, and Thou seest these things and Thou dost suffer them, and Thou dost not say to us what we are to do to them in regard to these.'

## Chapter 10.

1. Then said the Most High, the Holy and Great One spake, and sent **Uriel** to the son of Lamech, and said to him: 2. '<Go to Noah and> tell him in my name "Hide thyself!", and reveal to him the end that is approaching: that the whole earth will be destroyed, and a deluge is about to come upon the whole earth, and will destroy all that is on it. 3. And now instruct him that he may escape and his seed may be preserved for all the generations of the world.'[20] 4. And again the Lord said to Raphael: 'Bind Azâzêl hand and foot,

---

[20] The preservation of Noah's seed (genome) was crucial to the fulfillment of Messianic prophecy concerning a promised child who would one day emerge from the virgin womb of a daughter of Eve to save mankind from their sins and condemnation with the dragon. Had the offspring of Adam and Eve been entirely eradicated in the deluge, then the Messiah could never have been born, and mankind would be hopelessly condemned forever. (See Genesis 3, Revelation 12.)

and cast him into the darkness: and make an opening in the desert, which is in Dûdâêl, and cast him therein.[21] 5. And place upon him rough and jagged rocks, and cover him with darkness, and let him abide there forever, and cover his face that he may not see light.[22] 6. And on the day of the great judgment he shall be cast into the fire.[23] 7. And heal the earth which the angels have corrupted, and proclaim the healing of the earth, that they may heal the plague, and that all the children of men may not perish through all the secret things that the Watchers have **disclosed** and have taught their sons.[24] 8. And the whole earth has been corrupted through the works that were taught by Azâzêl: to him ascribe all sin.'[25] 9. And to Gabriel said the Lord: 'Proceed against the bastards and the reprobates, and against the children of fornication: and destroy [the children of fornication and] the children of the Watchers from amongst men [and cause them to go forth]: send them one against the other that they may destroy each other in battle: for length of days shall they not have. 10. And no request that they (*i.e.* their fathers) make of thee shall be granted

---

[21] The location of Dudael is a mystery. Some scholars believe that Dudael refers to a rocky terrace in the wilderness east of Jerusalem called Bet-hudedun, while others maintain that it is located somewhere in the Eastern Desert of upper Egypt.

[22] Azazel was the chief instructor of mankind. Among other dangerous secrets, he taught men the arts of weaponsmithing and warfare and was therefore held personally responsible for the carnage that ensued. He seems to have been a particularly sadistic character, inciting a murderous bloodlust in the world that had not previously existed. As manslaughter is the gravest of all crimes, Azazel was punished most severely among his brethren.

[23] Cast into the fire prepared for the devil and his angels (See Mathew 25:41.)

[24] The genetic matrix of life on Planet Earth was corrupted through the miscegenous mischief of the Watchers, which may have included cross-species genetic engineering. It is plausible that the plague that Raphael is instructed to heal refers to the propagation of their alien DNA in the gene pools of diverse species, including most catastrophically, homo sapiens. Not surprisingly, the name *Raphael* is derived from the root *rapha*, which means "to heal" or "to mend."

[25] The imputation of sin to Azazel, which derives exclusively from the Book of Enoch, became an important sacrificial ritual conducted on the Day of Atonement by the Aaronic Priesthood. The procedures of the rite are set forth thusly in Leviticus: "Then [Aaron] shall take the two goats and set them before the Lord at the entrance of the tent of meeting. And Aaron shall cast lots over the two goats, one lot for the Lord and the other lot for Azazel. And Aaron shall present the goat on which the lot fell for the Lord and use it as a sin offering, but the goat on which the lot fell for Azazel shall be presented alive before the Lord to make atonement over it, that it may be sent away into the wilderness to Azazel" (Leviticus 16:7–10, ESV).

unto their fathers on their behalf; for they hope to live an eternal life, and that each one of them will live five hundred years.'[26] 11. And the Lord said unto Michael: 'Go, **bind** Semjâzâ and his associates who have united themselves with women so as to have defiled themselves with them in all their uncleanness. 12. And, when their sons have slain one another, and they have seen the destruction of their beloved ones, bind them fast for seventy generations in the **valleys** of the earth, till the day of their judgment and of their consummation, till the judgment that is forever and ever is consummated.[27] 13. In those days they shall be led off to the abyss of fire: <and> to the torment and the prison in which they shall be confined forever. 14. And whosoever shall be **condemned** and destroyed will from thenceforth be bound together with them to the end of all generations.[28] 15. And destroy all the spirits of the reprobate, and the children of the Watchers, because they have wronged mankind. 16. Destroy all wrong from the face of the earth, and let every evil work come to an end and let the plant of righteousness and truth appear: {and it shall prove a blessing: the works of righteousness and truth shall} be planted in truth and joy for evermore.

17. And then shall all the righteous escape, and shall live till they beget thousands of children, and all the days of their youth and their

---

[26] Apparently, the sons of the Watchers had desired a lifespan of five hundred years followed by a resurrection and eternal life in heaven. Isaiah may be referencing the immutable destruction of the giants (Rephaim) when he writes: "Dead—they do not live, Rephaim, they do not rise, therefore You have inspected and destroy them, indeed, you destroy all their memory" (Isaiah 26:14, LSV).

[27] Some commentators believe that when seventy generations has elapsed, the Watchers will be released from their incarceration in the bowels of the earth to wreak havoc in the world once again during the end times. This position seems untenable, as the Watchers are explicitly bound *until* the day of their judgment, which is presumably the same day that all the living and the dead will be judged when Christ returns. Attempts to calculate the duration of the Watchers' prison sentence is somewhat futile as there is no consensus among scholars regarding the length of a generation, which varies throughout the biblical text. Moreover, seventy generations may not represent a literal calculation of time but a symbolization for the completion of time (the number seven is symbolic of completion in Hebrew cosmology).

[28] The notion that that unrighteous men will be condemned with fallen angels is affirmed by Jesus during the Olivet Discourse: "You that are accursed, depart from me into the eternal fire prepared for the devil and his angels" (Matthew 25:41, NRSV).

**old age** shall they complete in peace.[29]

18. And then shall the whole earth be tilled in righteousness, and shall all be planted with trees and be full of blessing. 19. And all desirable trees shall be planted on it, and they shall plant vines on it: and the vine which they plant thereon shall yield wine in abundance, and as for all the seed which is sown thereon each measure (of it) shall bear a thousand, and each measure of olives shall yield ten presses of oil. 20. And cleanse thou the earth from all oppression, and from all unrighteousness, and from all sin, and from all godlessness: and all the uncleanness that is wrought upon the earth destroy from off the earth. 21. {And all the children of men shall become righteous,} and all nations shall offer adoration and shall praise Me, and all shall worship Me. 22. And the earth shall be cleansed from all defilement, and from all sin, and from all punishment, and from all torment, and I will never again send (them) upon it from generation to generation and forever.

## Chapter 11.

1. And in those days I will open the store chambers of blessing which are in the heaven, so as to send them down {upon the earth} over the work and labor of the children of men. 2. And truth and peace shall be associated together throughout all the days of the world and throughout all the generations **of men**.'

## Chapter 12.

1. Before these things Enoch was hidden, and no one of the children of men knew where he was hidden, and where he abode, and what had become of him.[30] 2. And his activities had to do with the Watchers, and his days were with the holy ones.

3. And I, Enoch, was blessing the Lord of **majesty** and the King of the ages, and lo! the Watchers called me—Enoch the scribe—and

---

[29] The righteous who escape to beget thousands of children is clearly in reference of Noah and his family, who are predestined to survive the impending deluge and repopulate the earth.

[30] This sudden absence of Enoch among the sons of Adam may provide context for the enigmatic entry in Genesis 5:24: "Enoch walked with God; and he was not, for God took him" (NASB).

said to me:[31] 4. 'Enoch, thou scribe of righteousness,[32] go, †declare†
to the Watchers of the heaven who have left the high heaven, the holy
eternal place, and have defiled themselves with women, and have
done as the children of the earth do, and have taken unto themselves
wives: "Ye have wrought great destruction on the earth: 5. and ye shall
have no peace nor forgiveness of sin: and inasmuch as †they† delight
themselves in †their† children, 6. the murder of †their† beloved ones
shall †they† see, and over the destruction of †their† children shall
†they† lament, and shall make supplication unto eternity, but mercy
and peace shall ye not attain."'

## Chapter 13.

1. And Enoch went and said: 'Azâzêl, thou shalt have no peace: a
severe sentence has gone forth against thee to put thee in bonds: 2.
and thou shalt not have toleration nor †request† granted to thee,
because of the unrighteousness which thou hast taught, and because
of all the works of godlessness and unrighteousness and sin which
thou hast shown to men.' 3. Then I went and spoke to them all
together, and they were all afraid, and fear and trembling seized them.
4. And they besought me to draw up a petition for them that they
might find forgiveness, and to read their petition in the presence of
the Lord of heaven.[33] 5. For from thenceforward they could not speak

---

[31] Notice that Enoch is not summoned by Yahweh but by the Watchers of heaven, who are
convening to judge the actions of their apostate brethren on earth. This scene is reminiscent
of Daniel 4, in which a council of Watchers presides in judgment over Nebuchadnezzar,
the haughty king of Babylon. Just as Daniel acted as the intermediary in the case of Nebuchadnezzar, so Enoch acted as the intermediary in the case of the apostate Watchers. That
Enoch is called a scribe suggests that he was already the author of some unknown manuscript previous to penning the book which bears his name.

[32] It is interesting that Enoch is called a scribe of righteousness. The name Enoch (חֲנוֹךְ) means
"initiated" or "initiating," which corresponds to what was revealed to him and what he transcribed for posterity. Enoch was initiated into the mysteries of the gospel of Christ, the Son
of God who was to be born into the world as a Son of Man (a kinsman redeemer) in order
to deliver mankind from condemnation with the devil and his angels (i.e., the Watchers).
The Book of Enoch is, essentially, a revelation of Jesus Christ.

[33] As mankind was given dominion of Planet Earth (see Genesis 1:26–28), it was appropriate that a son of Adam should be chosen to act as an intermediary between the council of
heaven and the apostate Watchers, who had transgressed in Adam's realm. For more insight
on the politics of dominion in the biblical narrative, see Timothy Alberino, *Birthright: The
Coming Posthuman Apocalypse and the Usurpation of Adam's Dominion on Planet Earth.*

(with Him) nor lift up their eyes to heaven for shame of their sins for which they had been condemned. 6. Then I wrote out their petition, and the prayer †in regard to their spirits and their deeds individually and in regard to their requests that they should have forgiveness and length <of day>†. 7. And I went off and sat down at the waters of Dan, in the land of Dan, to the south of the west of Hermon: I read their petition till I fell asleep.[34] 8. And behold a dream came to me, and visions fell down upon me, and I saw visions of chastisement, {and a voice came bidding (me)} to tell it to the sons of heaven, and reprimand them. 9. And when I awaked, I came unto them, and they were all sitting gathered together, weeping in 'Abelsjâîl, which is between Lebanon and Sênêsêr, with their faces covered.[35] 10. And I recounted before them all the visions which I had seen in sleep, and I began to speak the words of righteousness, and to reprimand the heavenly Watchers.

## Chapter 14.

1. The book of the words of righteousness, and of the reprimand of the eternal Watchers in accordance with the command of the Holy Great One, in that vision. 2. I saw in my sleep what I will now say with a tongue of flesh and with the breath of my mouth: which the Great One has given to men to converse therewith and understand with the heart. 3. As He has created and given <to man the power of understanding the word of wisdom, so hath He created me also and

---

[34] That Enoch chooses to read aloud the petition of the apostate Watchers at the waters of Dan is perhaps more portentous than it may first appear. Located in upper Galilee and extending through Caesarea Philippi to Mount Hermon, the land of Dan has always been considered as sacred territory to the ancient people of the Levant; even the Greeks and Romans, recognizing its significance, erected various shrines and temples around the base of Hermon. It was widely believed that this area acted as a mystical gate to heaven and hell, through which contact with these realms could be effectuated. It was here, on the southern slopes of Hermon, that Jesus transfigured before his disciples (see Matthew 17, Mark 9, Luke 9), and here also where he stood in front of the *Paneion*, a sacred grotto dedicated to the Greek god Pan, and declared that the gates of hell would not prevail against his church (see Matthew 16).

[35] Lebanon likely refers to Mount Lebanon, and Seneser (Senir) is another name for Mount Hermon. It just so happens that an imposing megalithic complex is located between these two mountains—Baalbek. It is conceivable that the megalithic foundations of Baalbek are the remnants of an enormous temple built for the Watchers in the pre-Flood world.

given> me the power of reprimanding the Watchers, the children of heaven.[36] 4. I wrote out your petition, and in my vision it appeared thus, that your petition will not be granted unto you <throughout all the days of eternity, and that judgment has been finally passed upon you: yea (your petition) will not be granted unto you>. 5. And from henceforth you shall not ascend into heaven unto all eternity, and {in bonds} of the earth the decree has gone forth to bind you for all the days of the world.[37] 6. And (that) previously you shall have seen the destruction of your beloved sons and you shall have no pleasure in them, but they shall fall before you by the sword. 7. And your petition on their behalf shall not be granted, nor yet on your own: even though you weep and pray and **speak all the words** contained in the writing which I have written. 8. And the vision was shown to me thus: behold, in the vision clouds invited me and a mist summoned me, and the course of the stars and the lightning sped and **hastened** me, and the winds in the vision caused me to fly and lifted me upward, and bore me into heaven.[38] 9. And I went in till I drew nigh to a wall which is built of crystals and surrounded by tongues of fire: and it began to affright me.[39] 10. And I went into the tongues of fire and drew nigh to a large house which was built of crystals: and the walls of the house were like a tesselated floor (made) of crystals, and its

---

[36] Enoch's power to reprimand the Watchers is a function of his authority as a son of Adam on earth. While instructing the Corinthians in regard to how they ought to judge one another, Paul alludes to the remarkable authority invested in mankind: "Do you not know," he writes, "that we are to judge angels? How much more, then, matters pertaining to this life!" (1 Corinthians 6:3, ESV). The angels to whom Paul refers are likely these same Watchers who unlawfully interloped into man's domain and will be subject to judgment by the sons of Adam at the end of the age. (See Timothy Alberino, *Birthright: The Coming Posthuman Apocalypse and the Usurpation of Adam's Dominion on Planet Earth.*)

[37] Here again we read that the Watchers will be bound until the consummation of time ("all the days of the world"), which negates the notion that they will be released from their bondage before the great judgment.

[38] The tradition that Enoch ascended bodily into heaven, long held by the Christian church, is likely misconstrued from his visions of heaven, which he received in a dream while sleeping beside the Dan River. Jesus of Nazareth, who identified himself as the Son of Man from the oracles of Enoch, leaves no room for doubt regarding the matter: "No one has ascended into heaven except he who descended from heaven, the Son of Man" (John 3:13, ESV).

[39] Enoch's visions of heaven are intended to authenticate his message to the Watchers, who would have recognized the scenes and symbolism and understood their meaning.

groundwork was of crystal. 11. Its ceiling was like the path of the stars and the lightnings, and between them were fiery cherubim, and their heaven was (clear as) water. 12. A flaming fire surrounded the walls, and its portals blazed with fire. 13. And I entered into that house, and it was hot as fire and cold as ice: there were no delights of life therein: fear covered me, and trembling gat hold upon me. 14. And as I quaked and trembled, I fell upon my face. And I beheld a vision, 15. and lo! there was a second house, greater than the former, and the entire portal stood open before me, and it was built of flames of fire. 16. And in every respect it so excelled in splendor and magnificence and extent that I cannot describe to you its splendor and its extent. 17. And its floor was of fire, and above it were lightnings and the path of the stars, and its ceiling also was flaming fire. 18. And I looked and saw ‹therein› a lofty throne: its appearance was as crystal, and the wheels thereof as the shining sun, and there was the **vision** of cherubim. 19. And from underneath the throne came streams of flaming fire so that I could not look thereon. 20. And the Great Glory sat thereon, and His raiment shone more brightly than the sun and was whiter than any snow.[40] 21. None of the angels could enter and could behold His face by reason of the magnificence and glory, and no flesh could behold Him. 22. The flaming fire was round about Him, and a great fire stood before Him, and none around could draw nigh Him:[41] ten thousand times ten thousand (stood) before Him, yet He needed no counselor.[42] 23. And the most holy ones who were nigh to Him did not leave by night nor depart from Him.[43] 24. And until then I had been prostrate on my face, trembling: and the

---

[40] Daniel beholds a similar vision of the throne of God in heaven: "The Ancient of Days was seated; His garment was white as snow, and the hair of His head was like pure wool. His throne was a fiery flame, its wheels a burning fire; a fiery stream issued and came forth from before Him. A thousand thousands ministered to Him; ten thousand times ten thousand stood before Him" (Daniel 7:9–10, NKJV).

[41] Enoch's vision of the Great Glory, before whom no man could draw nigh or even behold, was likely the source text for Paul's affirmation, "He who is the blessed and only Potentate, the King of kings and Lord of lords, who alone has immortality, dwelling in unapproachable light, whom no man has seen or can see" (1 Timothy 6:16, NKJV).

[42] See Daniel 7:10 and Revelation 5:11.

[43] Probably the cherubim. (See Revelation 4:8.)

Lord called me with His own mouth, and said to me: 'Come hither, Enoch, and hear my word.' 25. {And one of the holy ones came to me and waked me}, and He made me rise up and approach the door: and I bowed my face downwards.

## Chapter 15.

1. And He answered and said to me, and I heard His voice: 'Fear not, Enoch, thou righteous man and scribe of righteousness: approach hither and hear my voice. 2. And go, say to ‹the Watchers of heaven,› who have sent thee to intercede ‹for them: "You should intercede› for men, and not men for you: 3. wherefore have ye left the high, holy, and eternal heaven, and lain with women, and defiled yourselves with the daughters of men and taken to yourselves wives, and done like the children of earth, and begotten giants (as your) sons?[44] 4. And though ye were holy, spiritual, living the eternal life, you have defiled yourselves with the blood of women, and have begotten (children) with the blood of flesh, and, **as the children** of men, have lusted after flesh and blood as those {also} do who die and perish. 5. Therefore have I given them wives also that they might impregnate them, and beget children by them, that thus nothing might be wanting to them on earth. 6. But you were {formerly} spiritual, living the eternal life, and immortal for all generations of the world. 7. And therefore I have not appointed wives for you; for as for the spiritual ones of the heaven, in heaven is their dwelling. 8. And now, the giants, who are produced from the spirits and flesh, shall be called evil spirits upon the earth, and on the earth shall be their dwelling. 9. Evil spirits have proceeded from their bodies; because they are born from **men**, ‹and› from the holy Watchers is their beginning and primal origin; {they shall be evil spirits on earth, and} evil spirits shall they be called.[45] [10. As for the spirits of heaven, in heaven shall be their dwelling,

---

[44] This verse provides the context for Jude's reference to the "angels who did not keep their proper domain, but left their own abode, [whom] he has reserved in everlasting chains under darkness for the judgment of the great day" (Jude 1:6, ESV).

[45] This is the origin of demons in Hebrew cosmology. In the New Testament these evil spirits are called "unclean spirits" and are the same that were exorcised from the bodies of their human hosts by Jesus and his disciples.

but as for the spirits of the earth which were born upon the earth, on the earth shall be their dwelling.] 11. And the spirits of the giants **afflict**, oppress, destroy, attack, do battle, and work destruction on the earth, and cause trouble: they take no food, {but nevertheless hunger} and thirst, and cause offences.[46] 12. And these spirits shall rise up against the children of men and against the women, because they have proceeded {from them}.

Chapter 16.

1. From the days of the slaughter and destruction and death {of the giants}, from the souls of whose flesh the spirits, having gone forth, shall destroy without incurring judgment—thus shall they destroy until the day of the consummation, the great {judgment} in which the age shall be consummated over the Watchers and the godless, yea, shall be wholly consummated."[47] 2. And now as to the Watchers who have sent thee to intercede for them, who had been <aforetime> in heaven, (say to them): 3. "You have been in heaven, but {all} the mysteries had not yet been revealed to you, and you knew worthless ones, and these in the hardness of your hearts you have made known to the women, and through these mysteries women and men work much evil on earth." 4. Say to them therefore: "You have no peace.'"

---

[46] A terrible curse was placed upon the unsanctioned hybrid offspring of the Watchers; upon death, their spirits would persist in the world as vagabond wraiths. Doomed to wander the earth disembodied, but still afflicted with the desires of the flesh, the evil spirits of the giants would forever seek to possess human bodies in order to alleviate their insatiable hunger and unquenchable thirst.

[47] The cursed spirits of the giants are doomed to roam the earth in a condition of disembodiment until the appointed day of judgment when they will be held accountable for their evil deeds and punished together with their fathers. It is in light of this verse from the Book of Enoch that we may understand the shock and horror of the demons who confronted Jesus of Nazareth on the shores of Galilee: "'What do you want with us, Son of God?' they shouted. 'Have you come here to torture us before the appointed time?" (Matthew 8:29, NIV). This legion of demons, who had possessed the bodies of two unfortunate men, immediately recognized Jesus as the Son of God, and thus, the great judge who will preside over the judgment of the last day, which they knew had not yet come. (See Matthew 8).

*Enoch's Journeys through the Earth and Sheol*

## Chapter 17.

1. And they took {and} brought me to a place in which those who were there were like flaming fire, and when they wished, they appeared as men.[48] 2. And they brought me to the place of darkness, and to a mountain the point of whose summit reached to heaven. 3. And I saw the places of the luminaries {and the treasuries of the stars} and of the thunder, {and} in the **uttermost depths**, where were a fiery bow and arrows and their quiver, ‹and a fiery sword› and all the lightnings. 4. And they took me to the living waters, and to the fire of the west, which receives every setting of the sun. 5. And I came to a river of fire in which the fire flows like water and discharges itself into the great sea towards the west. 6. I saw the great rivers and came to the great {river and to the great} darkness, and went to the place where no flesh walks. 7. I saw the mountains of the darkness of winter and the place whence all the waters of the deep flow. 8. I saw the mouths of all the rivers of the earth and the mouth of the deep.

## Chapter 18.

1. I saw the treasuries of all the winds; I saw how He had furnished with them the whole creation and the firm foundations of the earth. 2. And I saw the cornerstone of the earth: I saw the four winds which bear {the earth and} the firmament of the heaven. 3. ‹And I saw how the winds stretch out the vaults of heaven,› and have their station between heaven and earth: ‹these are the pillars of the heaven.› 4. I saw the winds of heaven which turn and bring the circumference of the sun and all the stars to their setting. 5. I saw the winds on the earth carrying the clouds: I saw ‹the paths of the angels: I saw› at the end of the earth the firmament of the heaven above. 6. And I proceeded and saw a place which burns day and night, where there are seven mountains of magnificent stones, three towards the east, and three

---

[48] It is important to recognize that Enoch's journeys through the earth and Sheol are happening within the context of a visionary experience; hence, the things he is shown are subject to interpretation and not to be taken literally.

towards the south.[49] 7. And as for those towards the east <one> was of colored stone, and one of pearl, and one of **jacinth**, and those towards the south of red stone. 8. But the middle one reached to heaven like the throne of God, of alabaster, and the summit of the throne was of sapphire. 9. And I saw a flaming fire. And beyond these mountains 10. is a region, the end of the great earth: there the heavens were completed. 11. And I saw a deep abyss, with columns <of heavenly fire, and among them I saw columns> of fire fall, which were beyond measure alike towards the height and towards the depth.[50] 12. And beyond that abyss I saw a place which had no firmament of the heaven above, and no firmly founded earth beneath it: there was no water upon it, and no birds, but it was a waste and horrible place. 13. I saw there seven stars like great burning mountains,[51] and to me, when I inquired regarding them, 14. the angel said: 'This place is the end of heaven and earth: this has become a prison for the stars and the host of heaven. 15. And the stars which roll over the fire are they which have transgressed the commandment of the Lord in the beginning of their rising, because they did not come forth at their appointed times. 16. And He was wroth with them, and bound them till the time when their guilt should be consummated (even) {for ten thousand years.}'

## Chapter 19.

1. And Uriel said to me: 'Here shall stand the angels who have connected themselves with women, and their spirits, assuming many different forms, are defiling mankind, and shall lead them astray into sacrificing to demons <as gods,> (here shall they stand), till <the day of> the great judgment in which they shall be judged till they are made an end of. 2. And the women also of the angels who went

---

[49] The seven mountains of magnificent stones may refer to planets. (See Ezekiel 28:14.)

[50] Probably a vision of Tartarus.

[51] Represented in the seven-headed dragon from Revelation 12, these seven burning stars may refer to the original seven fallen angels who first rebelled against the King of heaven in the pre-Adamic world. (See Timothy Alberino, *Birthright: The Coming Posthuman Apocalypse and the Usurpation of Adam's Dominion on Planet Earth.*)

astray shall become sirens.'[52] 3. And I, Enoch, alone saw the vision, the ends of all things: and no man shall see as I have seen.

## Chapter 20.

1. And these are the names of the holy angels who watch. 2. Uriel, one of the holy angels, who is over the world and over Tartarus. 3. Raphael, one of the holy angels, who is over the spirits of men. 4. Raguel, one of the holy angels who †takes vengeance on† the world of the luminaries. 5. Michael, one of the holy angels, to wit, he that is set over the best part of mankind <and> over chaos. 6. Saraqâêl, one of the holy angels, who is set over the spirits, who sin in the spirit. 7. Gabriel, one of the holy angels, who is over Paradise and the serpents and the cherubim. 8. Remiel, one of the holy angels, whom God set over those who rise.

## Chapter 21.

1. And I proceeded to where things were chaotic. 2. And I saw there something horrible: I saw neither a heaven above nor a firmly founded earth, but a place chaotic and horrible. 3. And there I saw seven stars of the heaven bound together in it, like great mountains and burning with fire. 4. Then I said: 'For what sin are they bound, and on what account have they been cast in hither?' 5. Then said Uriel, one of the holy angels, who was with me, and was chief over them, and said: 'Enoch, why dost thou ask, and why art thou eager for the truth? 6. These are of the number of the stars {of heaven} which have transgressed the commandment of the Lord, and are bound here till ten thousand years, the time entailed by their sins, are consummated.' 7. And from thence I went to another place, which was still more horrible than the former, and I saw a horrible thing: a great fire there which burnt and blazed, and the place was cleft as far as the abyss, being full of great descending columns of fire: neither its extent or magnitude could I see, nor could I conjecture.

---

[52] The wives were apparently willing participants in their husband's (the Watchers) transgressions and were punished accordingly, which supports the supposition that they were not taken by force but eager to wed the extraterrestrial interlopers.

8. Then I said: 'How fearful is the place and how terrible to look upon!' 9. Then Uriel answered me, one of the holy angels who was with me, and said unto me: 'Enoch, why hast thou such fear and affright?' And I answered: 'Because of this fearful place, and because of the spectacle of the pain.' 10. And he said <unto me>: 'This place is the prison of the angels, and here they will be imprisoned forever.'

## Chapter 22.

1. And thence I went to another place, and he showed me in the west {another} great and high mountain [and] of hard rock.

| E | G<sup>g</sup> |

| E | Gᵍ |
|---|---|
| 2. And there was in it †four† **hollow** places, deep and wide and very smooth. †How† smooth are **the hollow places** and deep and dark to look at. | 2. And there were †four† hollow places in it, deep and very smooth: †three† of them were dark and one bright; and there was a fountain of water in its midst. And I said: '†How† smooth are these hollow places, and deep and dark to view.' |

3. Then Raphael answered, one of the holy angels who was with me, and said unto me: 'These hollow places have been created for this very purpose, that the spirits of the souls of the dead should assemble therein, yea that all the souls of the children of men should assemble here. And these places **have been made** to receive them till the day of their judgment and till their appointed period [till the period appointed], till the great judgment (comes) upon them.'[53]

| E | Gᵍ |
|---|---|
| 5. I saw the spirits of the children of men who were dead, and their voice went forth to heaven and made suit. | 5. I saw <the spirit of> **a dead man** making suit, and his voice went forth to heaven and made suit. |

---

[53] Evinced in the verses that follow, Enoch's vision of Sheol provides the context for Christ's parable of the rich man and Lazarus in Luke 16.

6. Then I asked Raphael the angel who was with me, and I said unto him: 'This spirit—whose is it whose voice goeth forth and maketh suit?'

6. And I asked Raphael the angel who was with me, and I said unto him: 'This spirit which maketh suit, whose is it, whose voice goeth forth and maketh suit to heaven?'

7. And he answered me saying: 'This is the spirit which went forth from Abel, whom his brother Cain slew, and he makes his suit against him till his seed is destroyed from the face of the earth, and his seed is annihilated from amongst the seed of men.'

| E | G<sup>g</sup> |

8. Then I asked regarding it, and regarding all the **hollow places**: 'Why is one separated from the other?'

8. Then I asked regarding all the **hollow places**: 'Why is one separated from the other?'

9. And he answered me and said unto me: 'These three have been made that the spirits of the dead might be separated. And such a division has been made <for> the spirits of the righteous, in which there is the **bright** spring of water. 10. **And** such has been made for sinners when they die and are buried in the earth and judgment has not been executed on them in their lifetime. 11. Here their spirits shall be set apart in this great pain till the great day of judgment and punishment and torment of those who †curse† forever,

9. And he answered me saying: 'These three have been made that the spirits of the dead might be separated. And **this** division has been made for the spirits of the righteous, in which there is the bright spring of water. 10. And **this** has been made for sinners when they die and are buried in the earth and judgment has not been executed upon them in their lifetime. 11. Here their spirits shall be set apart in this great pain, till the great day of judgment, scourgings, and torments of the accursed forever,

and retribution for their spirits.[54] There He shall bind them forever. 12. And such a division has been made for the spirits of those who make their suit, who make disclosures concerning their destruction, when they were slain in the days of the sinners. 13. Such has been made for the spirits of men who were not righteous but sinners, who were complete in transgression, and of the transgressors they shall be companions: but their spirits shall not be slain in the day of judgment nor shall they be raised from thence.' 14. Then I blessed the Lord of glory and said: 'Blessed be my Lord, the Lord of righteousness, who ruleth forever.'

**so that** (there may be) retribution for their spirits. There He shall bind them forever. 12. And this division has been made for the spirits of those who make their suit, who make disclosures concerning their destruction, when they were slain in the days of the sinners. 13. And this has been made for the spirits of men who shall not be righteous but sinners, who are godless, and of the lawless they shall be companions: but their spirits shall not be punished in the day of judgment nor shall they be raised from thence.' 14. Then I blessed the Lord of Glory and said: 'Blessed art Thou, Lord of righteousness, who rulest over the world.'

## Chapter 23.

1. From thence I went to another place to the west of the ends of the earth. 2. And I saw a <burning> fire which ran without resting, and paused not from its course day or night but (ran) regularly. 3. And I asked saying: 'What is this which rests not?' 4. Then Raguel, one of the holy angels who was with me, answered me <and said unto me>: 'This course {of fire} <which thou hast seen> is the fire in the west which †persecutes† all the luminaries of heaven.'

---

[54] The division of Sheol into a pleasant place of rest for the righteous dead and a hellish place of torment for the unrighteous dead is a distinctive feature of Second Temple Judaism, to which these passages may belong.

## Chapter 24.

1. ‹And from thence I went to another place of the earth›, and he showed me a mountain range of fire which burnt ‹day and› night. 2. And I went beyond it and saw seven magnificent mountains all differing each from the other, and the stones (thereof) were magnificent and beautiful, magnificent as a whole, of glorious appearance and fair exterior: ‹three towards› the east, ‹one› founded on the other, and three towards the south, ‹one› upon the other, and deep rough ravines, no one of which joined with any other. 3. And the seventh mountain was in the midst of these, and it excelled them in height, resembling the seat of a throne: and fragrant trees encircled the throne. 4. And amongst them was a tree such as I had never yet smelt, neither was any amongst them nor were others like it: it had a fragrance beyond all fragrance, and its leaves and blooms and wood wither not forever: and its fruit ‹is beautiful, and its fruit› resembles the dates of a palm.[55] 5. Then I said: '{How} beautiful is this tree, and fragrant, and its leaves are fair, and its blooms ‹very› delightful in appearance.' 6. Then answered Michael, one of the holy ‹and honored› angels who was with me, and was their leader,

## Chapter 25.

1. And he said unto me: 'Enoch, why dost thou ask me regarding the fragrance of the tree, and {why} dost thou wish to learn the truth?' 2. Then I answered him, ‹saying›: 'I wish to know about everything, but especially about this tree.' 3. And he answered, saying: 'This high mountain ‹which thou hast seen›, whose summit is like the throne of God, is His throne, where the Holy Great One, the Lord of Glory, the Eternal King will sit, when He shall come down to visit the earth with goodness. 4. And as for this fragrant tree no mortal is permitted to touch it till the great judgment, when He shall take vengeance on all and bring (everything) to its consummation forever. It shall then be given to the righteous and holy. 5. Its fruit **shall be** for food to

---

[55] As in the biblical text, the abode of Yahweh is depicted in the Book of Enoch as both a mountain and a garden.

the elect: it shall be transplanted to the holy place, to the temple of the Lord, the Eternal King.

6. Then shall they rejoice with joy and be glad. And into the holy place shall they enter; and its fragrance shall be in their bones, and they shall live a long life on earth, such as thy fathers lived: and in their days shall no <sorrow or> plague or torment or calamity touch them.'[56]

7. Then blessed I the God of Glory, the Eternal King, who hath prepared such things for the righteous, and hath created them and promised to give to them.

## Chapter 26.

1. And I went from thence to the middle of the earth, and I saw a blessed place {in which there were trees} with branches abiding and blooming [of a dismembered tree]. 2. And there I saw a holy mountain, <and> underneath the mountain to the east there was a stream and it flowed towards the south. 3. And I saw towards the east another mountain higher than this, and between them a deep and narrow ravine: in it also ran a stream {underneath} the mountain. 4. And to the west thereof there was another mountain, lower than the former and of small elevation, and a ravine {deep and dry} between them: and another deep and dry ravine was at the extremities of the three {mountains}. 5. And all the ravines were deep <and narrow>, (being formed) of hard rock, and trees were not planted upon them. 6. And I marveled <at the rocks, and I marveled> at the ravine, yea, I marveled very much.

## Chapter 27.

1. Then said I: 'For what object is this blessed land, which is entirely filled with trees, and this accursed valley <between?>' 2. <Then Uriel, one of the holy angels who was with me, answered and said: 'This> accursed valley is for those who are accursed forever: here shall all

---

[56] In Hebrew cosmology, the tree of life represents the rectification of the human condition (i.e., sin and death) and the restoration of the Edenic order on Planet Earth. (See Revelation 22:1–2.)

{the accursed} be gathered together who utter with their lips against the Lord unseemly words and of His glory speak hard things.

| E | G$^g$ |
|---|---|
| Here shall they be gathered together, and here shall be their place of judgment. 3. In the last days there shall be upon them the spectacle of righteous judgment in the presence of the righteous forever: here shall the merciful bless the Lord of Glory, the Eternal King. | Here shall they be gathered together, and here shall be the place of their habitation. 3. In the last times, in the days of the true judgment in the presence of the righteous forever: here shall the **godly** bless the Lord of Glory, the Eternal King. |

4. In the days of judgment over the former, they shall bless Him for the mercy in accordance with which He has assigned them (their lot).' 5. Then I blessed the Lord of Glory and set forth His {glory} and lauded Him gloriously.

## Chapter 28.

1. And thence I went ‹towards the east›, into the midst ‹of the mountain range› of the desert, and I saw a wilderness and it was solitary, full of trees **and plants**. 2. ‹And› water gushed forth from above. 3. Rushing like a copious watercourse [which flowed] towards the northwest it caused **clouds** and dew to ascend on every side.

## Chapter 29.

1. And thence I went to another place in the desert, and approached to the east of this mountain range. 2. And ‹there› I saw **aromatic** trees exhaling the fragrance of frankincense and myrrh, and the trees also were similar to the almond tree.

## Chapter 30.

1. And beyond these, I went afar to the east, and I saw another place, a valley (full) of water. 2. And {therein there was} a tree, the color (?) of fragrant trees such as the mastic. 3. And on the sides of those valleys I saw fragrant cinnamon. And beyond these I proceeded to the east.

## Chapter 31.

1. And I saw other mountains, and amongst them were {groves of} trees, and there flowed forth from them nectar, which is named sarara and galbanum. 2. And beyond these mountains I saw another mountain {to the east of the ends of the earth}, <whereon were aloe trees>, and all the trees were full **of stacte**, being like almond trees. 3. And when one **burnt** it, it smelt sweeter than any fragrant odor.

## Chapter 32.

E

1. And after these fragrant odors, as I looked towards the north over the mountains I saw seven mountains full of choice nard and fragrant trees and cinnamon and pepper.

G^g

1. To the northeast I beheld seven mountains full of choice nard and mastic and cinnamon and pepper.

2. And thence I went over the summits of {all} these mountains, far towards the east {of the earth} and passed above the Erythraean sea, and went far from it, and passed over <the angel> Zotîêl.

E

3. And I came to the Garden of Righteousness, and saw beyond those trees many large trees growing there and of goodly fragrance, large, very beautiful and glorious, and the tree of wisdom whereof they eat and know great wisdom.[57]

G^g

3. And I came to the Garden of Righteousness, and from afar off trees more numerous than these trees and great—†two† trees there, very great, beautiful, and glorious, and magnificent, and the tree of knowledge, whose holy fruit they eat and know great wisdom.

---

[57] The Garden of Righteousness is an epithet for the Garden of Eden. Here, presumably, the angels (and/or perhaps the resurrected righteous) are permitted to partake of the tree of knowledge.

4. {That tree is in height like the fir, and its leaves are} like (those of) the Carob tree: and its fruit is like the clusters of the vine, very beautiful: and the fragrance of the tree penetrates afar. 5. Then I said: '{How} beautiful is the tree, and how attractive is its look!' 6. Then Raphael, the holy angel who was with me, answered me <and said>: 'This is the tree of wisdom, of which thy father old (in years) and thy aged mother, who were before thee, have eaten, and they learnt wisdom and their eyes were opened, and they knew that they were naked and they were driven out of the garden.'

## Chapter 33.

1. And from thence I went to the ends of the earth and saw there great beasts, and each differed from the other; and (I saw) birds also differing in appearance and beauty and voice, the one differing from the other. 2. And to the east of those beasts I saw the ends of the earth whereon the heaven rests, and the portals of the heaven open. 3. And I saw how the stars of heaven come forth, and I counted the portals out of which they proceed, and wrote down all their outlets, of each individual star by itself, according to their number and their names, their courses and their positions, and their times and their months, as Uriel the holy angel who was with me showed me. 4. He showed all things to me and wrote them down for me: also their names he wrote for me, and their laws and their companies.

## Chapter 34.

1. And from thence I went towards the north to the ends of the earth, and there I saw a great and glorious device at the ends of the whole earth. 2. And here I saw three portals of heaven open in the heaven: through each of them proceed north winds: when they blow there is cold, hail, frost, snow, dew, and rain. 3. And out of one portal they blow for good: but when they blow through the other two portals, †it is with violence and affliction on the earth, and they blow with violence.†

## Chapter 35.

1. And from thence I went towards the west to the ends of the earth, and saw there three portals of the heaven open such as I had seen in the †east†, the same number of portals, and the same number of outlets.

## Chapter. 36.

1. And from thence I went to the south to the ends of the earth, and saw there three open portals of the heaven: and thence there come dew, rain, †and wind†. 2. And from thence I went to the east to the ends of the heaven, and saw here the three eastern portals of heaven open and small portals above them. 3. Through each of these small portals pass the stars of heaven and run their course to the west on the path which is shown to them. 4. And as often as I saw I blessed always the Lord of Glory, and I continued to bless the Lord of Glory who has wrought great and glorious wonders, to show the greatness of His work to the angels and to **spirits** and to men, that they might praise His work and all His creation: that they might see the work of His might and praise the great work of His hands and bless Him forever.

### The Watchers descend on Mount Hermon.

We should resist the temptation to envision the Watchers descending from heaven with feathery wings flapping in the wind. Except in the context of prophetic iconography (which is subject to interpretation), the angels in the Book of Enoch, as those in the biblical narrative, are never depicted with wings. They are, however, clearly in possession of extraordinary scientific knowledge and, presumably, mechanical technology derived from the same. We might, then, imagine the Watchers appearing in the atmosphere above Mount Hermon at the helms of advanced aerospace vehicles, what we would describe today as *UFOs*, perhaps even through the facilitation of a portal (i.e., a traversable wormhole) instantly bridging the distance between far-flung galactic domains or parallel dimensions.

In the cosmologies of the Ancient Near East, Mount Hermon was considered to be an *axis mundi*—a cosmic gateway where the realms of heaven, Earth, and the underworld converged, and through which contact with the gods could be effectuated. The Sumerians believed that the gods occasionally reposed in a luxurious garden on the summit of Hermon while deliberating matters relating to mankind. The Canaanites, likewise, imagined *El*, the supreme deity in their pantheon, holding court with his divine assembly at the same location. In the Hebrew tradition, Mount Hermon was thought to conceal a mystical entrance into the netherworld. Not coincidentally, it was upon the high slopes of Hermon that Jesus of Nazareth transfigured before his disciples, who beheld a vision of the deceased patriarchs Moses and Elijah, and at the base of Hermon where he declared that the gates of hell would not prevail against his church (see Matthew 16–17).

For more insight into this perspective, read *Birthright: The Coming Posthuman Apocalypse and the Usurpation of Adam's Dominion on Planet Earth*, by Timothy Alberino.

## The Watchers wed the daughters of men.

The sexual desire of the angels in the Book of Enoch, and its referent in Genesis 6, has provoked much controversy among theologians over the centuries. The situation presents a paradox: how can spiritual beings be subject to carnal passions and accomplish procreation? Sensual impulses imply sexual organs and reproductive biology, which, according to convention, angels do not have. Whatever solution to the problem may be proposed must account for the critical first cause: the children of heaven *lusted* after the daughters of men. Aside from sexual attraction, the fact that these angels were reproductively compatible with human females suggest they possess a physiology similar to our own.

It is interesting that the Watchers saw fit to wed the women they desired rather than simply fornicate with them. This procedure reveals that they were after more than sex. It would seem that marriage to the daughters of men was part of a mutually beneficial transaction. The bargain was simple: in exchange for their maidens, the Watchers would teach the sons of Adam—or perhaps more precisely, the sons of Cain—the knowledge they were already striving to learn.

Some commentors speculate that the Watchers were reptilian in appearance. This is almost certainly not true. As sons of God, they bore the semblance of strikingly handsome young men, much like the angels who supped with Lot before Sodom's destruction (see Genesis 19). This would explain the seeming eagerness of the women to wed the Watchers (as attested in other apocryphal texts). It is hard to imagine a beautiful woman falling head over heels for a reptilian freak.

For more insight into this perspective, read *Birthright: The Coming Posthuman Apocalypse and the Usurpation of Adam's Dominion on Planet Earth*, by Timothy Alberino.

### The Watchers impart forbidden knowledge.

Much like Prometheus, the great Titan of Greek mythology who stole fire from the gods, the Watchers imparted forbidden knowledge to mankind, which fomented unimaginable chaos and carnage on earth. In exchange for their maidens, men were taught the dark arts of sorcery, astrology, pharmacy, and metallurgy. The function of these arcane sciences betrays the intent of the Promethean benefactors, who did not give them in good faith for the betterment of society, but as a means to beguile the sons of Adam into idolatry, self-destruction, and enmity with God. Endless speculation could be made regarding the technologies that might have been derived from the forbidden knowledge, but we may assume, at the very least, that antediluvian battlefields bore witness to the bloodlust of frenzied berserkers entranced with mind-altering psychedelics and armed to the hilt with mechanical instruments of bodily destruction.

It should be noted that the Watchers also instructed their wives and sons in the secrets of heaven. We may assume that they saved the best and most advantageous knowledge for their own families, who were intended to establish dynastic kingdoms and rule the world in a unified empire of the gods. The gigantic stature and superior technology of the Nephilim would have guaranteed their dominion over the thrones of men.

It is feasible that the technology of the gods in the Golden Age was, in certain aspects, equivalent or superior to that of modern society. The antediluvian world was likely composed of a bronze or iron age civilization dominated by a technologically advanced race of hybrid demigods.

For more insight into this perspective, read *Birthright: The Coming Posthuman Apocalypse and the Usurpation of Adam's Dominion on Planet Earth*, by Timothy Alberino.

## The Watchers' wives give birth to giants.

Procreation was an essential part of the Watchers' plan. By breeding with human females, they could produce their own hybrid offspring, who would be human enough to legally inherit Adam's birthright (dominion of Planet Earth), and powerful enough to take it by force.

One may wonder how the Watchers' wives were able to carry to term and deliver gigantic babies, a feat which would have surely proven fatal for both mother and child. According to some apocryphal traditions, the wombs of these women were indeed split open by the massive fetuses, but this scenario is not necessary to make sense of the phenomenon. Just like human babies born today with the genetic disorder of giantism, the size and weight of the hybrid babies may have been typical at birth, but as the infants progressed through childhood, they experienced accelerated growth, resulting in exceedingly large adults. However, in stark contrast to the genetic disorder of giantism, which weakens the heart and causes a cascade of debilitating conditions, the Nephilim were superhumanly enhanced with the exotic DNA of their angelic fathers.

For more insight into this perspective, read *Birthright: The Coming Posthuman Apocalypse and the Usurpation of Adam's Dominion on Planet Earth*, by Timothy Alberino.

## The giants devour men.

It must have been truly terrifying for those who watched in wonder as the children of the gods grew to colossal size and began to consume all the acquisitions from the land. Enoch records that men were forced to feed the giants, and when they could no longer satisfy their enormous appetites, the giants began to feed on men.

Perhaps initially, the consumption of human flesh was chaotic and indiscriminate. The giants would simply eat the men and women who failed to provide them with enough food. But one could imagine another, more organized procedure developing over time.

In order to ensure the survival of their offspring, the Watchers, who were no doubt venerated as living deities, might have instituted a ritual of appeasement in which a quota of men and women was required from each community. These unfortunate individuals would be ceremoniously offered up for consumption by the semi-divine sons of the gods. The man-devouring giants of the antediluvian world would later provide the mythological pretext for human sacrifice. Postdiluvian cultures, remembering the sanguinary appetite of the gods, would reenact the ritual of appeasement in their temples and sacred places, even feeding their screaming children into the gaping mouths of smoldering idols to be consumed alive in the flames.

For more insight into this perspective, read *Birthright: The Coming Posthuman Apocalypse and the Usurpation of Adam's Dominion on Planet Earth*, by Timothy Alberino.

**The giants go to war with one another.**

As punishment for their transgressions, the Watchers were forced to behold the destruction of their beloved sons, who were incited to violence and war with one another. When conceptualizing this scene, we should not imagine brutish giants beating each other over the heads with wooden clubs. These were the mighty Nephilim going to battle with technological armaments forged from the forbidden knowledge of their extraterrestrial fathers.

The fratricidal conflict between the giants should be framed within the context of a global empire. Much like the gods of the Greek pantheon, the Watchers, having apportioned the earth among themselves, established their respective kingdoms in their allotted realms (two hundred in all), which were governed by their hybrid sons. The civil war that fractured the empire of the gods in the antediluvian world is vividly illustrated in the Sanskrit epics of India (the *Ramayana* and *Mahabharata*), which depict Hindu deities and mortal men fighting heroic battles with high-tech weaponry, including extraordinary flying machines called *vimanas*. Remarkably, these ancient Sanskrit texts provide detailed blueprints describing the design and function of the *vimanas,* which were propelled by mercury vortex engines.

For more insight into this perspective, read *Birthright: The Coming Posthuman Apocalypse and the Usurpation of Adam's Dominion on Planet Earth*, by Timothy Alberino.

### The Flood ensues.

The Noahic Flood of biblical fame cannot be properly understood without the Book of Enoch in view. In the absence of Enoch, one is left to ponder the actions of a capricious and vengeful God who sorely regrets creating the human species. From this perspective, it is solely the depravity of mankind that provokes the near total liquidation of all terrestrial life on Planet Earth, a situation that seems excessively punitive, arbitrary, and illogical. It may surprise the reader to learn, however, that this was not the Hebraic perspective.

In the minds of the ancient Hebrews, who were well acquainted with the Enochian tale, the provocation of the Great Flood was not merely the unbridled depravity of mankind, but the mutagenic corruption of all flesh perpetrated by the Watchers. The aqueous cataclysm was intended to cleanse the earth of the Watchers' abominable seed and reset the genomic matrix of life through the people and animals preserved on the Ark.

Had God not sent the Flood to cleanse the earth of the mutagenic corruption, then every species would have ultimately been eradicated, and the kinsman redeemer of mankind, the promised seed of the woman (see Genesis 3), could never have been born from the loins of Adam. In this view, the Flood was not capricious and vengeful, but judicious and merciful. God did not determine to destroy the life He had created on Planet Earth, but to preserve it, and in doing so, to safeguard the birth of Jesus Christ, who would emerge from the womb of Mary to redeem the sons and daughters of Adam through his death on the cross.

For more insight into this perspective, read *Birthright: The Coming Posthuman Apocalypse and the Usurpation of Adam's Dominion on Planet Earth*, by Timothy Alberino.

# THE PARABLES

## Chapter 37.

1. The second vision which he saw, the vision of wisdom—which Enoch, the son of Jared, the son of Mahalalel, the son of Cainan, the son of Enos, the son of Seth, the son of Adam, saw. 2. And this is the beginning of the words of wisdom which I lifted up my voice to speak and say to those which dwell on earth: Hear, ye men of old time, and see, ye that come after, the words of the Holy One which I will speak before the Lord of Spirits. 3. It were better to declare (them only) to the men of old time, but even from those that come after we will not withhold the beginning of wisdom. 4. Till the present day such wisdom has never been given **by** the Lord of Spirits as I have received according to my insight, according to the good pleasure of the Lord of Spirits by whom the lot of eternal life has been given to me. 5. Now three parables were imparted to me, and I lifted up my voice and recounted them to those that dwell on the earth.

### *The First Parable*

## Chapter 38.

1. The First Parable. When the congregation of the righteous shall appear, and sinners shall be judged for their sins, and shall be driven from the face of the earth,

2. And when the Righteous One shall appear before the eyes of the righteous, whose elect works hang upon the Lord of Spirits, and light shall appear to the righteous and the elect who dwell on the earth, where then will be the dwelling of the sinners, and where the resting place of those who have denied the Lord of Spirits? It had been good for them if they had not been born.

3. When the secrets of the righteous shall be revealed and the sinners judged, and the godless driven from the presence of the righteous and elect,

4. From that time those that possess the earth shall no longer be powerful and exalted: and they shall not be able to behold the face of the holy, for the Lord of Spirits **has caused His light to appear** on the face of the holy, righteous, and elect.

5. Then shall the kings and the mighty perish and be given into the hands of the righteous and holy.

6. And thenceforward none shall seek for themselves mercy from the Lord of Spirits: for their life is at an end.

## Chapter 39.

[1. And it †shall come to pass in those days that elect and holy children† will descend from the high heaven, and their seed will become one with the children of men. 2. And in those days Enoch received books of zeal and wrath, and books of disquiet and expulsion.] And mercy shall not be accorded to them, saith the Lord of Spirits.

3. And in those days a whirlwind carried me off from the earth, and set me down at the end of the heavens.

4. And there I saw another vision, the dwelling places of the holy, and the resting places of the righteous.

5. Here mine eyes saw their dwellings with His righteous angels, and their resting places with the holy. And they petitioned and interceded and prayed for the children of men, and righteousness flowed before them as water, and mercy like dew upon the earth: thus it is amongst them forever and ever.

6a. And in that place mine eyes saw the Elect One of righteousness and of faith,

7a. And I saw his dwelling place under the wings of the Lord of Spirits.

6b. And righteousness shall prevail in his days, and the righteous and elect shall be without number before him forever and ever.

7*b*. And all the righteous and elect before him shall be †strong† as fiery lights, and their mouth shall be full of blessing, and their lips shall extol the name of the Lord of Spirits, and righteousness before him shall never fail, [and uprightness shall never fail before him].

8. There I wished to dwell, and my spirit longed for that dwelling place: and there heretofore hath been my portion, for so hath it been established concerning me before the Lord of Spirits.

9. In those days I praised and extolled the name of the Lord of Spirits with blessings and praises, because He hath destined me for blessing and glory according to the good pleasure of the Lord of Spirits. 10. For a long time my eyes regarded that place, and I blessed Him and praised Him, saying: 'Blessed is He, and may He be blessed from the beginning and forevermore. 11. And before Him there is no ceasing. He knows before the world was created what is forever and what will be from generation to generation. 12. Those who sleep not bless Thee: they stand before Thy glory and bless, praise, and extol, saying: "Holy, holy, holy, is the Lord of Spirits: He filleth the earth with spirits."' 13. And here my eyes saw all those who sleep not: they stand before Him and bless and say: 'Blessed be Thou, and blessed be the name of the Lord forever and ever.' 14. And my face was changed; for I could no longer behold.

## Chapter 40.

1. And after that, I saw thousands of thousands and ten thousand times ten thousand, I saw a multitude beyond number and reckoning, who stood before the Lord of Spirits. 2. And on the four sides of the Lord of Spirits I saw four presences, different from those that sleep not, and I learnt their names: for the angel that went with me made known to me their names, and showed me all the hidden things.

3. And I heard the voices of those four presences as they uttered praises before the Lord of glory. 4. The first voice blesses the Lord of Spirits forever and ever. 5. And the second voice I heard blessing the Elect One and the elect ones who hang upon the Lord of Spirits. 6. And the third voice I heard **pray and intercede** for those who dwell

on the earth and **supplicate** in the name of the Lord of Spirits. 7. And I heard the fourth voice fending off the Satans and forbidding them to come before the Lord of Spirits to accuse them who dwell on the earth. 8. After that I asked the angel of peace who went with me, who showed me everything that is hidden: 'Who are these four presences which I have seen and whose words I have heard and written down?' 9. And he said to me: 'This first is Michael, the merciful and long-suffering: and the second, who is set over all the diseases and all the wounds of the children of men, is Raphael: and the third, who is set over all the powers, is Gabriel: and the fourth, who is set over the repentance unto hope of those who inherit eternal life, is named Phanuel.' And these are the four angels of the Lord of Spirits and the four voices I heard in those days.

## Chapter 41.

1. And after that I saw all the secrets of the heavens, and how the kingdom is divided, and how the actions of men are weighed in the balance. 2. And there I saw the mansions of the elect and the mansions of the holy, and mine eyes saw there all the sinners being driven from thence which deny the name of the Lord of Spirits and being dragged off: and they could not abide because of the punishment which proceeds from the Lord of Spirits.

3. And there mine eyes saw the secrets of the lightning and of the thunder, and the secrets of the winds, how they are divided to blow over the earth, and the secrets of the clouds and dew, and there I saw from whence they proceed in that place and from whence they saturate the dusty earth. 4. And there I saw closed chambers out of which the winds are divided, the chamber of the hail and winds, the chamber of the mist, and of the clouds, and the cloud thereof hovers over the earth from the beginning of the world. 5. And I saw the chambers of the sun and moon, whence they proceed and whither they come again, and their glorious return, and how one is superior to the other, and their stately orbit, and how they do not leave their orbit, and they add nothing to their orbit and they take nothing from

it, and they keep faith with each other, in accordance with the oath by which they are bound together. 6. And first the sun goes forth and traverses his path according to the commandment of the Lord of Spirits, and mighty is His name forever and ever. 7. And after that I saw the hidden and the visible path of the moon, and she accomplishes the course of her path in that place by day and by night—the one holding a position opposite to the other before the Lord of Spirits. And they give thanks and praise and rest not; for unto them is their thanksgiving rest.

8. For the sun changes oft for a blessing or a curse, and the course of the path of the moon is light to the righteous, and darkness to the sinners in the name of the Lord, who made a separation between the light and the darkness, and divided the spirits of men, and strengthened the spirits of the righteous, in the name of His righteousness.

9. For no angel hinders and no power is able to hinder; for He appoints a judge for them all and He judges them all before Him.

## Chapter 42.

1. Wisdom found no place where she might dwell; then a dwelling place was assigned to her in the heavens.

2. Wisdom went forth to make her dwelling among the children of men, and found no dwelling place: Wisdom returned to her place and took her seat among the angels.

3. And unrighteousness went forth from her chambers: whom she sought not she found, and dwelt with them, as rain in a desert, and dew on a thirsty land.

## Chapter 43.

1. And I saw other lightnings and the stars of heaven, and I saw how He called them all by their names and they hearkened unto Him. 2. And I saw how they are weighed in a righteous balance according to their proportions of light: (I saw) the width of their spaces and the day of their appearing, and how their revolution produces lightning: and (I saw) their revolution according to the number of the angels,

and (how) they keep faith with each other. 3. And I asked the angel who went with me who showed me what was hidden: 'What are these?' 4. And he said to me: 'The Lord of Spirits hath showed thee their parabolic meaning (lit. 'their parable'): these are the names of the holy who dwell on the earth and believe in the name of the Lord of Spirits forever and ever.'

## Chapter 44.

Also another phenomenon I saw in regard to the lightnings: how some of the stars arise and become lightnings and cannot part with their new form.

## *The Second Parable*

## Chapter 45.

1. And this is the Second Parable concerning those who deny the name of the dwelling of the holy ones and the Lord of Spirits.

2. And into the heaven they shall not ascend, and on the earth they shall not come: such shall be the lot of the sinners who have denied the name of the Lord of Spirits, who are thus preserved for the day of suffering and tribulation.

3. On that day Mine Elect One shall sit on the throne of glory and shall **try** their works, and their places of rest shall be innumerable. And their souls shall grow strong within them when they see Mine elect ones, and those who have called upon My glorious name:

4. Then will I cause Mine Elect One to dwell among them. And I will transform the heaven and make it an eternal blessing and light,

5. And I will transform the earth and make it a blessing: and I will cause Mine elect ones to dwell upon it: but the sinners and evil doers shall not set foot thereon.

6. For I have provided and satisfied with peace My righteous ones, and have caused them to dwell before Me: but for the sinners there is judgment impending with Me, so that I shall destroy them from the face of the earth.

## Chapter 46.

1. And there I saw One, who had a head of days, and His head was white like wool, and with Him was another being whose countenance had the appearance of a man, and his face was full of graciousness, like one of the holy angels.

2. And I asked the **angel** who went with me and showed me all the hidden things, concerning that Son of Man, who he was, and whence he was, (and) why he went with the Head of Days?

3. And he answered and said unto me: 'This is the Son of Man who hath righteousness, with whom dwelleth righteousness, and who revealeth all the treasures of that which is hidden, because the Lord of Spirits hath chosen him, and whose lot hath the preeminence before the Lord of Spirits in uprightness forever.

4. And this Son of Man whom thou hast seen shall †raise up† the kings and the mighty from their seats, [and the strong from their thrones] and shall loosen the reins of the strong, and break the teeth of the sinners;

5. [And he shall put down the kings from their thrones and kingdoms] because they do not extol and praise him, nor humbly acknowledge whence the kingdom was bestowed upon them.

6. And he shall put down the countenance of the strong, and shall fill them with shame. And darkness shall be their dwelling, and worms shall be their bed, and they shall have no hope of rising from their beds, because they do not extol the name of the Lord of Spirits.

7. And these are they who †judge† the stars of heaven, [and raise their hands against the Most High], †and tread upon the earth and dwell upon it†. And all their deeds manifest unrighteousness, and their power rests upon their riches, and their faith is in the †gods† which they have made with their hands, and they deny the name of the Lord of Spirits,

8. And they persecute the houses of His congregations, and the faithful who hang upon the name of the Lord of Spirits.'

## Chapter 47.

1. And in those days shall have ascended the prayer of the righteous, and the blood of the righteous from the earth before the Lord of Spirits.

2. In those days the holy ones who dwell above in the heavens shall unite with one voice and supplicate and pray [and praise, and give thanks and bless the name of the Lord of Spirits] on behalf of the blood of the righteous which has been shed, and that the prayer of the righteous may not be in vain before the Lord of Spirits, that judgment may be done unto them, and that they may not have to suffer forever.

3. In those days I saw the Head of Days when He seated himself upon the throne of His glory, and the books of the living were opened before Him: and all His host which is in heaven above and His counselors stood before Him,

4. And the hearts of the holy were filled with joy; because the number of the righteous **had been offered**, and the prayer of the righteous had been heard, and the blood of the righteous been required before the Lord of Spirits.

## Chapter 48.

1. And in that place I saw the fountain of righteousness, which was inexhaustible: and around it were many fountains of wisdom; and all the thirsty drank of them, and were filled with wisdom and their dwellings were with the righteous and holy and elect.

2. And at that hour that Son of Man was named in the presence of the Lord of Spirits, and his name before the Head of Days.

3. Yea, before the sun and the signs were created, before the stars of the heaven were made, his name was named before the Lord of Spirits.

4. He shall be a staff to the righteous whereon to stay themselves and not fall, and he shall be the light of the Gentiles, and the hope of those who are troubled of heart.

5. All who dwell on earth shall fall down and worship before him,

and will praise and bless and celebrate with song the Lord of Spirits.

6. And for this reason hath he been chosen and hidden before Him, before the creation of the world and for evermore.

7. And the wisdom of the Lord of Spirits hath revealed him to the holy and righteous; for he hath preserved the lot of the righteous; because they have hated and despised this world of unrighteousness, and have hated all its works and ways in the name of the Lord of Spirits: for in his name they are saved, and according to his good pleasure hath it been in regard to their life.

8. In those days downcast in countenance shall the kings of the earth have become, and the strong who possess the land because of the works of their hands; for on the day of their anguish and affliction they shall not (be able to) save themselves.

9. And I will give them over into the hands of Mine elect: as straw in the fire so shall they burn before the face of the holy: as lead in the water shall they sink before the face of the righteous, and no trace of them shall any more be found.

10. And on the day of their affliction there shall be rest on the earth, and before them they shall fall and not rise again: and there shall be no one to take them with his hands and raise them: for they have denied the Lord of Spirits and His Anointed. The name of the Lord of Spirits be blessed.

## Chapter 49.

1. For wisdom is poured out like water, and glory faileth not before him for evermore.

2. For he is mighty in all the secrets of righteousness, and unrighteousness shall disappear as a shadow, and have no continuance; because the Elect One standeth before the Lord of Spirits, and his glory is forever and ever, and his might unto all generations.

3. And in him dwells the spirit of wisdom, and the spirit which gives insight, and the spirit of understanding and of might, and the spirit of those who have fallen asleep in righteousness.

4. And he shall judge the secret things, and none shall be able to utter a lying word before him; for he is the Elect One before the Lord of Spirits according to His good pleasure.

## Chapter 50.

1. And in those days a change shall take place for the holy and elect, and the light of days shall abide upon them, and glory and honor shall turn to the holy,

2. On the day of affliction on which evil shall have been treasured up against the sinners. And the righteous shall be victorious in the name of the Lord of Spirits: and He will cause the others to witness (this), that they may repent and forgo the works of their hands.

3. They shall have no honor through the name of the Lord of Spirits, yet through His name shall they be saved, and the Lord of Spirits will have compassion on them, for His compassion is great.

4. And He is righteous also in His judgment, and in the presence of His glory unrighteousness also shall not maintain itself: at His judgment the unrepentant shall perish before Him.

5. And from henceforth I will have no mercy on them, saith the Lord of Spirits.

## Chapter 51.

1. And in those days shall the earth also give back that which has been entrusted to it, and Sheol also shall give back that which it has received, and hell shall give back that which it owes.

5a. For in those days the Elect One shall arise,

2. And he shall choose the righteous and holy from among them: for the day has drawn nigh that they should be saved.

3. And the Elect One shall in those days sit on My throne, and his mouth shall **pour** forth all the secrets of wisdom and counsel: for the Lord of Spirits hath given (them) to him and hath glorified him.

4. And in those days shall the mountains leap like rams, and the hills also shall skip like lambs satisfied with milk, and the faces of [all] the

angels in heaven shall be lighted up with joy.

5b. And the earth shall rejoice,

c. And the righteous shall dwell upon it,

d. And the elect shall walk thereon.

## Chapter 52.

1. And after those days in that place where I had seen all the visions of that which is hidden—for I had been carried off in a whirlwind and they had borne me towards the west—2. there mine eyes saw all the secret things of heaven that shall be, a mountain of iron, and a mountain of copper, and a mountain of silver, and a mountain of gold, and a mountain of soft metal, and a mountain of lead.

3. And I asked the angel who went with me, saying, 'What things are these which I have seen in secret?' 4. And he said unto me: 'All these things which thou hast seen shall serve the dominion of His Anointed that he may be potent and mighty on the earth.'

5. And that angel of peace answered, saying unto me: 'Wait a little and there shall be revealed unto thee all the secret things, which surround the Lord of Spirits.

6. And these mountains which thine eyes have seen, the mountain of iron, and the mountain of copper, and the mountain of silver, and the mountain of gold, and the mountain of soft metal, and the mountain of lead, all these shall be in the presence of the Elect One, as wax before the fire, and like the water which streams down from above [upon those mountains], and they shall become powerless before his feet.

7. And it shall come to pass in those days that none shall be saved, either by gold or by silver, and none be able to escape.

8. And there shall be no iron for war, nor shall one clothe oneself with a breastplate. Bronze shall be of no service, and tin [shall be of no service and] shall not be esteemed, and lead shall not be desired.

9. And all these things shall be [denied and] destroyed from the surface of the earth, when the Elect One shall appear before the face of the Lord of Spirits.'

## Chapter 53.

1. There mine eyes saw a deep valley with open mouths, and all who dwell on the earth and sea and islands shall bring to him gifts and presents and tokens of homage, but that deep valley shall not become full.

2. And their hands commit lawless deeds, and the sinners devour all whom they lawlessly **oppress**: yet the sinners shall be destroyed before the face of the Lord of Spirits, and they shall be banished from off the face of His earth, and they shall perish forever and ever.

3. For I saw all the angels of punishment abiding (there) and preparing all the instruments of Satan. 4. And I asked the angel of peace who went with me: 'For whom are they preparing these instruments?' 5. And he said unto me: 'They prepare these for the kings and the mighty of this earth, that they may thereby be destroyed.

6. And after this the Righteous and Elect One shall cause the house of his congregation to appear: henceforth they shall be no more hindered in the name of the Lord of Spirits.

7. And these mountains shall not stand as the earth before his righteousness, but the hills shall be as a fountain of water, and the righteous shall have rest from the oppression of sinners.'

## Chapter 54.

1. And I looked and turned to another part of the earth, and saw there a deep valley with burning fire. 2. And they brought the kings and the mighty, and began to cast them into this deep valley. 3. And there mine eyes saw how they made these their instruments, iron chains of immeasurable weight. 4. And I asked the angel of peace who went with me, saying: 'For whom are these chains being prepared?' 5. And he said unto me: 'These are being prepared for the hosts of Azâzêl, so that they may take them and cast them into the abyss of complete

condemnation, and they shall cover their jaws with rough stones as the Lord of Spirits commanded.

6. And Michael, and Gabriel, and Raphael, and Phanuel shall take hold of them on that great day, and cast them on that day into the burning furnace, that the Lord of Spirits may take vengeance on them for their unrighteousness in becoming subject to Satan and leading astray those who dwell on the earth.'

*(54:7–55:2. Noahic fragment on the first world judgment.)*

7. 'And in those days shall punishment come from the Lord of Spirits, and He will open all the chambers of waters which are above the heavens, and of the fountains which are beneath the earth. 8. And all the waters shall be joined with the waters: that which is above the heavens is the masculine, and the water which is beneath the earth is the feminine. 9. And they shall destroy all who dwell on the earth and those who dwell under the ends of the heaven. 10. And **when** they have recognized their unrighteousness which they have wrought on the earth, then by these shall they perish.'

## Chapter 55.

1. And after that the Head of Days repented and said: 'In vain have I destroyed all who dwell on the earth.' 2. And He sware by His great name: 'Henceforth I will not do so to all who dwell on the earth, and I will set a sign in the heaven: and this shall be a pledge of good faith between Me and them forever, so long as heaven is above the earth. And this is in accordance with My command.'

3. 'When I have desired to take hold of them by the hand of the angels on the day of tribulation and pain **because of** this, I will cause My chastisement and My wrath to abide upon them, saith God, the Lord of Spirits. 4. Ye †mighty kings† who dwell on the earth, ye shall have to behold Mine Elect One, how he sits on the throne of glory and judges Azâzêl, and all his associates, and all his hosts in the name of the Lord of Spirits.'

## Chapter 56.

1. And I saw there the hosts of the angels of punishment going, and they held scourges and chains of iron and bronze. 2. And I asked the angel of peace who went with me, saying: 'To whom are these who hold the scourges going?' 3. And he said unto me: 'To their elect and beloved ones, that they may be cast into the chasm of the abyss of the valley.

4. And then that valley shall be filled with their elect and beloved, and the days of their lives shall be at an end, and the days of their leading astray shall not thenceforward be reckoned.

5. And in those days the angels shall return and hurl themselves to the east upon the Parthians and Medes: they shall stir up the kings, so that a spirit of unrest shall come upon them, and they shall rouse them from their thrones, that they may break forth as lions from their lairs, and as hungry wolves among their flocks.

6. And they shall go up and tread under foot the land of His elect ones, [and the land of His elect ones shall be before them a threshing floor and a highway]:

7. But the city of my righteous shall be a hindrance to their horses. And they shall begin to fight among themselves, and their right hand shall be strong against themselves, and a man shall not know his brother, nor a son his father or his mother, till there be no number of the corpses through their slaughter, and their punishment be not in vain.

8. In those days Sheol shall open its jaws, and they shall be swallowed up therein, and their destruction shall be at an end; Sheol shall devour the sinners in the presence of the elect.'

## Chapter 57.

1. And it came to pass after this that I saw another host of wagons, and men riding thereon, and coming on the winds from the east, and from the west to the south. 2. And the noise of their wagons was heard, and when this turmoil took place the holy ones from heaven

remarked it, and the pillars of the earth were moved from their place, and the sound thereof was heard from the one end of heaven to the other, in one day. 3. And they shall all fall down and worship the Lord of Spirits. And this is the end of the second Parable.

## *The Third Parable*

### Chapter 58.

1. And I began to speak the third Parable concerning the righteous and elect.

2. Blessed are ye, ye righteous and elect, for glorious shall be your lot.

3. And the righteous shall be in the light of the sun, and the elect in the light of eternal life: the days of their life shall be unending, and the days of the holy without number.

4. And they shall seek the light and find righteousness with the Lord of Spirits: there shall be peace to the righteous in the name of the Eternal Lord.

5. And after this it shall be said to the holy in heaven that they should seek out the secrets of righteousness, the heritage of faith: for it has become bright as the sun upon earth, and the darkness is past.

6. And there shall be a light that never **endeth**, and to a limit (lit. 'number') of days they shall not come, for the darkness shall first have been destroyed, [and the light established before the Lord of Spirits] and the light of uprightness established forever before the Lord of Spirits.

### Chapter 59.

[1. In those days mine eyes saw the secrets of the lightnings, and of the lights, and the judgments they execute (lit. 'their judgment'): and they lighten for a blessing or a curse as the Lord of Spirits willeth. 2. And there I saw the secrets of the thunder, and how when it resounds above in the heaven, the sound thereof is heard, and he caused me to see the **judgments** executed on the earth, whether they be for well-being and blessing, or for a curse, according to the word of the Lord of Spirits. 3. And after that all the secrets of the lights and lightnings were shown to me, and they lighten for blessing and for satisfying.]

## Chapter 60. *Book of Noah—a Fragment*

1. In the year five hundred, in the seventh month, on the fourteenth day of the month in the life of †Enoch†. In that Parable I saw how a mighty quaking made the heaven of heavens to quake, and the host of the Most High, and the angels, a thousand thousands and ten thousand times ten thousand, were disquieted with a great disquiet. 2. And the Head of Days sat on the throne of His glory, and the angels and the righteous stood around Him.

3. And a great trembling seized me, and fear took hold of me, and my loins gave way, and dissolved were my reins, and I fell upon my face.

4. And Michael sent another angel from among the holy ones and he raised me up, and when he had raised me up my spirit returned; for I had not been able to endure the look of this host, and the commotion and the quaking of the heaven. And Michael said unto me: 'Why art thou disquieted with such a vision? Until this day lasted the day of His mercy; and He hath been merciful and long-suffering towards those who dwell on the earth. 6. And when the day, and the power, and the punishment, and the judgment come, which the Lord of Spirits hath prepared for those who worship not the righteous **law**, and for those who deny the righteous judgment, and for those who take His name in vain—that day is prepared; for the elect a covenant, but for sinners an inquisition. When the punishment of the Lord of Spirits shall rest upon them, it shall rest in order that the punishment of the Lord of Spirits may not come in vain, and it shall slay the children with their mothers and the children with their fathers. Afterwards the judgment shall take place according to His mercy and His patience.'

7. And on that day were two monsters parted, a female monster named Leviathan, to dwell in the abysses of the ocean over the fountains of the waters.

8. But the male is named Behemoth, who occupied with his breast a waste wilderness named †Dûidâin†, on the east of the garden where the elect and righteous dwell, where my grandfather was taken up, the seventh from Adam, the first man whom the Lord of Spirits created. 9. And I besought the other angel that he should show me the might of those monsters, how they were parted on one day and cast, the one into the abysses of the sea, and the other unto the dry land of the wilderness. 10. And he said to me: 'Thou son of man, herein thou dost seek to know what is hidden.'

11. And the other angel who went with me and showed me what was hidden told me, what is first and last in the heaven in the height, and beneath the earth in the depth, and at the ends of the heaven, and on the foundation of the heaven. 12. And the chambers of the winds, and how the winds are divided, and how they are weighed, and (how) the **portals** of the winds are reckoned, each according to the power of the wind, and the power of the lights of the moon, and according to the power that is fitting: and the divisions of the stars according to their names, and how all the divisions are divided. 13. And the thunders according to the places where they fall, and all the divisions that are made among the lightnings that it may lighten, and their host that they may at once obey. 14. For the thunder has †places of rest† (which) are assigned (to it) while it is waiting for its peal; and the thunder and lightning are inseparable, and although not one and undivided, they both go together through the spirit and separate not. 15. For when the lightning lightens, the thunder utters its voice, and the spirit enforces a pause during the peal, and divides equally between them; for the treasury of their peals is like the sand, and each one of them as it peals is held in with a bridle, and turned back by the power of the spirit, and pushed forward according to the many quarters of the earth. 16. And the spirit of the sea is masculine and strong, and according to the might of his strength he draws it back with a rein, and in like manner it is driven forward and disperses amid all the mountains of the earth. 17. And the spirit of the hoar frost is his own angel, and the spirit of the hail is a good angel.

18. And the spirit of the snow has forsaken (his chamber) on account of his strength—there is a special spirit therein, and that which ascends from it is like smoke, and its name is frost. 19. And the spirit of the mist is not united with them in their chambers, but it has a special chamber; for its course is †glorious† both in light and in darkness, and in winter and in summer, and in its chamber is an angel. 20. And the spirit of the dew has its dwelling at the ends of the heaven, and is connected with the chambers of the rain, and its course is in winter and summer: and its clouds and the clouds of the mist are connected, and the one gives to the other. 21. And when the spirit of the rain goes forth from its chamber, the angels come and open the chamber and lead it out, and when it is diffused over the whole earth it unites with the water on the earth. And whensoever it unites with the water on the earth. . . . 22. For the waters are for those who dwell on the earth; for they are nourishment for the earth from the Most High who is in heaven: therefore there is a measure for the rain, and the angels take it in charge. 23. And these things I saw towards the Garden of the Righteous. 24. And the angel of peace who was with me said to me: 'These two monsters, prepared conformably to the greatness of God, shall feed. . .'

## Chapter 61.

1. And I saw in those days how long cords were given to those angels, and they took to themselves wings and flew, and they went towards the north.

2. And I asked the angel, saying unto him: 'Why have those (angels) taken these cords and gone off?' And he said unto me: 'They have gone to measure.'

3. And the angel who went with me said unto me: 'These shall bring the measures of the righteous, and the ropes of the righteous to the righteous, that they may stay themselves on the name of the Lord of Spirits forever and ever.

4. The elect shall begin to dwell with the elect, and those are the measures which shall be given to faith and which shall strengthen righteousness.

5. And these measures shall reveal all the secrets of the depths of the earth, and those who have been destroyed by the desert, and those who have been devoured by the beasts, and those who have been devoured by the fish of the sea, that they may return and stay themselves on the day of the Elect One; for none shall be destroyed before the Lord of Spirits, and none can be destroyed.

6. And all who dwell above in the heaven received a command and power and one voice and one light like unto fire.

7. And that One (with) their first words they blessed, and extolled and lauded with wisdom, and they were wise in utterance and in the spirit of life.

8. And the Lord of Spirits placed the Elect One on the throne of glory. And he shall judge all the works of the holy above in the heaven, and in the balance shall their deeds be weighed.

9. And when he shall lift up his countenance to judge their secret ways according to the word of the name of the Lord of Spirits, and their path according to the way of the righteous judgment of the Lord of Spirits, then shall they all with one voice speak and bless and glorify and extol and sanctify the name of the Lord of Spirits.

10. And He will summon all the host of the heavens, and all the holy ones above, and the host of God, the cherubim, seraphim, and ophanim, and all the angels of power, and all the angels of principalities, and the Elect One, and the other powers on the earth (and) over the water. 11. On that day shall they raise one voice, and bless and glorify and exalt in the spirit of faith, and in the spirit of wisdom, and in the spirit of patience, and in the spirit of mercy, and in the spirit of judgment and of peace, and in the spirit of goodness, and shall all say with one voice: "Blessed is He, and may the name of the Lord of Spirits be blessed forever and ever."

12. All who sleep not above in heaven shall bless Him: all the holy ones who are in heaven shall bless Him, and all the elect who dwell in the garden of life: and every spirit of light who is able to bless, and glorify, and extol, and hallow Thy blessed name, and all flesh shall beyond measure glorify and bless Thy name forever and ever.

13. For great is the mercy of the Lord of Spirits, and He is long-suffering, and all His works and all that He has created He has revealed to the righteous and elect, in the name of the Lord of Spirits.'

## Chapter 62.

1. And thus the Lord commanded the kings and the mighty and the exalted, and those who dwell on the earth, and said: 'Open your eyes and lift up your horns if ye are able to recognize the Elect One.'

2. And the Lord of Spirits seated him on the throne of His glory, and the spirit of righteousness was poured out upon him, and the word of his mouth slays all the sinners, and all the unrighteous are destroyed from before his face. 3. And there shall stand up in that day all the kings and the mighty, and the exalted and those who hold the earth, and they shall see and recognize how he sits on the throne of his glory, and righteousness is judged before him, and no lying word is spoken before him.

4. Then shall pain come upon them as on a woman in travail, [and she has pain in bringing forth] when her child enters the mouth of the womb, and she has pain in bringing forth.

5. And one portion of them shall look on the other and they shall be terrified, and they shall be downcast of countenance, and pain shall seize them, when they see that Son of Man sitting on the throne of his glory.

6. And the kings and the mighty and all who possess the earth shall bless and glorify and extol him who rules over all, who was hidden.

7. For from the beginning the Son of Man was hidden, And the Most High preserved him in the presence of His might, and revealed him to the elect.

8. And the congregation of the elect and holy shall be sown, and all the elect shall stand before him on that day.

9. And all the kings and the mighty and the exalted and those who rule the earth shall fall down before him on their faces, and worship and set their hope upon that Son of Man, and petition him and supplicate for mercy at his hands.

10. Nevertheless that Lord of Spirits will so press them that they shall hastily go forth from His presence, and their faces shall be filled with shame, and the darkness shall grow deeper on their faces.

11. And **He will deliver** them to the angels for punishment, to execute vengeance on them because they have oppressed His children and His elect.

12. And they shall be a spectacle for the righteous and for His elect: they shall rejoice over them, because the wrath of the Lord of Spirits resteth upon them, and His sword is drunk with their blood.

13. And the righteous and elect shall be saved on that day, and they shall never thenceforward see the face of the sinners and unrighteous.

14. And the Lord of Spirits will abide over them, and with that Son of Man shall they eat and lie down and rise up forever and ever.

15. And the righteous and elect shall have risen from the earth, and ceased to be of downcast countenance.

16. And they shall have been clothed with garments of glory, and these shall be the garments of life from the Lord of Spirits: and your garments shall not grow old, nor your glory pass away before the Lord of Spirits.

## Chapter 63.

1. In those days shall the mighty and the kings who possess the earth implore (Him) to grant them a little respite from His angels of punishment to whom they were delivered, that they might fall down and worship before the Lord of Spirits, and confess their sins before Him. 2. And they shall bless and glorify the Lord of Spirits, and say: 'Blessed is the Lord of Spirits and the Lord of kings, and the

Lord of the mighty and the Lord of the rich, and the Lord of glory and the Lord of wisdom;

3. And splendid in every secret thing is Thy power from generation to generation, and Thy glory forever and ever: deep are all Thy secrets and innumerable, and Thy righteousness is beyond reckoning.

4. We have now learnt that we should glorify and bless the Lord of kings and Him who is king over all kings.'

5. And they shall say: 'Would that we had rest to glorify and give thanks and confess our faith before His glory!

6. And now we long for a little rest, but find it not: we follow hard upon (it) and obtain (it) not: and light has vanished from before us, and darkness is our dwelling place forever and ever:

7. For we have not believed before Him, nor glorified the name of the Lord of Spirits, [nor glorified our Lord] but our hope was in the scepter of our kingdom, and in our glory.

8. And in the day of our suffering and tribulation He saves us not, and we find no respite for confession, that our Lord is true in all His works, and in His judgments and His justice; and His judgments have no respect of persons.

9. And we pass away from before His face on account of our works, and all our sins are reckoned up in righteousness.'

10. Now they will say unto themselves: 'Our souls are full of unrighteous gain, but it does not prevent us from descending from the midst thereof into the †burden† of Sheol.'

11. And after that their faces shall be filled with darkness and shame before that Son of Man, and they shall be driven from his presence, and the sword shall abide before his face in their midst.

12. Thus spake the Lord of Spirits: 'This is the ordinance and judgment with respect to the mighty and the kings and the exalted and those who possess the earth before the Lord of Spirits.'

## Chapter 64.

1. And other forms I saw hidden in that place. 2. I heard the voice of the angel saying: 'These are the angels who descended to the earth, and revealed what was hidden to the children of men, and seduced the children of men into committing sin.'

## Chapter 65.

1. And in those days Noah saw the earth that it had sunk down and its destruction was nigh. 2. And he arose from thence and went to the ends of the earth, and cried aloud to his grandfather Enoch: and Noah said three times with an embittered voice: 'Hear me, hear me, hear me.' 3. And I said unto him: 'Tell me what it is that is falling out on the earth that the earth is in such evil plight and shaken, lest perchance I shall perish with it.' 4. And thereupon there was a great commotion on the earth, and a voice was heard from heaven, and I fell on my face. 5. And Enoch my grandfather came and stood by me, and said unto me: 'Why hast thou cried unto me with a bitter cry and weeping?

6. And a command has gone forth from the presence of the Lord concerning those who dwell on the earth that their ruin is accomplished because they have learnt all the secrets of the angels, and all the violence of the Satans, and all their powers—the most secret ones—and all the power of those who practice sorcery, and the power of witchcraft, and the power of those who make molten images for the whole earth: 7. and how silver is produced from the dust of the earth, and how soft metal originates in the earth. 8. For lead and tin are not produced from the earth like the first: it is a fountain that produces them, and an angel stands therein, and that angel is preeminent.' 9. And after that my grandfather Enoch took hold of me by my hand and raised me up, and said unto me: 'Go, for I have asked the Lord of Spirits as touching this commotion on the earth. 10. And He said unto me: "Because of their unrighteousness their judgment has been determined upon and shall not be **withheld** by Me forever. Because of the **sorceries** which they have searched out

and learnt, the earth and those who dwell upon it shall be destroyed."

11. And these—they have no **place of repentance** forever, because they have shown them what was hidden, and they are the damned: but as for thee, my son, the Lord of Spirits knows that thou art pure, and guiltless of this reproach concerning the secrets.

12. And He has destined thy name to be among the holy, and will preserve thee amongst those who dwell on the earth, and has destined thy righteous seed both for kingship and for great honors, and from thy seed shall proceed a fountain of the righteous and holy without number forever.'

## Chapter 66.

1. And after that he showed me the angels of punishment who are prepared to come and let loose all the powers of the waters which are beneath in the earth in order to bring judgment and destruction on all who [abide and] dwell on the earth. 2. And the Lord of Spirits gave commandment to the angels who were going forth, that they should not cause **the waters** to rise but should hold them in check; for those angels were over the powers of the waters. 3. And I went away from the presence of Enoch.

## Chapter 67.

1. And in those days the word of God came unto me, and He said unto me: 'Noah, thy lot has come up before Me, a lot without blame, a lot of love and uprightness. 2. And now the angels are making a wooden (building), and when they have completed that task, I will place My hand upon it and preserve it, and there shall come forth from it the seed of life, and a change shall set in so that the earth will not remain without inhabitant. 3. And I will make fast thy seed before me forever and ever, and I will spread abroad those who dwell with thee: it shall not **be unfruitful** on the face of the earth, but it shall be blessed and multiply on the earth in the name of the Lord.'

4. And He will imprison those angels, who have shown unrighteousness, in that burning valley which my grandfather Enoch had formerly shown to me in the west among the mountains of gold

and silver and iron and soft metal and tin. 5. And I saw that valley in which there was a great convulsion and a convulsion of the waters. 6. And when all this took place, from that fiery molten metal and from the convulsion thereof in that place, there was produced a smell of sulfur, and it was connected with those waters, and that valley of the angels who had led astray (mankind) burned beneath that land. 7. And through its valleys proceed streams of fire, where these angels are punished who had led astray those who dwell upon the earth.

8. But those waters shall in those days serve for the kings and the mighty and the exalted, and those who dwell on the earth, for the healing of the body, but for the punishment of the spirit; now their spirit is full of lust, that they may be punished in their body, for they have denied the Lord of Spirits and see their punishment daily, and yet believe not in His name. 9. And in proportion as the burning of their bodies becomes severe, a corresponding change shall take place in their spirit forever and ever; for before the Lord of Spirits none shall utter an idle word. 10. For the judgment shall come upon them, because they believe in the lust of their body and deny the Spirit of the Lord. 11. And those same waters will undergo a change in those days; for when those angels **are** punished in these waters, these water springs shall change their temperature, and when the angels ascend, this water of the springs shall change and become cold. 12. And I heard Michael answering and saying: 'This judgement wherewith the angels are judged is a testimony for the kings and the mighty who possess the earth.' 13. Because these waters of judgment minister to the healing of the body of the **kings** and the lust of their body; therefore they will not see and will not believe that those waters will change and become a fire which burns forever.

## Chapter 68.

1. And after that my grandfather Enoch gave me the teaching of all the secrets in the book in the Parables which had been given to him; and he put them together for me in the words of the book of the Parables. 2. And on that day Michael answered Raphael and

said: 'The power of the spirit transports and **makes me to tremble** because of the severity of the judgment of the secrets, the judgment of the angels: who can endure the severe judgement which has
been executed, and before which they melt away?' 3. And Michael
answered again, and said to Raphael: 'Who is he whose heart is not
softened concerning it, and whose reins are not troubled by this
word of judgment (that) has gone forth upon them because of those
who have thus led them out?' 4. And it came to pass when he stood
before the Lord of Spirits, Michael said thus to Raphael: 'I will not
take their part under the eye of the Lord; for the Lord of Spirits has
been angry with them because they do as if they were the Lord. 5.
Therefore all that is hidden shall come upon them forever and ever;
for neither angel nor man shall have his portion (in it), but alone they
have received their judgment forever and ever.'

## Chapter 69.

1. And after this judgement they shall terrify and **make** them **to
tremble** because they have shown this to those who dwell on
the earth.

2. And behold the names of those angels [and these are their names:
the first of them is Samjâzâ, the second Artâqîfâ, and the third Armên,
the fourth Kôkabêl, the fifth †Tûrâêl†, the sixth Rûmjâl, the seventh
Dânjâl, the eighth †Nêqâêl†, the ninth Barâqêl, the tenth Azâzêl, the
eleventh Armârôs, the twelfth Batarjâl, the thirteenth †Busasêjal†,
the fourteenth Hanânêl, the fifteenth †Tûrêl†, and the sixteenth
Sîmâpêsîêl, the seventeenth Jetrêl, the eighteenth Tûmâêl, the nineteenth Tûrêl, the twentieth †Rûmâêl†, the twenty-first †Azâzêl†. 3.
And these are the chiefs of their angels and their names, and their
chief ones over hundreds and over fifties and over tens].

4. The name of the first Jeqôn: that is, the one who led astray [all]
the sons of **God**, and brought them down to the earth, and led them
astray through the daughters of men. 5. And the second was named
Asbeêl: he imparted to the holy sons of **God** evil counsel, and led
them astray so that they defiled their bodies with the daughters of

men. 6. And the third was named Gâdreêl: he it is who showed the children of men all the blows of death, and he led astray Eve, and showed [the weapons of death to the sons of men] the shield and the coat of mail, and the sword for battle, and all the weapons of death to the children of men. 7. And from his hand they have proceeded against those who dwell on the earth from that day and for evermore. 8. And the fourth was named Pênêmûe: he taught the children of men the bitter and the sweet, and he taught them all the secrets of their wisdom. 9. And he instructed mankind in writing with ink and paper, and thereby many sinned from eternity to eternity and until this day. 10. For men were not created for such a purpose, to give confirmation to their good faith with pen and ink. 11. For men were created exactly like the angels, to the intent that they should continue pure and righteous, and death, which destroys everything, could not have taken hold of them; but through this their knowledge they are perishing, and through this power †it is consuming me.† 12. And the fifth was named Kâsdejâ: this is he who showed the children of men all the wicked smitings of spirits and demons, and the smitings of the embryo in the womb, that it may pass away, and [the smitings of the soul] the bites of the serpent, and the smitings which befall through the noontide heat, the son of the serpent named Tabâ'êt. 13. And this is the **task** of Kâsbeêl, the chief of the oath which he showed to the holy ones when he dwelt high above in glory, and its name is Bîqâ. 14. This (angel) requested Michael to show him the hidden name, that he might enunciate it in the oath, so that those might quake before that name and oath who revealed all that was in secret to the children of men. 15. And this is the power of this oath, for it is powerful and strong, and he placed this oath Akâe in the hand of Michael. 16. And these are the secrets of this oath ... and they are strong through his oath: and the heaven was suspended before the world was created, and forever.

17. And through it the earth was founded upon the water, and from the secret recesses of the mountains come beautiful waters, from the creation of the world and unto eternity.

18. And through that oath the sea was created, and †as its foundation† He set for it the sand against the time of (its) anger, and it dare not pass beyond it from the creation of the world unto eternity.

19. And through that oath are the depths made fast, and abide and stir not from their place from eternity to eternity.

20. And through that oath the sun and moon complete their course, and deviate not from their ordinance from eternity to eternity.

21. And through that oath the stars complete their course, and He calls them by their names, and they answer Him from eternity to eternity.

[22. And in like manner the spirits of the water, and of the winds, and of all zephyrs, and (their) paths from all the quarters of the winds. 23. And there are preserved the voices of the thunder and the light of the lightnings: and there are preserved the chambers of the hail and the chambers of the hoar frost, and the chambers of the mist, and the chambers of the rain and the dew. 24. And all these believe and give thanks before the Lord of Spirits, and glorify (Him) with all their power, and their food is in every act of thanksgiving: they thank and glorify and extol the name of the Lord of Spirits forever and ever.]

25. And this oath is mighty over them, and through it [they are preserved and] their paths are preserved, and their course is not destroyed.

*Close of the Third Parable*

26. And there was great joy amongst them, and they blessed and glorified and extolled, because the name of that Son of Man had been revealed unto them.

27. And he sat on the throne of his glory, and the sum of judgment was given unto the Son of Man, and he caused the sinners to pass away and be destroyed from off the face of the earth, and those who have led the world astray.

28. With chains shall they be bound, and in their assemblage place of destruction shall they be imprisoned, and all their works vanish

from the face of the earth.

29. And from henceforth there shall be nothing corruptible, for that Son of Man has appeared, and has seated himself on the throne of his glory, and all evil shall pass away before his face, and the word of that Son of Man shall go forth and be strong before the Lord of Spirits. This is the third Parable of Enoch.

## Chapter 70.

1. And it came to pass after this that his name during his lifetime was raised aloft to that Son of Man and to the Lord of Spirits from amongst those who dwell on the earth. 2. And he was raised aloft on the chariots of the spirit and his name vanished among them. 3. And from that day I was no longer numbered amongst them; and he set me between the two winds, between the north and the west, where the angels took the cords to measure for me the place for the elect and righteous. 4. And there I saw the first fathers and the righteous who from the beginning dwell in that place.

## Chapter 71.

1. And it came to pass after this that my spirit was translated and it ascended into the heavens: and I saw the **holy sons of God**. They were stepping on flames of fire: their garments were white [and their raiment], and their faces shone like snow.

2. And I saw two streams of fire, and the light of that fire shone like hyacinth, and I fell on my face before the Lord of Spirits.

3. And the angel Michael [one of the archangels] seized me by my right hand, and lifted me up and led me forth into all the secrets, and he showed me all the secrets of righteousness.

4. And he showed me all the secrets of the ends of the heaven, and all the chambers of all the stars, and all the luminaries, whence they proceed before the face of the holy ones.

5. And he translated my spirit into the heaven of heavens, and I saw there as it were a structure built of crystals, and between those crystals tongues of living fire.

6. And my spirit saw the girdle which girt that house of fire, and on its four sides were streams full of living fire, and they girt that house.

7. And round about were seraphim, cherubim, and ophanim: and these are they who sleep not, and guard the throne of His glory.

8. And I saw angels who could not be counted, a thousand thousands, and ten thousand times ten thousand, encircling that house, and Michael, and Raphael, and Gabriel, and Phanuel, and the holy angels who are above the heavens, go in and out of that house.

9. And they came forth from that house, and Michael and Gabriel, Raphael and Phanuel, and many holy angels without number.

10. And with them the Head of Days, His head white and pure as wool, and His raiment indescribable.

11. And I fell on my face, and my whole body became relaxed, and my spirit was transfigured; and I cried with a loud voice, ... with the spirit of power, and blessed and glorified and extolled.

12. And these blessings which went forth out of my mouth were well pleasing before that Head of Days. 13. And that Head of Days came with Michael and Gabriel, Raphael and Phanuel, thousands and ten thousands of angels without number.

[Lost passage wherein the Son of Man was described as accompanying the Head of Days, and Enoch asked one of the angels (as in 46:3) concerning the Son of Man as to who he was.]

14. And he (*i.e.* the angel) came to me and greeted me with his voice, and said unto me: '**This is** the Son of Man who is born unto righteousness; and righteousness abides over **him**, and the righteousness of the Head of Days forsakes **him** not.'

15. And he said unto me: 'He proclaims unto thee peace in the name of the world to come; for from hence has proceeded peace since the creation of the world, and so shall it be unto thee forever and forever and ever.

16. And all shall walk in **his** ways since righteousness never forsakes **him**: with **him** will be their dwelling places, and with **him** their

heritage, and they shall not be separated from him forever and ever and ever.

17. And so there shall be length of days with that Son of Man, and the righteous shall have peace and an upright way, in the name of the Lord of Spirits forever and ever.'

# Book of the Course of the Heavenly Luminaries

### Chapter 72.

1. The book of the courses of the luminaries of the heaven, the relations of each, according to their classes, their dominion and their seasons, according to their names and places of origin, and according to their months, which Uriel, the holy angel, who was with me, who is their guide, showed me; and he showed me all their laws exactly as they are, and how it is with regard to all the years of the world and unto eternity, till the new creation is accomplished which dureth till eternity. 2. And this is the first law of the luminaries: the luminary the Sun has its rising in the eastern portals of the heaven, and its setting in the western portals of the heaven. 3. And I saw six portals in which the sun rises, and six portals in which the sun sets: and the moon rises and sets in these portals, and the leaders of the stars and those whom they lead: six in the east and six in the west, and all following each other in accurately corresponding order: also many windows to the right and left of these portals. 4. And first there goes forth the great luminary, named the Sun, and his circumference is like the circumference of the heaven, and he is quite filled with illuminating and heating fire. 5. The chariot on which he ascends, the wind drives, and the sun goes down from the heaven and returns through the north in order to reach the east, and is so guided that he comes to the appropriate (lit. 'that') portal and shines in the face of the heaven. 6. In this way he rises in the first month in the great portal, which is the fourth [those six portals in the cast]. 7. And in that fourth portal from which the sun rises in the first month are twelve window openings, from which proceed a flame when they are opened in their season. 8. When

the sun rises in the heaven, he comes forth through that fourth portal thirty mornings in succession, and sets accurately in the fourth portal in the west of the heaven. 9. And during this period the day becomes daily longer and the night nightly shorter to the thirtieth morning. 10. On that day the day is longer than the night by a ninth part, and the day amounts exactly to ten parts and the night to eight parts. 11. And the sun rises from that fourth portal, and sets in the fourth and returns to the fifth portal of the east thirty mornings, and rises from it and sets in the fifth portal. 12. And then the day becomes longer by †two† parts and amounts to eleven parts, and the night becomes shorter and amounts to seven parts. 13. And it returns to the east and enters into the sixth portal, and rises and sets in the sixth portal one and thirty mornings on account of its sign. 14. On that day the day becomes longer than the night, and the day becomes double the night, and the day becomes twelve parts, and the night is shortened and becomes six parts. 15. And the sun mounts up to make the day shorter and the night longer, and the sun returns to the east and enters into the sixth portal, and rises from it and sets thirty mornings. 16. And when thirty mornings are accomplished, the day decreases by exactly one part, and becomes eleven parts, and the night seven. 17. And the sun goes forth from that sixth portal in the west, and goes to the east and rises in the fifth portal for thirty mornings, and sets in the west again in the fifth western portal. 18. On that day the day decreases by †two† parts, and amounts to ten parts and the night to eight parts. 19. And the sun goes forth from that fifth portal and sets in the fifth portal of the west, and rises in the fourth portal for one and thirty mornings on account of its sign, and sets in the west. 20. On that day the day is equalized with the night, [and becomes of equal length], and the night amounts to nine parts and the day to nine parts. 21. And the sun rises from that portal and sets in the west, and returns to the east and rises thirty mornings in the third portal and sets in the west in the third portal. 22. And on that day the night becomes longer than the day, and night becomes longer than night, and day shorter than day till the thirtieth morning, and the night amounts exactly to ten parts and the day to eight parts. 23. And the sun rises from that third portal and sets in the third portal in the west and returns to the east, and for thirty mornings rises in the second portal in the east, and in like manner sets in the second portal in the west of the heaven. 24. And on that day the night amounts to eleven parts and the day to seven parts. 25. And the sun rises on that day from that second portal and sets in the west in the second portal, and returns to the east into the first portal for one and thirty mornings, and sets in the first portal in the west of the heaven. 26. And on that day the night becomes longer and amounts to the double of the day: and the night amounts exactly to twelve parts and the day to six. 27. And the sun has (therewith) traversed the divisions of his orbit and turns again on those divisions of his orbit, and enters that portal thirty mornings and sets also in the west opposite to it. 28. And on that night has the night decreased in length by a †ninth† part, and the night has become eleven parts and the day seven parts. 29. And the sun has returned and entered into the second portal in the east, and returns on those his divisions of his orbit for thirty mornings, rising and setting. 30. And on that day the night decreases in length, and the night amounts to ten parts and the day to eight. 31. And on that day the sun rises from that portal, and sets in the west, and returns to the east, and rises in the third portal for one and thirty mornings, and sets in the west of the heaven. 32. On that day the night decreases and amounts to nine parts, and the day to nine parts, and the night is equal to the day and the year is exactly as to its days three hundred and sixty-four. 33. And the length of the day and of the night, and the shortness of the day and of the night arise—through the course of the sun these distinctions are made (lit. 'they are separated'). 34. So it comes that its course becomes daily longer, and its course nightly shorter. 35. And this is the law and the course of the sun, and his return as often as he returns sixty times and rises, *i.e.* the great luminary which is named the Sun, forever and ever. 36. And that which (thus) rises is the great luminary, and is so named according to its appearance, according as the Lord commanded. 37. As he rises, so he sets and decreases not, and rests not, but runs day and night, and his light is sevenfold brighter than that of the moon; but as regards size they are both equal.

## Chapter 73.

1. And after this law I saw another law dealing with the smaller luminary, which is named the Moon. 2. And her circumference is like the circumference of the heaven, and her chariot in which she rides is driven by the wind, and light is given to her in (definite) measure. 3. And her rising and setting changes every month: and her days are like the days of the sun, and when her light is uniform (*i.e.* full) it amounts to the seventh part of the light of the sun. 4. And thus she rises. And her first phase in the east comes forth on the thirtieth morning: and on that day she becomes visible, and constitutes for you the first phase of the moon on the thirtieth day together with the sun in the portal where the sun rises. 5. And the one half of her goes forth by a seventh part, and her whole circumference is empty, without light, with the exception of one-seventh part of it, (and) the fourteenth part of her light. 6. And when she receives one-seventh part of the half of her light, her light amounts to one-seventh part and the half thereof. 7. And she sets with the sun, and when the sun rises the moon rises with him and receives the half of one part of light, and in that night in the beginning of her morning [in the commencement of the lunar day] the moon sets with the sun, and is invisible that night with the fourteen parts and the half of one of them. 8. And she rises on that day with exactly a seventh part, and comes forth and recedes from the rising of the sun, and in her remaining days she becomes bright in the (remaining) thirteen parts.

## Chapter 74.

1. And I saw another course, a law for her, (and) how according to that law she performs her monthly revolution. 2. And all these Uriel, the holy angel who is the leader of them all, showed to me, and their positions, and I wrote down their positions as he showed them to me, and I wrote down their months as they were, and the appearance of

their lights till fifteen days were accomplished. 3. In single seventh parts she accomplishes all her light in the east, and in single seventh parts accomplishes all her darkness in the west. 4. And in certain months she alters her settings, and in certain months she pursues her own peculiar course. 5. In two months the moon sets with the sun in those two middle portals the third and the fourth. 6. She goes forth for seven days, and turns about and returns again through the portal where the sun rises, and accomplishes all her light: and she recedes from the sun, and in eight days enters the sixth portal from which the sun goes forth. 7. And when the sun goes forth from the fourth portal she goes forth seven days, until she goes forth from the fifth and turns back again in seven days into the fourth portal and accomplishes all her light: and she recedes and enters into the first portal in eight days. 8. And she returns again in seven days into the fourth portal from which the sun goes forth. 9. Thus I saw their position— how the moons rose and the sun set in those days. 10. And if five years are added together the sun has an overplus of thirty days, and all the days which accrue to it for one of those five years, when they are full, amount to 364 days. 11. And the overplus of the sun and of the stars amounts to six days: in 5 years 6 days every year come to 30 days: and the moon falls behind the sun and stars to the number of 30 days. 12. And **the sun** and the stars bring in all the years exactly, so that they do not advance or delay their position by a single day unto eternity; but **complete** the years with perfect justice in 364 days. 13. In 3 years there are 1092 days, and in 5 years 1820 days, so that in 8 years there are 2912 days. 14. For the moon alone the days amount in 3 years to 1062 days, and in 5 years she falls 50 days behind: [*i.e.* to the sum (of 1770) there is to be added (1000 and) 62 days.] 15. And in 5 years there are 1770 days, so that for the moon the days in 8 years amount to 2832 days. 16. [For in 8 years she falls behind to the amount of 80 days], all the days she falls behind in 8 years are 80. 17. And the year is accurately completed in conformity with their world stations and the stations of the sun, which rise from the portals through which it (the sun) rises and sets 30 days.

## Chapter 75.

1. And the leaders of the heads of the thousands, who are placed over the whole creation and over all the stars, have also to do with the four intercalary days, being inseparable from their office, according to the reckoning of the year, and these render service on the four days which are not reckoned in the reckoning of the year. 2. And owing to them men go wrong therein, for those luminaries truly render service on the world stations, one in the first portal, one in the third portal of the heaven, one in the fourth portal, and one in the sixth portal, and the exactness of the year is accomplished through its separate three hundred and sixty-four stations. 3. For the signs and the times and the years and the days the angel Uriel showed to me, whom the Lord of glory hath set forever over all the luminaries of the heaven, in the heaven and in the world, that they should rule on the face of the heaven and be seen on the earth, and be leaders for the day and the night, *i.e.* the sun, moon, and stars, and all the ministering creatures which make their revolution in all the chariots of the heaven. 4. In like manner twelve doors Uriel showed me, open in the circumference of the sun's chariot in the heaven, through which the rays of the sun break forth: and from them is warmth diffused over the earth, when they are opened at their appointed seasons. 5. [And for the winds and the spirit of the †dew† when they are opened, standing open in the heavens at the ends.] 6. As for the twelve portals in the heaven, at the ends of the earth, out of which go forth the sun, moon, and stars, and all the works of heaven in the east and in the west. 7. There are many windows open to the left and right of them, and one window at its (appointed) season produces warmth, corresponding (as these do) to those doors from which the stars come forth according as He has commanded them, and wherein they set corresponding to their number. 8. And I saw chariots in the heaven, running in the world, above those portals in which revolve the stars that never set. 9. And one is larger than all the rest, and it is that that makes its course through the entire world.

## Chapter 76.

1. And at the ends of the earth I saw twelve portals open to all the **quarters** (of the heaven), from which the winds go forth and blow over the earth. 2. Three of them are open on the face (*i.e.* the east) of the heavens, and three in the west, and three on the right (*i.e.* the south) of the heaven, and three on the left (*i.e.* the north). 3. And the three first are those of the east, and three are of †the north, and three [after those on the left] of the south†, and three of the west. 4. Through four of these come winds of blessing and prosperity, and from those eight come hurtful winds: when they are sent, they bring destruction on all the earth and on the water upon it, and on all who dwell thereon, and on everything which is in the water and on the land.

5. And the first wind from those portals, called the east wind, comes forth through the first portal which is in the east, inclining towards the south: from it come forth desolation, drought, heat, and destruction. 6. And through the second portal in the middle comes what is fitting, and from it there come rain and fruitfulness and prosperity and dew; and through the third portal which lies toward the north come cold and drought.

7. And after these come forth the south winds through three portals: through the first portal of them inclining to the east comes forth a hot wind. 8. And through the middle portal next to it there come forth fragrant smells, and dew and rain, and prosperity and health. 9. And through the third portal lying to the west come forth dew and rain, locusts and desolation.

10. And after these the north winds: from the seventh portal in the east come dew and rain, locusts and desolation. 11. And from the middle portal come in a direct direction health and rain and dew and prosperity; and through the third portal in the west come cloud and hoar frost, and snow and rain, and dew and locusts.

12. And after these [four] are the west winds: through the first portal adjoining the north come forth dew and hoar frost, and cold and

snow and frost. 13. And from the middle portal come forth dew and rain, and prosperity and blessing; and through the last portal which adjoins the south come forth drought and desolation, and burning and destruction. 14. And the twelve portals of the four **quarters** of the heaven are therewith completed, and all their laws and all their plagues and all their benefactions have I shown to thee, my son Methuselah.

## Chapter 77.

1. And the first **quarter** is called the east, because it is the first: and the second, the south, because the Most High **will descend** there, yea, there in quite a special sense will He who is blessed forever **descend**. 2. And the west **quarter** is named the diminished, because there all the luminaries of the heaven wane and go down. 3. And the fourth **quarter**, named the north, is divided into three parts: the first of them is for the dwelling of men: and the second contains seas of water, and the abysses and forests and rivers, and darkness and clouds; and the third part contains the garden of righteousness.

4. I saw seven high mountains, higher than all the mountains which are on the earth: and thence comes forth hoar frost, and days, seasons, and years pass away. 5. I saw seven rivers on the earth larger than all the rivers: one of them coming from the †west† pours its waters into the Great Sea. 6. And these two come from the north to the sea and pour their waters into the Erythraean Sea in the east. 7. And the remaining four come forth on the side of the north to their own sea, <two of them to> the Erythraean Sea, and two into the Great Sea and discharge themselves there [and some say: into the desert]. 8. Seven great islands I saw in the sea and in the mainland: two in the mainland and five in the Great Sea.

## Chapter 78.

1. And the names of the sun are the following: the first Orjârês, and the second Tômâs. 2. And the moon has four names: the first name is Asônjâ, the second Eblâ, the third Benâsê, and the fourth Erâe. 3. These are the two great luminaries: their circumference is like

the circumference of the heaven, and the size of the circumference of both is alike. 4. In the circumference of the sun there are seven portions of light which are added to it more than to the moon, and in definite measures it is s transferred till the seventh portion of the sun is exhausted. 5. And they set and enter the portals of the west, and make their revolution by the north, and come forth through the eastern portals on the face of the heaven. 6. And when the moon rises one-fourteenth part appears in the heaven: [the light becomes full in her]: on the fourteenth day she accomplishes her light. 7. And fifteen parts of light are transferred to her till the fifteenth day (when) her light is accomplished, according to the sign of the year, and she becomes fifteen parts, and the moon grows by (the addition of) fourteenth parts. 8. And in her waning (the moon) decreases on the first day to fourteen parts of her light, on the second to thirteen parts of light, on the third to twelve, on the fourth to eleven, on the fifth to ten, on the sixth to nine, on the seventh to eight, on the eighth to seven, on the ninth to six, on the tenth to five, on the eleventh to four, on the twelfth to three, on the thirteenth to two, on the fourteenth to the half of a seventh, and all her remaining light disappears wholly on the fifteenth. 9. And in certain months the month has twenty-nine days and once twenty-eight. 10. And Uriel showed me another law: when light is transferred to the moon, and on which side it is transferred to her by the sun. 11. During all the period during which the moon is growing in her light, she is transferring it to herself when opposite to the sun during fourteen days [her light is accomplished in the heaven], and when she is illumined throughout, her light is accomplished full in the heaven. 12. And on the first day she is called the new moon, for on that day the light rises upon her. 13. She becomes full moon exactly on the day when the sun sets in the west, and from the east she rises at night, and the moon shines the whole night through till the sun rises over against her and the moon is seen over against the sun. 14. On the side whence the light of the moon comes forth, there again she wanes till all the light vanishes and all the days of the month are at an end, and her circumference is empty, void of light. 15. And three months she makes of thirty days, and at her time she makes three months of twenty-nine days each, in which she accomplishes her waning in the first period of time, and in the first portal for one hundred and seventy-seven days. 16. And in the time of her going out she appears for three months (of) thirty days each, and for three months she appears (of) twenty-nine each. 17. At night she appears like a man for twenty days each time, and by day she appears like the heaven, and there is nothing else in her save her light.

## Chapter 79.

1. And now, my son, I have shown thee everything, and the law of all the stars of the heaven is completed. 2. And he showed me all the laws of these for every day, and for every season of bearing rule, and for every year, and for its going forth, and for the order prescribed to it every month and every week: 3. and the waning of the moon which takes place in the sixth portal: for in this sixth portal her light is accomplished, and after that there is the beginning of the waning: 4. <and the waning> which takes place in the first portal in its season, till one hundred and seventy-seven days are accomplished: reckoned according to weeks, twenty-five (weeks) and two days. 5. She falls behind the sun and the order of the stars exactly five days in the course of one period, and when this place which thou seest has been traversed. 6. Such is the picture and sketch of every luminary which Uriel the archangel, who is their leader, showed unto me.

## Chapter 80.

1. And in those days the angel Uriel answered and said to me: 'Behold, I have shown thee everything, Enoch, and I have revealed everything to thee that thou shouldst see this sun and this moon, and the leaders of the stars of the heaven and all those who turn them, their tasks and times and departures.

2. And in the days of the sinners the years shall be shortened, and their seed shall be tardy on their lands and fields and all things on the earth shall alter, and shall not appear in their time: and the rain shall be kept back, and the heaven shall withhold (it).

3. And in those times the fruits of the earth shall be backward, and shall not grow in their time, and the fruits of the trees shall be withheld in their time.

4. And the moon shall alter her order, and not appear at her time.

5. [And in those days the **sun** shall be seen and he shall journey in the **evening** †on the extremity of the great chariot in† the west] and shall shine more brightly than accords with the order of light.

6. And many chiefs of the stars shall transgress the order (prescribed); and these shall alter their orbits and tasks, and not appear at the seasons prescribed to them.

7. And the whole order of the stars shall be concealed from the sinners, and the thoughts of those on the earth shall err concerning them, [and they shall be altered from all their ways], yea, they shall err and take them to be gods.

8. And evil shall be multiplied upon them, and punishment shall come upon them so as to destroy all.'

## Chapter 81.

1. And he said unto me: 'Observe, Enoch, these heavenly tablets, and read what is written thereon, and mark every individual fact.'

2. And I observed the heavenly tablets, and read everything which was written (thereon) and understood everything, and read the book of all the deeds of mankind, and of all the children of flesh that shall be upon the earth to the remotest generations. 3. And forthwith I blessed the great Lord, the King of glory forever, in that He has made all the works of the world. And I extolled the Lord because of His patience, and blessed Him because of the children of men.

4. And after that I said: 'Blessed is the man who dies in righteousness and goodness, concerning whom there is no book of unrighteousness written, and against whom no day of judgment shall be found.'

5. And those seven holy ones brought me and placed me on the earth before the door of my house, and said to me: 'Declare everything to thy son Methuselah, and show to all thy children that no flesh is

righteous in the sight of the Lord, for He is their Creator. 6. One year we will leave thee with thy son, till thou givest thy (last) commands, that thou mayest teach thy children and record (it) for them, and testify to all thy children; and in the second year they shall take thee from their midst.

7. Let thy heart be strong, for the good shall announce righteousness to the good; the righteous with the righteous shall rejoice, and shall offer congratulation to one another.

8. But the sinners shall die with the sinners, and the apostate go down with the apostate.

9. And those who practice righteousness shall die on account of the deeds of men, and be taken away on account of the doings of the godless.'

10. And in those days they ceased to speak to me, and I came to my people, blessing the Lord of the world.

## Chapter 82.

1. And now, my son Methuselah, all these things I am recounting to thee and writing down for thee, and I have revealed to thee everything, and given thee books concerning all these: so preserve, my son Methuselah, the books from thy father's hand, and (see) that thou deliver them to the generations of the world.

2. I have given wisdom to thee and to thy children, [and thy children that shall be to thee], that they may give it to their children for generations, this wisdom (namely) that passeth their thought.

3. And those who understand it shall not sleep, but shall listen with the ear that they may learn this wisdom, and it shall please those that eat thereof better than good food.

4. Blessed are all the righteous, blessed are all those who walk in the way of righteousness and sin not as the sinners in the reckoning of all their days in which the sun traverses the heaven, entering into and departing from the portals for thirty days with the heads of thousands of the order of the stars, together with the four which are

114

intercalated which divide the four portions of the year, which lead them and enter with them four days. 5. Owing to them men shall be at fault and not reckon them in the **whole reckoning of the year**: yea, men shall be at fault, and not recognize them accurately. 6. For they belong to the reckoning of the year and are truly recorded (thereon) forever, one in the first portal and one in the third, and one in the fourth and one in the sixth, and the year is completed in three hundred and sixty-four days.

7. And the account thereof is accurate and the recorded reckoning thereof exact; for the luminaries, and months and festivals, and years and days, has Uriel shown and revealed to me, **to whom** the Lord of the whole creation of the world hath **subjected** the host of heaven. 8. And he has power over night and day in the heaven to cause the light to give light to men—sun, moon, and stars, and all the powers of the heaven which revolve in their circular chariots. 9. And these are the orders of the stars, which set in their places, and in their seasons and festivals and months.

10. And these are the names of those who lead them, who watch **that they** enter at their times, in their orders, in their seasons, in their months, in their periods of dominion, and in their positions. 11. Their four leaders who divide the four parts of the year enter first; and after them the twelve leaders of the orders who divide the months; and for the three hundred and sixty (days) there are heads over thousands who divide the days; and for the four intercalary days there are the leaders which sunder the four parts of the year. 12. And these heads over thousands are intercalated between leader and leader, each behind a station, but their leaders make the division. 13. And these are the names of the leaders who divide the four parts of the year which are ordained: Mîlkî'êl, Hel'emmêlêk, and Mêl'êjal, and Nârêl. 14. And the names of those who lead them: Adnâr'êl, and Îjâsûsa'êl, and 'Elômê'êl—these three follow the leaders of the orders, and there is one that follows the three leaders of the orders which follow those leaders of stations that divide the four parts of the year.

15. In the beginning of the year Melkejâl rises first and rules, who is named †Tam'âinî, and sun† and all the days of his dominion whilst he bears rule are ninety-one days. 16. And these are the signs of the days which are to be seen on earth in the days of his dominion: sweat, and heat, and calms; and all the trees bear fruit, and leaves are produced on all the trees, and the harvest of wheat, and the rose flowers, and all the flowers which come forth in the field, but the trees of the winter season become withered. 17. And these are the names of the leaders which are under them: Berka'êl, Zêlebs'êl, and another who is added a head of a thousand, called Hîlûjâsêph: and the days of the dominion of this (leader) are at an end.

18. The next leader after him is Hêl'emmêlêk, whom one names the shining sun, and all the days of his light are ninety-one days. 19. And these are the signs of (his) days on the earth: glowing heat and dryness, and the trees ripen their fruits and produce all their fruits ripe and ready, and the sheep pair and become pregnant, and all the fruits of the earth are gathered in, and everything that is in the fields, and the winepress: these things take place in the days of his dominion. 20. These are the names, and the orders, and the leaders of those heads of thousands: Gîdâ'îjal, Kê'êl, and Hê'êl, and the name of the head of a thousand which is added to them, Asfâ'êl': and the days of his dominion are at an end.

# The Dream Visions

## Chapter 83.

1. And now, my son Methuselah, I will show thee all my visions which I have seen, recounting them before thee. 2. Two visions I saw before I took a wife, and the one was quite unlike the other: the first when I was learning to write, the second before I took thy mother, (when) I saw a terrible vision. And regarding them I prayed to the Lord. 3. I had laid me down in the house of my grandfather Mahalalel, (when) I saw in a vision how the heaven collapsed and was borne off and fell to the earth. 4. And when it fell to the earth I saw how the earth was swallowed up in a great abyss, and mountains were suspended on mountains, and hills sank down on hills, and high trees were rent from their stems, and hurled down and sunk in the abyss. 5. And thereupon a word fell into my mouth, and I lifted up (my voice) to cry aloud, and said: 'The earth is destroyed.' 6. And my grandfather Mahalalel waked me as I lay near him, and said unto me: 'Why dost thou cry so, my son, and why dost thou make such lamentation?' 7. And I recounted to him the whole vision which I had seen, and he said unto me: 'A terrible thing hast thou seen, my son, and of grave moment is thy dream-vision as to the secrets of all the sin of the earth: it must sink into the abyss and be destroyed with a great destruction. 8. And now, my son, arise and make petition to the Lord of glory, since thou art a believer, that a remnant may remain on the earth, and that He may not destroy the whole earth. 9. My son, from heaven all this will come upon the earth, and upon the earth there will be great destruction.' 10. After that I arose and prayed and implored and besought, and wrote down my prayer for the generations of the world, and I will show everything to thee, my son Methuselah.

11. And when I had gone forth below and seen the heaven, and the sun rising in the east, and the moon setting in the west, and a few stars, and the whole earth, and everything as †He had known† it in the beginning, then I blessed the Lord of judgment and extolled Him because He had made the sun to go forth from the windows of the east, †and he† ascended and rose on the face of the heaven, and set out and kept traversing the path shown unto him.

## Chapter 84.

1. And I lifted up my hands in righteousness and blessed the Holy and Great One, and spake with the breath of my mouth, and with the tongue of flesh, which God has made for the children of the flesh of men, that they should speak therewith, and He gave them breath and a tongue and a mouth that they should speak therewith:

2. 'Blessed be Thou, O Lord, King, great and mighty in Thy greatness, Lord of the whole creation of the heaven, King of kings and God of the whole world. And Thy power and kingship and greatness abide forever and ever, and throughout all generations Thy dominion: and all the heavens are Thy throne forever, and the whole earth Thy footstool forever and ever.

3. For Thou hast made and Thou rulest all things, and nothing is too hard for Thee, wisdom departs not **from the place of Thy throne**, **nor turns away** from Thy presence. And Thou knowest and seest and hearest everything, and there is nothing hidden from Thee [for Thou seest everything].

4. And now the angels of Thy heavens are guilty of trespass, and upon the flesh of men abideth Thy wrath until the great day of judgment.

5. And now, O God and Lord and Great King, I implore and beseech Thee to fulfil my prayer, to leave me a posterity on earth, and not destroy all the flesh of man, and make the earth without inhabitant, so that there should be an eternal destruction.

6. And now, my Lord, destroy from the earth the flesh which has aroused Thy wrath, but the flesh of righteousness and uprightness

establish as a plant of the eternal seed, and hide not Thy face from the prayer of Thy servant, O Lord.'

## The Animal Apocalypse

### *Adam, Eve, and the Offspring of Cain and Seth*

### Chapter 85.

1. And after this I saw another dream, and I will show the whole dream to thee, my son. 2. And Enoch lifted up (his voice) and spake to his son Methuselah: 'To thee, my son, will I speak: hear my words— incline thine ear to the dream-vision of thy father. 3. Before I took thy mother Edna, I saw in a vision on my bed, and behold a bull came forth from the earth, and that bull was white; and after it came forth a heifer, and along with this (latter) came forth two bulls, one of them black and the other red. 4. And that black bull gored the red one and pursued him over the earth, and thereupon I could no longer see that red bull. 5. But that black bull grew and that heifer went with him, and I saw that many oxen proceeded from him which resembled and followed him. 6. And that cow, that first one, went from the presence of that first bull in order to seek that red one, but found him not, and lamented with a great lamentation over him and sought him. 7. And I looked till that first bull came to her and quieted her, and from that time onward she cried no more. 8. And after that she bore another white bull, and after him she bore many bulls and black cows.

9. And I saw in my sleep that white bull likewise grow and become a great white bull, and from him proceeded many white bulls, and they resembled him. 10. And they began to beget many white bulls, which resembled them, one following the other, (even) many.

The Fall of the Angels and the Demoralization of Mankind

### Chapter 86.

1. And again I saw with mine eyes as I slept, and I saw the heaven above, and behold a star fell from heaven, and it arose and ate and pastured amongst those oxen. 2. And after that I saw the large and

the black oxen, and behold they all changed their stalls and pastures and their cattle, and began to live with each other. 3. And again I saw in the vision, and looked towards the heaven, and behold I saw many stars descend and cast themselves down from heaven to that first star, and they became bulls amongst those cattle and pastured with them [amongst them]. 4. And I looked at them and saw, and behold they all let out their privy members, like horses, and began to cover the cows of the oxen, and they all became pregnant and bare elephants, camels, and asses. 5. And all the oxen feared them and were affrighted at them, and began to bite with their teeth and to devour, and to gore with their horns. 6. And they began, moreover, to devour those oxen; and behold all the children of the earth began to tremble and quake before them and to flee from them.

### The Advent of the Seven Archangels
### Chapter 87.

1. And again I saw how they began to gore each other and to devour each other, and the earth began to cry aloud. 2. And I raised mine eyes again to heaven, and I saw in the vision, and behold there came forth from heaven beings who were like white men: and four went forth from that place and three with them. 3. And those three that had last come forth grasped me by my hand and took me up, away from the generations of the earth, and raised me up to a lofty place, and showed me a tower raised high above the earth, and all the hills were lower. 4. And one said unto me: 'Remain here till thou seest everything that befalls those elephants, camels, and asses, and the stars and the oxen, and all of them.'

### The Punishment of the Fallen Angels by the Archangels
### Chapter 88.

1. And I saw one of those four who had come forth first, and he seized that first star which had fallen from the heaven, and bound it hand and foot and cast it into an abyss: now that abyss was narrow and deep, and horrible and dark. 2. And one of them drew a sword,

and gave it to those elephants and camels and asses: then they began to smite each other, and the whole earth quaked because of them. 3. And as I was beholding in the vision, lo, one of those four who had come forth stoned (them) from heaven, and gathered and took all the great stars whose privy members were like those of horses, and bound them all hand and foot, and cast them in an abyss of the earth.

### The Deluge and the Deliverance of Noah

### Chapter 89.

1. And one of those four went to that white bull and instructed him in a secret, without his being terrified: he was born a bull and became a man, and built for himself a great vessel and dwelt thereon; and three bulls dwelt with him in that vessel and they were covered in. 2. And again I raised mine eyes towards heaven and saw a lofty roof, with seven water torrents thereon, and those torrents flowed with much water into an enclosure. 3. And I saw again, and behold fountains were opened on the surface of that great enclosure, and that water began to swell and rise upon the surface, and I saw that enclosure till all its surface was covered with water. 4. And the water, the darkness, and mist increased upon it; and as I looked at the height of that water, that water had risen above the height of that enclosure, and was streaming over that enclosure, and it stood upon the earth. 5. And all the cattle of that enclosure were gathered together until I saw how they sank and were swallowed up and perished in that water. 6. But that vessel floated on the water, while all the oxen and elephants and camels and asses sank to the bottom with all the animals, so that I could no longer see them, and they were not able to escape, (but) perished and sank into the depths. 7. And again I saw in the vision till those water torrents were removed from that high roof, and the chasms of the earth were levelled up and other abysses were opened. 8. Then the water began to run down into these, till the earth became visible; but that vessel settled on the earth, and the darkness retired and light appeared. 9. But that white bull which had become a man came out of that vessel, and the three bulls with him, and one of those

three was white like that bull, and one of them was red as blood, and one black: and that white bull departed from them.

### From the Death of Noah to the Exodus

10. And they began to bring forth beasts of the field and birds, so that there arose different genera: lions, tigers, wolves, dogs, hyenas, wild boars, foxes, squirrels, swine, falcons, vultures, kites, eagles, and ravens; and among them was born a white bull. 11. And they began to bite one another; but that white bull which was born amongst them begat a wild ass and a white bull with it, and the wild asses multiplied. 12. But that bull which was born from him begat a black wild boar and a white sheep; and the former begat many boars, but that sheep begat twelve sheep. 13. And when those twelve sheep had grown, they gave up one of them to the asses, and those asses again gave up that sheep to the wolves, and that sheep grew up among the wolves. 14. And the Lord brought the eleven sheep to live with it and to pasture with it among the wolves: and they multiplied and became many flocks of sheep. 15. And the wolves began to fear them, and they oppressed them until they destroyed their little ones, and they cast their young into a river of much water: but those sheep began to cry aloud on account of their little ones, and to complain unto their Lord. 16. And a sheep which had been saved from the wolves fled and escaped to the wild asses; and I saw the sheep how they lamented and cried, and besought their Lord with all their might, till that Lord of the sheep descended at the voice of the sheep from a lofty abode, and came to them and pastured them. 17. And He called that sheep which had escaped the wolves, and spake with it concerning the wolves that it should admonish them not to touch the sheep. 18. And the sheep went to the wolves according to the word of the Lord, and another sheep met it and went with it, and the two went and entered together into the assembly of those wolves, and spake with them and admonished them not to touch the sheep from henceforth. 19. And thereupon I saw the wolves, and how they oppressed the sheep exceedingly with all their power; and the sheep

cried aloud. 20. And the Lord came to the sheep and they began to smite those wolves: and the wolves began to make lamentation; but the sheep became quiet and forthwith ceased to cry out. 21. And I saw the sheep till they departed from amongst the wolves; but the eyes of the wolves were blinded, and those wolves departed in pursuit of the sheep with all their power. 22. And the Lord of the sheep went with them, as their leader, and all His sheep followed Him: and His face was dazzling and glorious and terrible to behold. 23. But the wolves began to pursue those sheep till they reached a sea of water. 24. And that sea was divided, and the water stood on this side and on that before their face, and their Lord led them and placed Himself between them and the wolves. 25. And as those wolves did not yet see the sheep, they proceeded into the midst of that sea, and the wolves followed the sheep, and [those wolves] ran after them into that sea. 26. And when they saw the Lord of the sheep, they turned to flee before His face, but that sea gathered itself together, and became as it had been created, and the water swelled and rose till it covered those wolves. 27. And I saw till all the wolves who pursued those sheep perished and were drowned.

### Israel in the Desert, the Giving of the Law, the Entrance into Palestine

28. But the sheep escaped from that water and went forth into a wilderness, where there was no water and no grass; and they began to open their eyes and to see; and I saw the Lord of the sheep pasturing them and giving them water and grass, and that sheep going and leading them. 29. And that sheep ascended to the summit of that lofty rock, and the Lord of the sheep sent it to them. 30. And after that I saw the Lord of the sheep who stood before them, and His appearance was great and terrible and majestic, and all those sheep saw Him and were afraid before His face. 31. And they all feared and trembled because of Him, and they cried to that sheep with them [which was amongst them]: "We are not able to stand before our Lord or to behold Him." 32. And that sheep which led them

again ascended to the summit of that rock, but the sheep began to be blinded and to wander from the way which he had showed them, but that sheep was not thereof. 33. And the Lord of the sheep was wrathful exceedingly against them, and that sheep discovered it, and went down from the summit of the rock, and came to the sheep, and found the greatest part of them blinded and fallen away. 34. And when they saw it they feared and trembled at its presence, and desired to return to their folds. 35. And that sheep took other sheep with it, and came to those sheep which had fallen away, and began to slay them; and the sheep feared its presence, and thus that sheep brought back those sheep that had fallen away, and they returned to their folds. 36. And I saw in this vision till that sheep became a man and built a house for the Lord of the sheep, and placed all the sheep in that house. 37. And I saw till this sheep which had met that sheep which led them fell asleep: and I saw till all the great sheep perished and little ones arose in their place, and they came to a pasture, and approached a stream of water. 38. Then that sheep, their leader which had become a man, withdrew from them and fell asleep, and all the sheep sought it and cried over it with a great crying. 39. And I saw till they left off crying for that sheep and crossed that stream of water, and there arose the **two** sheep as leaders in the place of those which had led them and fallen asleep (lit. "had fallen asleep and led them"). 40. And I saw till the sheep came to a goodly place, and a pleasant and glorious land, and I saw till those sheep were satisfied; and that house stood amongst them in the pleasant land.

*From the Time of the Judges till the Building of the Temple*

41. And sometimes their eyes were opened, and sometimes blinded, till another sheep arose and led them and brought them all back, and their eyes were opened.

42. And the dogs and the foxes and the wild boars began to devour those sheep till the Lord of the sheep raised up [another sheep] a ram from their midst, which led them. 43. And that ram began to butt on either side those dogs, foxes, and wild boars till he had destroyed

them †all†. 44. And that sheep whose eyes were opened saw that ram, which was amongst the sheep, **till** it †forsook its glory† and began to butt those sheep, and trampled upon them, and behaved itself unseemly. 45. And the Lord of the sheep sent the **lamb** to another **lamb** and raised it to being a ram and leader of the sheep instead of that ram which had †forsaken its glory†. 46. And it went to it and spake to it alone, and raised it to being a ram, and made it the prince and leader of the sheep; but during all these things those dogs oppressed the sheep. 47. And the first ram pursued that second ram, and that second ram arose and fled before it; and I saw till those dogs pulled down the first ram. 48. And that second ram arose and led the [little] sheep. 49. And those sheep grew and multiplied; but all the dogs, and foxes, and wild boars feared and fled before it, and that ram butted and killed the wild beasts, and those wild beasts had no longer any power among the sheep and robbed them no more of ought. 48ᵇ. And that ram begat many sheep and fell asleep; and a little sheep became ram in its stead, and became prince and leader of those sheep.

50. And that house became great and broad, and it was built for those sheep: <and> a tower lofty and great was built on the house for the Lord of the sheep, and that house was low, but the tower was elevated and lofty, and the Lord of the sheep stood on that tower and they offered a full table before Him.

### The Two Kingdoms of Israel and Judah, to the Destruction of Jerusalem

51. And again I saw those sheep that they again erred and went many ways, and forsook that their house, and the Lord of the sheep called some from amongst the sheep and sent them to the sheep, but the sheep began to slay them. 52. And one of them was saved and was not slain, and it sped away and cried aloud over the sheep; and they sought to slay it, but the Lord of the sheep saved it from the sheep, and brought it up to me, and caused it to dwell there. 53. And many other sheep He sent to those sheep to testify unto them and lament

over them. 54. And after that I saw that when they forsook the house of the Lord and His tower they fell away entirely, and their eyes were blinded; and I saw the Lord of the sheep how He wrought much slaughter amongst them in their herds until those sheep invited that slaughter and betrayed His place. 55. And He gave them over into the hands of the lions and tigers, and wolves and hyenas, and into the hand of the foxes, and to all the wild beasts, and those wild beasts began to tear in pieces those sheep. 56. And I saw that He forsook that their house and their tower and gave them all into the hand of the lions, to tear and devour them, into the hand of all the wild beasts. 57. And I began to cry aloud with all my power, and to appeal to the Lord of the sheep, and to represent to Him in regard to the sheep that they were devoured by all the wild beasts. 58. But He remained unmoved, though He saw it, and rejoiced that they were devoured and swallowed and robbed, and left them to be devoured in the hand of all the beasts. 59. And He called seventy shepherds, and cast those sheep to them that they might pasture them, and He spake to the shepherds and their companions: "Let each individual of you pasture the sheep henceforward, and everything that I shall command you that do ye. 60. And I will deliver them over unto you duly numbered, and tell you which of them are to be destroyed— and them destroy ye." And He gave over unto them those sheep. 61. And He called another and spake unto him: "Observe and mark everything that the shepherds will do to those sheep; for they will destroy more of them than I have commanded them. 62. And every excess and the destruction which will be wrought through the shepherds, record (namely) how many they destroy according to my command, and how many according to their own caprice: record against every individual shepherd all the destruction he effects. 63. And read out before me by number how many they destroy, and how many they deliver over for destruction, that I may have this as a testimony against them, and know every deed of the shepherds, that I may **comprehend** and see what they do, whether or not they abide by my command which I have commanded them. 64. But they shall not know it, and thou shalt not declare it to them, nor admonish them, but only record against each individual all the destruction which the shepherds effect each in his time, and lay it all before me." 65. And I saw till those shepherds pastured in their season, and they began to slay and to destroy more than they were bidden, and they delivered those sheep into the hand of the lions. 66. And the lions and tigers ate and devoured the greater part of those sheep, and the wild boars ate along with them; and they burnt that tower and demolished that house. 67. And I became exceedingly sorrowful over that tower because that house of the sheep was demolished, and afterwards I was unable to see if those sheep entered that house.

### First Period of the Angelic Rulers—from the Destruction of Jerusalem to the Return from the Captivity

68. And the shepherds and their associates delivered over those sheep to all the wild beasts, to devour them, and each one of them received in his time a definite number: it was written by the other in a book how many each one of them destroyed of them. 69. And each one slew and destroyed many more than was prescribed; and I began to weep and lament on account of those sheep. 70. And thus in the vision I saw that one who wrote, how he wrote down every one that was destroyed by those shepherds, day by day, and carried up and laid down and showed actually the whole book to the Lord of the sheep— (even) everything that they had done, and all that each one of them had made away with, and all that they had given over to destruction. 71. And the book was read before the Lord of the sheep, and He took the book from his hand and read it and sealed it and laid it down.

### Second Period—from the Time of Cyrus to that of Alexander the Great

72. And forthwith I saw how the shepherds pastured for twelve hours, and behold three of those sheep turned back and came and entered and began to build up all that had fallen down of that house; but the wild boars tried to hinder them, but they were not able. 73. And they began again to build as before, and they reared up that tower, and

it was named the high tower; and they began again to place a table before the tower, but all the bread on it was polluted and not pure. 74. And as touching all this the eyes of those sheep were blinded so that they saw not, and (the eyes of) their shepherds likewise; and they delivered them in large numbers to their shepherds for destruction, and they trampled the sheep with their feet and devoured them. 75. And the Lord of the sheep remained unmoved till all the sheep were dispersed over the field and mingled with them (*i.e.* the beasts), and they (*i.e.* the shepherds) did not save them out of the hand of the beasts. 76. And this one who wrote the book carried it up, and showed it and read it before the Lord of the sheep, and implored Him on their account, and besought Him on their account as he showed Him all the doings of the shepherds, and gave testimony before Him against all the shepherds. 77. And he took the actual book and laid it down beside Him and departed.

### Third Period—from Alexander the Great to the Greco-Syrian Domination

### Chapter 90.

1. And I saw till that in this manner **thirty-five** shepherds undertook the pasturing (of the sheep), and they severally completed their periods as did the first; and others received them into their hands to pasture them for their period, each shepherd in his own period. 2. And after that I saw in my vision all the birds of heaven coming, the eagles, the vultures, the kites, the ravens; but the eagles led all the birds; and they began to devour those sheep, and to pick out their eyes and to devour their flesh. 3. And the sheep cried out because their flesh was being devoured by the birds, and as for me I looked and lamented in my sleep over that shepherd who pastured the sheep. 4. And I saw until those sheep were devoured by the dogs and eagles and kites, and they left neither flesh nor skin nor sinew remaining on them till only their bones stood there: and their bones too fell to the earth and the sheep became few. 5. And I saw until that twenty-three had undertaken the pasturing and completed in their several

periods fifty-eight times.

*Fourth Period—from the Greco-Syrian Domination
to the Maccabean Revolt*

6. But behold lambs were borne by those white sheep, and they began to open their eyes and to see, and to cry to the sheep. 7. Yea, they cried to them, but they did not hearken to what they said to them, but were exceedingly deaf, and their eyes were very exceedingly blinded. 8. And I saw in the vision how the ravens flew upon those lambs, and took one of those lambs, and dashed the sheep in pieces and devoured them. 9. And I saw till horns grew upon those lambs, and the ravens cast down their horns; and I saw till there sprouted a great horn of one of those sheep, and their eyes were opened. 10. And it †looked at† them [and their eyes opened], and it cried to the sheep, and the rams saw it and all ran to it. 11. And notwithstanding all this those eagles and vultures and ravens and kites still kept tearing the sheep and swooping down upon them and devouring them: still the sheep remained silent, but the rams lamented and cried out. 12. And those ravens fought and battled with it and sought to lay low its horn, but they had no power over it.

*The Last Assault of the Gentiles on the Jews
(where vv. 53–55 and 16–18 are doublets)*

13. And I saw till the †shepherds and† eagles and those vultures and kites came, and †they cried to the ravens† that they should break the horn of that ram, and they battled and fought with it, and it battled with them and cried that its help might come.

16. All the eagles and vultures and ravens and kites were gathered together, and there came with them all the sheep of the field, yea, they all came together, and helped each other to break that horn of the ram.

19. And I saw till a great sword was given to the sheep, and the sheep proceeded against all the beasts of the field to slay them, and all the beasts and the birds of the heaven fled before their face.

14. And I saw till that man, who wrote down the names of the shepherds [and] carried up into the presence of the Lord of the sheep [came and helped it and showed it everything: he had come down for the help of that ram].

15. And I saw till the Lord of the sheep came unto them in wrath, and all who saw Him fled, and they all fell †into His shadow† from before His face.

17. And I saw that man, who wrote the book according to the command of the Lord, till he opened that book concerning the destruction which those twelve last shepherds had wrought, and showed that they had destroyed much more than their predecessors, before the Lord of the sheep.

18. And I saw till the Lord of the sheep came unto them and took in His hand the staff of His wrath, and smote the earth, and the earth clove asunder, and all the beasts and all the birds of the heaven fell from among those sheep, and were swallowed up in the earth and it covered them.

### Judgment of the Fallen Angels, the Shepherds, and the Apostates

20. And I saw till a throne was erected in the pleasant land, and the Lord of the sheep sat Himself thereon, and **the other** took the sealed books and opened those books before the Lord of the sheep. 21. And the Lord called those men the seven first white ones, and commanded that they should bring before Him, beginning with the first star which led the way, **all the** stars whose privy members were like those of horses, and they brought them all before Him. 22. And He said to that man who wrote before Him, being one of those seven white ones, and said unto him: "Take those seventy shepherds to whom I delivered the sheep, and who taking them on their own authority slew more than I commanded them." 23. And behold, they were all bound, I saw, and they all stood before Him. 24. And

the judgment was held first over the stars, and they were judged and found guilty, and went to the place of condemnation, and they were cast into an abyss, full of fire and flaming, and full of pillars of fire. 25. And those seventy shepherds were judged and found guilty, and they were cast into that fiery abyss. 26. And I saw at that time how a like abyss was opened in the midst of the earth, full of fire, and they brought those blinded sheep, and they were all judged and found guilty and cast into this fiery abyss, and they burned; now this abyss was to the right of that house. 27. And I saw those sheep burning †and their bones burning†.

### The New Jerusalem, the Conversion of the Surviving Gentiles, the Resurrection of the Righteous, the Messiah

28. And I stood up to see till they folded up that old house; and carried off all the pillars, and all the beams and ornaments of the house were at the same time folded up with it, and they carried it off and laid it in a place in the south of the land. 29. And I saw till the Lord of the sheep brought a new house greater and loftier than that first, and set it up in the place of the first which had been folded up: all its pillars were new, and its ornaments were new and larger than those of the first, the old one which He had taken away, and all the sheep were within it.

30. And I saw all the sheep which had been left, and all the beasts on the earth, and all the birds of the heaven, falling down and doing homage to those sheep and making petition to and obeying them in every **thing**. 31. And thereafter those three who were clothed in white and had seized me by my hand [who had taken me up before], and the hand of that ram also seizing hold of me, they took me up and set me down in the midst of those sheep †before the judgment took place†. 32. And those sheep were all white, and their wool was abundant and clean. 33. And all that had been destroyed and dispersed, and all the beasts of the field, and all the birds of the heaven, assembled in that house, and the Lord of the sheep rejoiced with great joy because they were all good and had returned to His house. 34. And I

saw till they laid down that sword, which had been given to the sheep, and they brought it back into the house, and it was sealed before the presence of the Lord, and all the sheep were invited into that house, but it held them not. 35. And the eyes of them all were opened, and they saw the good, and there was not one among them that did not see. 36. And I saw that that house was large and broad and very full.

37. And I saw that a white bull was born, with large horns, and all the beasts of the field and all the birds of the air feared him and made petition to him all the time. 38. And I saw till all their generations were transformed, and they all became white bulls; and the first among them became a **lamb**, and that **lamb** became a great animal and had great black horns on its head; and the Lord of the sheep rejoiced over **it** and over all the oxen. 39. And I slept in their midst: and I awoke and saw everything. 40. This is the vision which I saw while I slept, and I awoke and blessed the Lord of righteousness and gave Him glory. 41. Then I wept with a great weeping, and my tears stayed not till I could no longer endure it: when I saw, they flowed on account of what I had seen; for everything shall come and be fulfilled; and all the deeds of men in their order were shown to me. 42. On that night I remembered the first dream, and because of it I wept and was troubled—because I had seen that vision.'

# Concluding Section
# of the Book

## Chapter 91.

1. The book written by Enoch—[Enoch indeed wrote this complete doctrine of wisdom, (which is) praised of all men and a judge of all the earth] for all my children who shall dwell on the earth; and for the future generations who shall observe uprightness and peace.

2. Let not your spirit be troubled on account of the times; for the Holy and Great One has appointed days for all things.

3. And the righteous one shall arise from sleep, [shall arise] and walk in the paths of righteousness, and all his path and conversation shall be in eternal goodness and grace.

4. He will be gracious to the righteous and give him eternal uprightness, and He will give him power so that he shall be (endowed) with goodness and righteousness, and he shall walk in eternal light.

5. And sin shall perish in darkness forever, and shall no more be seen from that day for evermore.

## Chapter 92.

1. 'And now, my son Methuselah, call to me all thy brothers, and gather together to me all the sons of thy mother, for the word calls me, and the spirit is poured out upon me, that I may show you everything that shall befall you forever.'

2. And there upon Methuselah went and summoned to him all his brothers and assembled his relatives. 3. And he spake unto all the children of righteousness and said: 'Hear, ye sons of Enoch, all the words of your father, and hearken aright to the voice of my mouth;

for I exhort you and say unto you, beloved: love uprightness and walk therein.

4. And draw not nigh to uprightness with a double heart, and associate not with those of a double heart, but walk in righteousness, my sons. and it shall guide you on good paths, and righteousness shall be your companion.

5. For I know that violence **must** increase on the earth, and a great chastisement be executed on the earth, and all unrighteousness come to an end: yea, it shall be cut off from its roots, and its whole structure be destroyed.

6. And unrighteousness shall again be consummated on the earth, and all the deeds of unrighteousness and of violence and transgression shall prevail in a twofold degree.

7. And when sin and unrighteousness and blasphemy and violence in all kinds of deeds increase, and apostasy and transgression and uncleanness increase, a great chastisement shall come from heaven upon all these, and the holy Lord will come forth with wrath and chastisement to execute judgment on earth.

8. In those days violence shall be cut off from its roots, and the roots of unrighteousness together with deceit, and they shall be destroyed from under heaven.

9. And all the idols of the heathen shall be abandoned, and the temples burned with fire, and they shall remove them from the whole earth, and they (*i.e.* the heathen) shall be cast into the judgment of fire, and shall perish in wrath and in grievous judgment forever.

10. And the righteous shall arise from their sleep, and wisdom shall arise and be given unto them.

[11. And after that the roots of unrighteousness shall be cut off, and the sinners shall be destroyed by the sword ... shall be cut off from the blasphemers in every place, and those who plan violence and those who commit blasphemy shall perish by the sword.]

12. And now I tell you, my sons, and show you the paths of

righteousness, and the paths of violence. Yea, I will show them to you again, that ye may know what will come to pass.

13. And now, hearken unto me, my sons, and walk in the paths of righteousness, and walk not in the paths of violence; for all who walk in the paths of unrighteousness shall perish forever.'

## Chapter 93.

1. And after that Enoch both †gave† and began to recount from the books. 2. And Enoch said: 'Concerning the children of righteousness and concerning the elect of the world, and concerning the plant of uprightness, I will speak these things, yea, I Enoch, will declare (them) unto you, my sons: according to that which appeared to me in the heavenly vision, and which I have known through the word of the holy angels, and have learnt from the heavenly tablets.'

3. And Enoch began to recount from the books and said: 'I was born the seventh in the first week, while judgment and righteousness still endured.

4. And after me there shall arise in the second week great wickedness, and deceit shall have sprung up; and in it there shall be the first end. And in it a man shall be saved; and after it is ended unrighteousness shall grow up, and a law shall be made for the sinners.

5. And after that in the third week, at its close, a man shall be elected as the plant of righteous judgment. And **his posterity** shall become the plant of righteousness for evermore.

6. And after that in the fourth week, at its close, visions of the holy and righteous shall be seen. And a law for all generations and an enclosure shall be made for them.

7. And after that in the fifth week, at its close, the house of glory and dominion shall be built forever.

8. And after that in the sixth week, all who live in it shall be blinded, and the hearts of all of them shall godlessly forsake wisdom. And in it a man shall ascend; and at its close the house of dominion shall be burnt with fire, and the whole race of the chosen root

shall be dispersed.

9. And after that in the seventh week, shall an apostate generation arise, and many shall be its deeds, and all its deeds shall be apostate.

10. And at its close shall be elected the elect righteous of the eternal plant of righteousness, to receive sevenfold instruction concerning all His creation.

[11. For who is there of all the children of men that is able to hear the voice of the Holy One without being troubled? And who can think His thoughts? And who is there that can behold all the works of heaven? 12. And how should there be one who could behold the heaven, and who is there that could understand the things of heaven and see a soul or a spirit and could tell thereof, or ascend and see all their ends and think them or do like them? 13. And who is there of all men that could know what is the breadth and the length of the earth, and to whom has been shown the measure of all of them? 14. Or is there anyone who could discern the length of the heaven and how great is its height, and upon what it is founded, and how great is the number of the stars, and where all the luminaries rest?]

12. And after that there shall be another, the eighth week, that of righteousness, and a sword shall be given to it that a righteous judgment may be executed on the oppressors, and sinners shall be delivered into the hands of the righteous.

13. And at its close they shall acquire houses through their righteousness, and a house shall be built for the Great King in glory for evermore,

14d. And all mankind shall look to the path of uprightness.

14a. And after that, in the ninth week, the righteous judgment shall be revealed to the whole world,

b. And all the works of the godless shall vanish from all the earth,

c. And the world shall be written down for destruction.

15. And after this, in the tenth week in the seventh part, there shall be the great eternal judgment in which He will execute vengeance

amongst the angels.

16. And the first heaven shall depart and pass away, and a new heaven shall appear, and all the powers of the heavens shall give sevenfold light.

17. And after that there will be many weeks without number forever, and all shall be in goodness and righteousness, and sin shall no more be mentioned forever.

## Chapter 94.

1. And now I say unto you, my sons, love righteousness and walk therein; for the paths of righteousness are worthy of acceptation, but the paths of unrighteousness shall suddenly be destroyed and vanish.

2. And to certain men of a generation shall the paths of violence and of death be revealed, and they shall hold themselves afar from them, and shall not follow them.

3. And now I say unto you the righteous: walk not on the paths of wickedness, nor on the paths of death, and draw not nigh to them, lest ye be destroyed.

4. But seek and choose for yourselves righteousness and an elect life, and walk in the paths of peace, and ye shall live and prosper.

5. And hold fast my words in the thoughts of your hearts, and suffer them not to be effaced from your hearts; for know that sinners will tempt men to **evilly-entreat** wisdom so that no place may be found for her, and no manner of temptation may minish.

6. Woe to those who build unrighteousness and oppression, and lay deceit as a foundation; for they shall be suddenly overthrown, and they shall have no peace.

7. Woe to those who build their houses with sin; for from all their foundations shall they be overthrown, and by the sword shall they fall. [And those who acquire gold and silver in judgment suddenly shall perish.]

8. Woe to you, ye rich, for ye have trusted in your riches, and from your riches shall ye depart, because ye have not remembered the Most

High in the days of your riches.

9. Ye have committed blasphemy and unrighteousness, and have become ready for the day of slaughter, and the day of darkness and the day of the great judgment.

10. Thus I speak and declare unto you: He who hath created you will overthrow you, and for your fall there shall be no compassion, and your Creator will rejoice at your destruction.

11. And your righteous ones in those days shall be a reproach to the sinners and the godless.

## Chapter 95.

1. Oh that mine eyes were [a cloud of] waters that I might weep over you, and pour down my tears as a cloud †of† waters: that so I might rest from my trouble of heart!

2. †Who has permitted you to practice reproaches and wickedness? And so judgment shall overtake you, sinners.†

3. Fear not the sinners, ye righteous; for again will the Lord deliver them into your hands, that ye may execute judgment upon them according to your desires.

4. Woe to you who fulminate anathemas which cannot be reversed: healing shall therefore be far from you because of your sins.

5. Woe to you who requite your neighbor with evil; for ye shall be requited according to your works.

6. Woe to you, lying witnesses, and to those who weigh out injustice, for suddenly shall ye perish.

7. Woe to you, sinners, for ye persecute the righteous; for ye shall be delivered up and persecuted because of injustice, and heavy shall its yoke be upon you.

## Chapter 96.

1. Be hopeful, ye righteous; for suddenly shall the sinners perish before you, and ye shall have lordship over them according to your desires.

[2. And in the day of the tribulation of the sinners, your children shall mount and rise as eagles, and higher than the vultures will be your nest, and ye shall ascend and enter the crevices of the earth, and the clefts of the rock forever as coneys before the unrighteous, and the sirens shall sigh because of you and weep.]

3. Wherefore fear not, ye that have suffered; for healing shall be your portion, and a bright light shall enlighten you, and the voice of rest ye shall hear from heaven.

4. Woe unto you, ye sinners, for your riches make you appear like the righteous, but your hearts convict you of being sinners, and this fact shall be a testimony against you for a memorial of (your) evil deeds.

5. Woe to you who devour the finest of the wheat, and drink **wine in large bowls**, and tread under foot the lowly with your might.

6. Woe to you who drink water **from every fountain**, for suddenly shall ye be consumed and wither away, because ye have forsaken the fountain of life.

7. Woe to you who work unrighteousness, and deceit and blasphemy: it shall be a memorial against you for evil.

8. Woe to you, ye mighty, who with might oppress the righteous; for the day of your destruction is coming. In those days many and good days shall come to the righteous—in the day of your judgment.

## Chapter 97.

1. Believe, ye righteous, that the sinners will become a shame, and perish in the day of unrighteousness.

2. Be it known unto you (ye sinners) that the Most High is mindful of your destruction, and the angels of heaven rejoice over your destruction.

3. What will ye do, ye sinners, and whither will ye flee on that day of judgment, when ye hear the voice of the prayer of the righteous?

4. Yea, ye shall fare like unto them, against whom this word shall be a testimony: "Ye have been companions of sinners."

5. And in those days the prayer of the righteous shall reach unto the Lord. And for you the days of your judgment shall come,

6. And all the words of your unrighteousness shall be read out before the Great Holy One; and your faces shall be covered with shame, and He will reject every work which is grounded on unrighteousness.

7. Woe to you, ye sinners, who live on the mid-ocean and on the dry land, whose remembrance is evil against you.

8. Woe to you who acquire silver and gold in unrighteousness, and say: "We have become rich with riches and have possessions, and have acquired everything we have desired.

9. And now let us do what we purposed: for we have gathered silver,

9d And many are the husbandmen in our houses.

9c And our granaries are (brim) full as with water."

10. Yea, and like water your lies shall flow away; for your riches shall not abide, but speedily ascend from you; for ye have acquired it all in unrighteousness, and ye shall be given over to a great curse.

## Chapter 98.

1. And now I swear unto you, to the wise and to the foolish, for ye shall have manifold experiences on the earth.

2. For ye men shall put on more adornments than a woman, and colored garments more than a virgin: in royalty and in grandeur and in power, and in silver and in gold and in purple, and in splendor and in food they shall be poured out as water.

3. Therefore they shall be wanting in doctrine and wisdom, and they shall perish thereby together with their possessions; and with all their glory and their splendor, and in shame and in slaughter and in great destitution, their spirits shall be cast into the furnace of fire.

4. I have sworn unto you, ye sinners, as a mountain has not become a slave, and a hill does not become the handmaid of a woman, even so sin has not been sent upon the earth, but man of himself has created it, and under a great curse shall they fall who commit it.

5. And barrenness has not been given to the woman, but on account of the deeds of her own hands she dies without children.

6. I have sworn unto you, ye sinners, by the Holy Great One, that all your evil deeds are revealed in the heavens, and that none of your deeds of oppression are covered and hidden.

7. And do not think in your spirit, nor say in your heart, that ye do not know and that ye do not see that every sin is every day recorded in heaven in the presence of the Most High. 8. From henceforth ye know that all your oppression wherewith ye oppress is written down every day till the day of your judgment.

9. Woe to you, ye fools, for through your folly shall ye perish: and ye transgress against the wise, and so good hap shall not be your portion. 10. And now, know ye that ye are prepared for the day of destruction: wherefore do not hope to live, ye sinners, but ye shall depart and die; for ye know no ransom; for ye are prepared for the day of the great judgment, for the day of tribulation and great shame for your spirits.

11. Woe to you, ye obstinate of heart, who work wickedness and eat blood: whence have ye good things to eat and to drink and to be filled? From all the good things which the Lord the Most High has placed in abundance on the earth; therefore ye shall have no peace. 12. Woe to you who love the deeds of unrighteousness: wherefore do ye hope for good hap unto yourselves? Know that ye shall be delivered into the hands of the righteous, and they shall cut off your necks and slay you, and have no mercy upon you. 13. Woe to you who rejoice in the tribulation of the righteous; for no grave shall be dug for you. 14. Woe to you who set at nought the words of the righteous; for ye shall have no hope of life. 15. Woe to you who write down lying and godless words; for they write down their lies that men may hear them and act godlessly towards (their) neighbor. 16. Therefore they shall have no peace, but die a sudden death.

## Chapter 99.

1. Woe to you who work godlessness, and glory in lying and extol them: ye shall perish, and no happy life shall be yours.

2. Woe to them who pervert the words of uprightness, and transgress the eternal law, and transform themselves into what they were not [into sinners]: they shall be trodden under foot upon the earth.

3. In those days make ready, ye righteous, to raise your prayers as a memorial, and place them as a testimony before the angels, that they may place the sin of the sinners for a memorial before the Most High.

4. In those days the nations shall be stirred up, and the families of the nations shall arise on the day of destruction.

5. And in those days the destitute shall go forth and carry off their children, and they shall abandon them, so that their children shall perish through them: yea, they shall abandon their children (that are still) sucklings, and not return to them, and shall have no pity on their beloved ones.

6. And again I swear to you, ye sinners, that sin is prepared for a day of unceasing bloodshed. 7. And they who worship stones, and grave images of gold and silver and wood <and stone> and clay, and those who worship impure spirits and demons, and all kinds of idols not according to knowledge, shall get no manner of help from them.

8. And they shall become godless by reason of the folly of their hearts, and their eyes shall be blinded through the fear of their hearts, and through visions in their dreams.

9. Through these they shall become godless and fearful; for they shall have wrought all their work in a lie, and shall have worshiped a stone: therefore in an instant shall they perish.

10. But in those days blessed are all they who accept the words of wisdom, and understand them, and observe the paths of the Most High, and walk in the path of His righteousness, and become not godless with the godless; for they shall be saved.

11. Woe to you who spread evil to your neighbors; for you shall be

slain in Sheol.

12. Woe to you who make deceitful and false measures, and (to them) who cause bitterness on the earth; for they shall thereby be utterly consumed.

13. Woe to you who build your houses through the grievous toil of others, and all their building materials are the bricks and stones of sin; I tell you ye shall have no peace.

14. Woe to them who reject the measure and eternal heritage of their fathers, and whose souls follow after idols; for they shall have no rest.

15. Woe to them who work unrighteousness and help oppression, and slay their neighbors until the day of the great judgment.

16. For He shall cast down your glory, and bring affliction on your hearts, and shall arouse **His fierce indignation**, and destroy you all with the sword; and all the holy and righteous shall remember your sins.

## Chapter 100.

1. And in those days in one place the fathers together with their sons shall be smitten, and brothers one with another shall fall in death, till the streams flow with their blood.

2. For a man shall not withhold his hand from slaying his sons and his son's sons, and the sinner shall not withhold his hand from his honored brother: from dawn till sunset they shall slay one another.

3. And the horse shall walk up to the breast in the blood of sinners, and the chariot shall be submerged to its height.

4. In those days the angels shall descend into the secret places, and gather together into one place all those who brought down sin, and the Most High will arise on that day of judgment, to execute great judgement amongst sinners.

5. And over all the righteous and holy He will appoint guardians from amongst the holy angels, to guard them as the apple of an eye, until He makes an end of all wickedness and all sin, and though the righteous sleep a long sleep, they have nought to fear.

6. And (then) the children of the earth shall see the wise **in security**, and shall understand all the words of this book, and recognize that their riches shall not be able to save them in the overthrow of their sins.

7. Woe to you, sinners, on the day of strong anguish, **ye who** afflict the righteous and burn them with fire: ye shall be requited according to your works.

8. Woe to you, ye obstinate of heart, who watch in order to devise wickedness: therefore shall fear come upon you, and there shall be none to help you.

9. Woe to you, ye sinners, on account of the words of your mouth, and on account of the deeds of your hands which your godlessness as wrought, in blazing flames burning worse than fire shall ye burn.

10. And now, know ye that from the angels He will inquire as to your deeds in heaven, from the sun and from the moon and from the stars in reference to your sins because upon the earth ye execute judgment on the righteous. 11. And He will summon to testify against you every cloud and mist and dew and rain; for they shall all be withheld because of you from descending upon you, and they shall be mindful of your sins. 12. And now give presents to the rain that it be not withheld from descending upon you, nor yet the dew, when it has received gold and silver from you that it may descend. 13. When the hoar frost and snow with their chilliness, and all the snow storms with all their plagues fall upon you, in those days ye shall not be able to stand before them.

## Chapter 101.

1. Observe the heaven, ye children of heaven, and every work of the Most High, and fear ye Him and work no evil in His presence. 2. If He closes the windows of heaven, and withholds the rain and the dew from descending on the earth on your account, what will ye do then? 3. And if He sends His anger upon you because of your deeds, ye cannot petition Him; for ye spake proud and insolent words against His righteousness: therefore ye shall have no peace. 4. And see ye not

the **sailors** of the ships, how their ships are tossed to and fro by the waves, and are shaken by the winds, and are in sore trouble? 5. And therefore do they fear because all their goodly possessions go upon the sea with them, and they have evil forebodings of heart that the sea will swallow them and they will perish therein.

6. Are not the entire sea and all its waters, and all its movements, the work of the Most High, and has He not set limits to its doings, and confined it throughout by the sand? 7. And at His reproof it is afraid and dries up, and all its fish die and all that is in it; but ye sinners that are on the earth fear Him not. 8. Has He not made the heaven and the earth, and all that is therein? Who has given understanding and wisdom to everything that moves on the earth and in the sea? 9. Do not the **sailors** of the ships fear the sea? Yet sinners fear not the Most High.

## Chapter 102.

1. In those days when He hath brought a grievous fire upon you, whither will ye flee, and where will ye find deliverance? And when He launches forth His word against you, will you not be affrighted and fear?

2. And all the luminaries shall be affrighted with great fear, and all the earth shall be affrighted and tremble and be alarmed.

3. And all the †angels shall execute their commands† and shall seek to hide themselves from the presence of the Great Glory, and the children of earth shall tremble and quake; and ye sinners shall be cursed forever, and ye shall have no peace.

4. Fear ye not, ye souls of the righteous, and be hopeful ye that have died in righteousness.

5. And grieve not if your soul into Sheol has descended in grief, and that in your life your body fared not according to your goodness, but **wait for** the day of the **judgment** of sinners, and for the day of cursing and chastisement.

6. And yet when ye die the sinners speak over you: "As we die, so die

the righteous, and what benefit do they reap for their deeds?

7. Behold, even as we, so do they die in grief and darkness, and what have they more than we? From henceforth we are equal.

8. And what will they receive and what will they see forever? Behold, they too have died, and henceforth forever shall they see no light."

9. I tell you, ye sinners, ye are content to eat and drink, and rob and sin, and strip men naked, and acquire wealth and see good days. 10. Have ye seen the righteous how their end falls out, that no manner of violence is found in them till their death? 11. "Nevertheless they perished and became as though they had not been, and their spirits descended into Sheol in tribulation."

## Chapter 103.

1. Now, therefore, I swear to you, the righteous, by the glory of the Great and Honored and Mighty One in dominion, and by His greatness I swear to you:

2. I know a mystery and have read the heavenly tablets, and have seen the holy books, and have found written therein and inscribed regarding them:

3. That all goodness and joy and glory are prepared for them and written down for the spirits of those who have died in righteousness, and that manifold good shall be given to you in recompense for your labors, and that your lot is abundantly beyond the lot of the living.

4. And the spirits of you who have died in righteousness shall live and rejoice, and their spirits shall not perish, nor their memorial from before the face of the Great One unto all the generations of the world: wherefore no longer fear their contumely.

5. Woe to you, ye sinners, when ye have died, if ye die in the wealth of your sins; and those who are like you say regarding you: "Blessed are the sinners: they have seen all their days.

6. And how they have died in prosperity and in wealth, and have not seen tribulation or murder in their life; and they have died in honor, and judgment has not been executed on them during their life."

7. Know ye, that their souls will be made to descend into Sheol, and they shall be wretched in their great tribulation.

8. And into darkness and chains and a burning flame where there is grievous judgment shall your spirits enter; and the great judgment shall be for all the generations of the world. Woe to you, for ye shall have no peace.

9. Say not in regard to the righteous and good who are in life: "In our troubled days we have toiled laboriously and experienced every trouble, and met with much evil and been consumed, and have become few and our spirit small.

10. And we have been destroyed and have not found any to help us even with a word: we have been tortured [and destroyed], and not hoped to see life from day to day.

11. We hoped to be the head and have become the tail: we have toiled laboriously and had no satisfaction in our toil; and we have become the food of the sinners and the unrighteous and they have laid their yoke heavily upon us.

12. They have had dominion over us that hated us †and smote us; and to those that hated us† we have bowed our necks, but they pitied us not.

13. We desired to get away from them that we might escape and be at rest, but found no place whereunto we should flee and be safe from them.

14. And we complained to the rulers in our tribulation, and cried out against those who devoured us; but they did not attend to our cries, and would not hearken to our voice.

15. And they helped those who robbed us and devoured us and those who made us few; and they concealed their oppression, and they did not remove from us the yoke of those that devoured us and dispersed us and murdered us, and they concealed their murder, and remembered not that they had lifted up their hands against us."

## Chapter 104.

1. I swear unto you, that in heaven the angels remember you for good before the glory of the Great One: and your names are written before the glory of the Great One. 2. Be hopeful; for aforetime ye were put to shame through ill and affliction; but now ye shall shine as the lights of heaven, ye shall shine and ye shall be seen, and the portals of heaven shall be opened to you. 3. And in your cry, cry for judgment, and it shall appear to you; for all your tribulation shall be visited on the rulers, and on all who helped those who plundered you. 4. Be hopeful, and cast not away your hope; for ye shall have great joy as the angels of heaven. 5. What shall ye be obliged to do? Ye shall not have to hide on the day of the great judgment and ye shall not be found as sinners, and the eternal judgment shall be far from you for all the generations of the world. 6. And now fear not, ye righteous, when ye see the sinners growing strong and prospering in their ways: be not companions with them, but keep afar from their violence; for ye shall become companions of the hosts of heaven. 7. And, although ye sinners say: "All our sins shall not be searched out and be written down," nevertheless they shall write down all your sins every day. 8. And now I show unto you that light and darkness, day and night, see all your sins. 9. Be not godless in your hearts, and lie not and alter not the words of uprightness, nor charge with lying the words of the Holy Great One, nor take account of your idols; for all your lying and all your godlessness issue not in righteousness, but in great sin. 10. And now I know this mystery, that sinners will alter and pervert the words of righteousness in many ways, and will speak wicked words, and lie, and practice great deceits, and write books concerning their words. 11. But when they write down truthfully all my words in their languages, and do not change or minish ought from my words, but write them all down truthfully—all that I first testified concerning them, 12. then, I know another mystery, that books will be given to the righteous and the wise to become a cause of joy and uprightness and much wisdom. 13. And to them shall the books be given, and they shall believe in them and rejoice over them, and then shall all

the righteous who have learnt therefrom all the paths of uprightness be recompensed.'

## Chapter 105.

1. In those days the Lord bade (them) to summon and testify to the children of earth concerning their wisdom: show (it) unto them; for ye are their guides, and a recompense over the whole earth. 2. For I and My Son will be united with them forever in the paths of uprightness in their lives; and ye shall have peace: rejoice, ye children of uprightness. Amen.

# FRAGMENT OF THE BOOK OF NOAH

## Chapter 106.

1. And after some days my son Methuselah took a wife for his son Lamech, and she became pregnant by him and bore a son. 2. And his body was white as snow and red as the blooming of a rose, and the hair of his head †and his long locks were white as wool, and his eyes beautiful†. And when he opened his eyes, he lighted up the whole house like the sun, and the whole house was very bright. 3. And thereupon he arose in the hands of the midwife, opened his mouth, and †conversed with† the Lord of righteousness. 4. And his father Lamech was afraid of him and fled, and came to his father Methuselah. 5. And he said unto him: 'I have begotten a strange son, diverse from and unlike man, and resembling the sons of the God of heaven; and his nature is different, and he is not like us, and his eyes are as the rays of the sun, and his countenance is glorious. 6. And it seems to me that he is not sprung from me but from the angels, and I fear that in his days a wonder may be wrought on the earth. 7. And now, my father, I am here to petition thee and implore thee that thou mayest go to Enoch, our father, and learn from him the truth, for his dwelling place is amongst the angels.' 8. And when Methuselah heard the words of his son, he came to me to the ends of the earth; for he had heard that I was there, and he cried aloud, and I heard his voice and I came to him. And I said unto him: 'Behold, here am I, my son, **wherefore** hast thou come to me?' 9. And he answered and said: 'Because of a great cause of anxiety have I come to thee, and because of a disturbing vision have I approached. 10. And now, my father, hear me: unto Lamech my son there hath been born a

son, the like of whom there is none, and his nature is not like man's nature, and the color of his body is whiter than snow and redder than the bloom of a rose, and the hair of his head is whiter than white wool, and his eyes are like the rays of the sun, and he opened his eyes and thereupon lighted up the whole house. 11. And he arose in the hands of the midwife, and opened his mouth and blessed the Lord of heaven. 12. And his father Lamech became afraid and fled to me, and did not believe that he was sprung from him, but that he was in the likeness of the angels of heaven; and behold I have come to thee that thou mayest make known to me the truth.' 13. And I, Enoch, answered and said unto him: 'The Lord will do a new thing on the earth, and this I have already seen in a vision, and make known to thee that in the generation of my father Jared some of the **angels** of heaven transgressed the word of the Lord. 14. And behold they commit sin and transgress the law, and have united themselves with women and commit sin with them, and have married some of them, and have begot children by them. 15. And they shall produce on the earth giants not according to the spirit, but according to the flesh, and there shall be a great punishment on the earth, and the earth shall be cleansed from all impurity. 16. Yea, there shall come a great destruction over the whole earth, and there shall be a deluge and a great destruction for one year. 17. And this son who has been born unto you shall be left on the earth, and his three children shall be saved with him: when all mankind that are on the earth shall die [he and his sons shall be saved]. 18. And now make known to thy son Lamech that he who has been born is in truth his son, and call his name Noah; for he shall be left to you, and he and his sons shall be saved from the destruction, which shall come upon the earth on account of all the sin and all the unrighteousness, which shall be consummated on the earth in his days. 19. And after that there shall be still more unrighteousness than that which was first consummated on the earth; for I know the mysteries of the holy ones; for He, the Lord, has showed me and informed me, and I have read (them) in the heavenly tablets.

## Chapter 107.

1. And I saw written on them that generation upon generation shall transgress, till a generation of righteousness arises, and transgression is destroyed and sin passes away from the earth, and all manner of good comes upon it. 2. And now, my son, go and make known to thy son Lamech that this son, which has been born, is in truth his son, and that (this) is no lie.' 3. And when Methuselah had heard the words of his father Enoch—for he had shown to him everything in secret—he returned and showed (them) to him and called the name of that son Noah; for he will comfort the earth after all the destruction.

# An Appendix to the Book of Enoch

## Chapter 108.

1. Another book which Enoch wrote for his son Methuselah and for those who will come after him, and keep the law in the last days. 2. Ye who have done good shall wait for those days till an end is made of those who work evil, and an end of the might of the transgressors. 3. And wait ye indeed till sin has passed away, for their names shall be blotted out of the book of life and out of the holy books, and their seed shall be destroyed forever, and their spirits shall be slain, and they shall cry and make lamentation in a place that is a chaotic wilderness, and **in the fire shall they burn**; for there is no earth there. 4. And I saw there something like an invisible cloud; for by reason of its depth I could not †look over†, and I saw a flame of fire blazing brightly, and things like shining mountains circling and sweeping to and from. 5. And I asked one of the holy angels who was with me and said unto him: 'What is this shining thing? For it is not a heaven but only the flame of a blazing fire, and the voice of weeping and crying and lamentation and strong pain.' 6. And he said unto me: 'This place which thou seest—here are cast the spirits of sinners and blasphemers, and of those who work wickedness, and of those who pervert everything that the Lord hath spoken through the mouth of the prophets—(even) the things that shall be. 7. For some of them are written and inscribed above in the heaven, in order that the angels may read them and know that which shall befall the sinners, and the spirits of the humble, and of those who have afflicted their bodies, and been recompensed by God; and of those who have been put to shame by wicked men: 8. who love God and loved neither gold nor

silver nor any of the good things which are in the world, but gave over their bodies to torture. 9. Who, since they came into being, longed not after earthly food, but regarded everything as a passing breath, and lived accordingly, and the Lord tried them much, and their spirits were found pure so that they should bless His name. 10. And all the blessings destined for them I have recounted in the books. And he hath assigned them their recompense, because they have been found to be such as loved heaven more than their life in the world, and though they were trodden under foot of wicked men, and experienced abuse and reviling from them and were put to shame, yet they blessed Me. 11. And now I will summon the spirits of the good who belong to the generation of light, and I will transform those who were born in darkness, who in the flesh were not recompensed with such honor as their faithfulness deserved. 12. And I will bring forth in shining light those who have loved My holy name, and I will seat each on the throne of his honor. 13. And they shall be resplendent for times without number; for righteousness is the judgement of God; for to the faithful He will give faithfulness in the habitation of upright paths. 14. And they shall see those who were born in darkness led into darkness, while the righteous shall be resplendent. 15. And the sinners shall cry aloud and see them resplendent, and they indeed shall go where days and seasons are prescribed for them.'

# 2
# ENOCH

Also known as the Slavonic Enoch
& the Book of the Secrets of Enoch
Translation by W. R. Morfill, 1896

# Book of the Secrets of Enoch

### Chapter 1.

1. There was a wise man, a great artificer, and the Lord conceived love for him and received him, that he should behold the uppermost dwellings and be an eye-witness of the wise and great and inconceivable and immutable realm of God Almighty, of the very wonderful and glorious and bright and many-eyed station of the Lord's servants, and of the inaccessible throne of the Lord, and of the degrees and manifestations of the incorporeal hosts, and of the ineffable ministration of the multitude of the elements, and of the various apparition and inexpressible singing of the host of Cherubim, and of the boundless light.

2. At that time, he said, 'When my one hundred and sixty-fifth year was completed, I begat my son Mathusal (Methuselah). 3. After this too I lived two hundred years and completed all the years of my life three hundred and sixty-five years. 4. On the first day of the month I was in my house alone and was resting on my bed and slept. 5. And when I was asleep, great distress came up into my heart, and I was weeping with my eyes in sleep, and I could not understand what this distress was, or what would happen to me. 6. And there appeared to me two men, exceeding big, so that I never saw such on earth; their faces were shining like the sun, their eyes too (were) like a burning light, and from their lips was fire coming forth with clothing and singing of various kinds in appearance purple, their wings brighter than gold, their hands whiter than snow. 7. They were standing at the head of my bed and began to call me by my name. 8. And I arose from my sleep and saw clearly those two men standing in front of me.

9. And I saluted them and was seized with fear and the appearance of my face was changed from terror, and those men said to me, 10. "Have courage, Enoch, do not fear; the eternal God sent us to you, and lo! You shalt today ascend with us into heaven, and you shall tell your sons and all your household all that they shall do without you on earth in your house and let no one seek you till the Lord return you to them."

11. And I made haste to obey them and went out from my house, and made to the doors, as it was ordered me, and summoned my sons Mathusal (Methuselah) and Regim and Gaidad and made known to them all the marvels those (men) had told me.'

## Chapter 2.

'Listen to me, my children, I know not whither I go, or what will befall me; now therefore, my children, I tell you: turn not from God before the face of the vain, who made not Heaven and earth, for these shall perish and those who worship them, and may the Lord make confident your hearts in the fear of him. And now, my children, let no one think to seek me until the Lord return me to you.'

## Chapter 3.

It came to pass when Enoch had told his sons, that the angels took him on to their wings and bore him up onto the first heaven and placed him on the clouds. And there I looked, and again I looked higher and saw the ether, and they placed me on the first heaven and showed me a very great Sea, greater than the earthly sea.

## Chapter 4.

They brought before my face the elders and rulers of the stellar orders and showed me two hundred angels, who rule the stars and (their) services to the heavens, and fly with their wings and come round all those who sail.

## Chapter 5.

And here I looked down and saw the treasure-houses of the snow, and the angels who keep their terrible store-houses, and the clouds whence they come out and into which they go.

## Chapter 6.

They showed me the treasure-house of the dew, like oil of the olive, and the appearance of its form, as of all the flowers of the earth; further many angels guarding the treasure-houses of these (things), and how they are made to shut and open.

## Chapter 7.

1. And those men took me and led me up on to the second heaven, and showed me darkness, greater than earthly darkness, and there I saw prisoners hanging, watched, awaiting the great and boundless judgment, and these angels (spirits) were dark-looking, more than earthly darkness, and incessantly making weeping through all hours. 2. And I said to the men who were with me, 'Wherefore are these incessantly tortured?' They answered me, "These are God's apostates, who obeyed not God's commands, but took counsel with their own will, and turned away with their prince, who also (is) fastened on the fifth heaven."

3. And I felt great pity for them, and they saluted me, and said to me, "Man of God, pray for us to the Lord," and I answered to them, 'Who am I, a mortal man, that I should pray for angels (spirits)? Who knows whither I go, or what will befall me? Or who will pray for me?'

## Chapter 8.

1. And those men took me thence, and led me up on to the third heaven, and placed me there; and I looked downwards, and saw the produce of these places, such as has never been known for goodness. 2. And I saw all the sweet-flowering trees and beheld their fruits, which were sweet-smelling, and all the foods borne (by them) bubbling with fragrant exhalation. 3. And in the midst of the trees that of life, in that place whereon the Lord rests, when he goes up into paradise; and this tree is of ineffable goodness and fragrance, and adorned more than every existing thing; and on all sides (it is) in form gold-looking and vermilion and fire-like and covers all, and it

has produce from all fruits. 4. Its root is in the garden at the earth's end. 5. And paradise is between corruptibility and incorruptibility.

6. And two springs come out which send forth honey and milk, and their springs send forth oil and wine, and they separate into four parts, and go round with quiet course, and go down into the Paradise of Eden, between corruptibility and incorruptibility. 7. And thence they go forth along the earth and have a revolution to their circle even as other elements. 8. And here there is no unfruitful tree, and every place is blessed. 9. And (there are) three hundred angels very bright, who keep the garden, and with incessant sweet singing and never-silent voices serve the Lord throughout all days and hours. 10. And I said, 'How very sweet is this place,' and those men said to me,

## Chapter 9.

"This place, O Enoch, is prepared for the righteous, who endure all manner of offence from those that exasperate their souls, who avert their eyes from iniquity, and make righteous judgment, and give bread to the hungering, and cover the naked with clothing, and raise up the fallen, and help injured orphans, and who walk without fault before the face of the Lord, and serve him alone, and for them is prepared this place for eternal inheritance."

## Chapter 10.

1. And those two men led me up onto the Northern side and showed me there a very terrible place, and (there were) all manner of tortures in that place; cruel darkness and unillumined gloom, and there is no light there, but murky fire constantly flaming aloft, and (there is) a fiery river coming forth, and that whole place is everywhere fire, and everywhere (there is) frost and ice, thirst and shivering, while the bonds are very cruel, and the angels (spirits) fearful and merciless, bearing angry weapons, merciless torture, and I said, 2. 'Woe, woe, how very terrible is this place?'

3. And those men said to me, "This place, O Enoch, is prepared for those who dishonor God, who on earth practice sin against nature, which is child-corruption after the sodomitic fashion, magic-making,

enchantments, and devilish witchcrafts, and who boast of their wicked deeds, stealing, lies, calumnies, envy, rancor, fornication, murder, and who accursed, steal the souls of men, who, seeing the poor take away their goods and themselves wax rich, injuring them for other men's goods; who being able to satisfy the empty, made the hungering to die; being able to clothe, stripped the naked; and who knew not their creator and bowed to the soulless (and lifeless) gods, who cannot see nor hear, vain gods, (who also) built hewn images and bow down to unclean handiwork, for all these is prepared this place among these, for eternal inheritance."

## Chapter 11.

1. Those men took me, and led me up on to the fourth heaven, and showed me all the successive goings, and all the rays of the light of sun and moon. 2. And I measured their goings and compared their light, and saw that the sun's light is greater than the moon's. 3. Its circle and the wheels on which it goes always, like the wind going past with very marvelous speed, and day and night it has no rest. 4. Its passage and return (are accompanied by) four great stars, (and) each star has under it a thousand stars, to the right of the sun's wheel, (and by) four to the left, each having under it a thousand stars, altogether eight thousand, issuing with the sun continually. 5. And by day fifteen myriads of angels attend it, and by night A thousand. 6. And six-winged ones issue with the angels before the sun's wheel into the fiery flames, and a hundred angels kindle the sun and set it alight.

## Chapter 12.

1. And I looked and saw other flying elements of the sun, whose names (are) Phoenixes and Chalkydri, marvelous and wonderful, with feet and tails in the form of a lion, and a crocodile's head, their appearance (is) empurpled, like the rainbow; their size (is) nine hundred measures, their wings (are like) those of angels, each (has) twelve, and they attend and accompany the sun, bearing heat and dew, as it is ordered them from God. 2. Thus (the sun) revolves and goes, and rises under the heaven, and its course goes under the earth

with the light of its rays incessantly.

## Chapter 13.

1. Those men bore me away to the east, and placed me at the sun's gates, where the sun goes forth according to the regulation of the seasons and the circuit of the months of the whole year, and the number of the hours day and night.

2. And I saw six gates open, each gate having sixty-one stadia and a quarter of one stadium, and I measured (them) truly, and understood their size (to be) so much, through which the sun goes forth, and goes to the west, and is made even, and rises throughout all the months, and turns back again from the six gates according to the succession of the seasons; thus (the period) of the whole year is finished after the returns of the four seasons.

## Chapter 14.

1. And again those men led me away to the western parts and showed me six great gates open corresponding to the eastern gates, opposite to where the sun sets, according to the number of the days three hundred and sixty-five and a quarter.

2. Thus again it goes down to the western gates, (and) draws away its light, the greatness of its brightness, under the earth; for since the crown of its shining is in heaven with the Lord, and guarded by four hundred angels, while the sun goes round on wheel under the earth, and stands seven great hours in night, and spends half (its course) under the earth, when it comes to the eastern approach in the eighth hour of the night, it brings its lights, and the crown of shining, and the sun flames forth more than fire.

## Chapter 15.

1. Then the elements of the sun, called Phoenixes and Chalkydri break into song, therefore every bird flutters with its wings, rejoicing at the giver of light, and they broke into song at the command of the Lord.

2. The giver of light comes to give brightness to the whole world, and

the morning guard takes shape, which is the rays of the sun, and the sun of the earth goes out, and receives its brightness to light up the whole face of the earth, and they showed me this calculation of the sun's going. 3. And the gates which it enters, these are the great gates of the calculation of the hours of the year; for this reason, the sun is a great creation, whose circuit (lasts) twenty-eight years, and begins again from the beginning.

## Chapter 16.

1. Those men showed me the other course, that of the moon, twelve great gates, crowned from west to east, by which the moon goes in and out of the customary times. 2. It goes in at the first gate to the western places of the sun, by the first gates with (thirty)-one (days) exactly, by the second gates with thirty-one days exactly, by the third with thirty days exactly, by the fourth with thirty days exactly, by the fifth with thirty-one days exactly, by the sixth with thirty-one days exactly, by the seventh with thirty days exactly, by the eighth with thirty-one days perfectly, by the ninth with thirty-one days exactly, by the tenth with thirty days perfectly, by the eleventh with thirty-one days exactly, by the twelfth with twenty-eight days exactly. 3. And it goes through the western gates in the order and number of the eastern, and accomplishes the three hundred and sixty-five and a quarter days of the solar year, while the lunar year has three hundred fifty-four, and there are wanting (to it) twelve days of the solar circle, which are the lunar epacts of the whole year.

4. Thus, too, the great circle contains five hundred and thirty-two years. 5. The quarter (of a day) is omitted for three years, the fourth fulfills it exactly. 6. Therefore they are taken outside of heaven for three years and are not added to the number of days, because they change the time of the years to two new months towards completion, to two others towards diminution. 7. And when the western gates are finished, it returns and goes to the eastern to the lights, and goes thus day and night about the heavenly circles, lower than all circles, swifter than the heavenly winds, and spirits and elements and angels flying;

each angel has six wings. 8. It has a sevenfold course in nineteen years.

## Chapter 17.

In the midst of the heavens I saw armed soldiers, serving the Lord, with tympana and organs, with incessant voice, with sweet voice, with sweet and incessant (voice) and various singing, which it is impossible to describe, and (which) astonishes every mind, so wonderful and marvelous is the singing of those angels, and I was delighted listening to it.

## Chapter 18.

1. The men took me on to the fifth heaven and placed me, and there I saw many and countless soldiers, called Grigori, of human appearance, and their size (was) greater than that of great giants and their faces withered, and the silence of their mouths perpetual, and there was no service on the fifth heaven, and I said to the men who were with me, 2. 'Wherefore are these very withered and their faces melancholy, and their mouths silent, and (wherefore) is there no service on this heaven?'

3. And they said to me, "These are the Grigori, who with their prince Satanail (Satan) rejected the Lord of light, and after them are those who are held in great darkness on the second heaven, and three of them went down on to earth from the Lord's throne to the place Ermon, and broke through their vows on the shoulder of the hill Ermon and saw the daughters of men how good they are, and took to themselves wives, and befouled the earth with their deeds, who in all times of their age made lawlessness and mixing, and giants are born and marvelous big men and great enmity. 4. And therefore God judged them with great judgment, and they weep for their brethren and they will be punished on the Lord's great day."

5. And I said to the Grigori, 'I saw your brethren and their works, and their great torments, and I prayed for them, but the Lord has condemned them (to be) under earth till (the existing) heaven and earth shall end forever.'

6. And I said, 'Wherefore do you wait, brethren, and do not serve before the Lord's face, and have not put your services before the Lord's face, lest you anger your Lord utterly?'

7. And they listened to my admonition, and spoke to the four ranks in heaven, and lo! As I stood with those two men four trumpets trumpeted together with great voice, and the Grigori broke into song with one voice, and their voice went up before the Lord pitifully and affectingly.

## Chapter 19.

1. And thence those men took me and bore me up on to the sixth heaven, and there I saw seven bands of angels, very bright and very glorious, and their faces shining more than the sun's shining, glistening, and there is no difference in their faces, or behavior, or manner of dress; and these make the orders, and learn the goings of the stars, and the alteration of the moon, or revolution of the sun, and the good government of the world. 2. And when they see evildoing, they make commandments and instruction, and sweet and loud singing, and all (songs) of praise.

3. These are the archangels who are above angels, measure all life in heaven and on earth, and the angels who are (appointed) over seasons and years, the angels who are over rivers and sea, and who are over the fruits of the earth, and the angels who are over every grass, giving food to all, to every living thing, and the angels who write all the souls of men, and all their deeds, and their lives before the Lord's face; in their midst are six Phoenixes and six Cherubim and six six-winged ones continually with one voice singing one voice, and it is not possible to describe their singing, and they rejoice before the Lord at his footstool.

## Chapter 20.

1. And those two men lifted me up thence on to the seventh heaven, and I saw there a very great light, and fiery troops of great archangels, incorporeal forces, and dominions, orders and governments, Cherubim and seraphim, thrones and many-eyed ones, nine regiments,

the Ioanit stations of light, and I became afraid, and began to tremble with great terror, and those men took me, and led me after them, and said to me, 2. "Have courage, Enoch, do not fear," and showed me the Lord from afar, sitting on His very high throne. For what is there on the tenth heaven, since the Lord dwells there?

3. On the tenth heaven is God, in the Hebrew tongue he is called Aravat. 4. And all the heavenly troops would come and stand on the ten steps according to their rank, and would bow down to the Lord, and would again go to their places in joy and felicity, singing songs in the boundless light with small and tender voices, gloriously serving Him.

## Chapter 21.

1. And the Cherubim and seraphim standing about the throne, the six-winged and many-eyed ones do not depart, standing before the Lord's face doing His will, and cover His whole throne, singing with gentle voice before the Lord's face, "Holy, holy, holy, Lord Ruler of Sabaoth, heavens and earth are full of Your glory."

2. When I saw all these things, those men said to me, "Enoch, thus far is it commanded us to journey with you," and those men went away from me and thereupon I saw them not.

3. And I remained alone at the end of the seventh heaven and became afraid, and fell on my face and said to myself, 'Woe is me, what has befallen me?' 4. And the Lord sent one of his glorious ones, the archangel Gabriel, and (he) said to me, "Have courage, Enoch, do not fear, arise before the Lord's face into eternity, arise, come with me."

5. And I answered him, and said in myself, 'My Lord, my soul is departed from me, from terror and trembling, and I called to the men who led me up to this place, on them I relied, and (it is) with them I go before the Lord's face.'

6. And Gabriel caught me up, as a leaf caught up by the wind, and placed me before the Lord's face. 7. And I saw the eighth heaven, which is called in the Hebrew tongue Muzaloth, changer of the

seasons, of drought, and of wet, and of the twelve constellations of the circle of the firmament, which are above the seventh heaven. 8. And I saw the ninth heaven, which is called in Hebrew Kuchavim, where are the heavenly homes of the twelve constellations of the circle of the firmament.

## Chapter 22.

1. On the tenth heaven, (which is called) Aravoth, I saw the appearance of the Lord's face, like iron made to glow in fire, and brought out, emitting sparks, and it burns. 2. Thus (in a moment of eternity) I saw the Lord's face, but the Lord's face is ineffable, marvelous, and very awful, and very, very terrible. 3. And who am I to tell of the Lord's unspeakable being, and of his very wonderful face? And I cannot tell the quantity of his many instructions, and various voices, the Lord's throne (is) very great and not made with hands, nor the quantity of those standing round Him, troops of Cherubim and seraphim, nor their incessant singing, nor his immutable beauty, and who shall tell of the ineffable greatness of His glory.

4. And I fell prone and bowed down to the Lord, and the Lord with His lips said to me, 5. "Have courage, Enoch, do not fear, arise, and stand before My face into eternity." 6. And the archangel Michael lifted me up, and led me to before the Lord's face.

7. And the Lord said to His servants tempting them, "Let Enoch stand before My face into eternity," and the glorious ones bowed down to the Lord, and said, "Let Enoch go according to Your word."

8. And the Lord said to Michael, "Go and take Enoch from out (of) his earthly garments, and anoint him with My sweet ointment, and put him into the garments of My glory." 9. And Michael did thus, as the Lord told him. He anointed me and dressed me, and the appearance of that ointment is more than the great light, and His ointment is like sweet dew, and its smell mild, shining like the sun's ray, and I looked at myself, and (I) was like (transfigured) one of his glorious ones.

10. And the Lord summoned one of His archangels by name Pravuil,

whose knowledge was quicker in wisdom than the other archangels, who wrote all the deeds of the Lord; and the Lord said to Pravuil, "Bring out the books from My store-houses, and a reed of quick-writing, and give (it) to Enoch, and deliver to him the choice and comforting books out of your hand."

## Chapter 23.

1. And he was telling me all the works of heaven, earth, and sea, and all the elements, their passages and goings, and the thunderings of the thunders, the sun and moon, the goings and changes of the stars, the seasons, years, days, and hours, the risings of the wind, the numbers of the angels, and the formation of their songs, and all human things, the tongue of every human song and life, the commandments, instructions, and sweet-voiced singing, and all things that it is fitting to learn. 2. And Pravuil told me, "All the things that I have told you, we have written. Sit and write all the souls of mankind, however many of them are born, and the places prepared for them to eternity; for all souls are prepared to eternity, before the formation of the world."

3. And all double thirty days and thirty nights, and I wrote out all things exactly and wrote three hundred and sixty-six books.

## Chapter 24.

1. And the Lord summoned me and said to me, "Enoch, sit down on my left with Gabriel." 2. And I bowed down to the Lord, and the Lord spoke to me, "Enoch, beloved, all (that) you see, all things that are standing finished I tell to you even before the very beginning, all that I created from non-being, and visible (physical) things from invisible (spiritual). 3. Hear, Enoch, and take in these My words, for not to My angels have I told My secret, and I have not told them their rise, nor My endless realm, nor have they understood My creating, which I tell you today. 4. For before all things were visible (physical), I alone used to go about in the invisible (spiritual) things, like the sun from east to west, and from west to east. 5. But even the sun has peace in itself, while I found no peace, because I was creating all

things, and I conceived the thought of placing foundations, and of creating visible (physical) creation.

## Chapter 25.

1. I commanded in the very lowest (parts), that visible (physical) things should come down from invisible (spiritual), and Adoil came down very great, and I beheld him, and lo! He had a belly of great light. 2. And I said to him, 'Become undone, Adoil, and let the visible (physical) (come) out of you.' 3. And he came undone, and a great light came out. And I (was) in the midst of the great light, and as there is born light from light, there came forth a great age, and showed all creation, which I had thought to create. 4. And I saw that (it was) good.

5. And I placed for myself a throne and took my seat on it, and said to the light, 'Go thence up higher and fix yourself high above the throne, and be a foundation to the highest things. 6. And above the light, there is nothing else, and then I bent up and looked up from My throne.

## Chapter 26.

1. And I summoned the very lowest a second time, and said, 'Let Archas come forth hard, and he came forth hard from the invisible (spiritual). 2. And Archas came forth, hard, heavy, and very red. 3. And I said, 'Be opened, Archas, and let there be born from you, and he came undone, an age came forth, very great and very dark, bearing the creation of all lower things, and I saw that (it was) good and said to him, 4. 'Go thence down below, and make yourself firm, and be a foundation for the lower things, and it happened and he went down and fixed himself, and became the foundation for the lower things, and below the darkness there is nothing else.

## Chapter 27.

1. And I commanded that there should be taken from light and darkness, and I said, 'Be thick, and it became thus, and I spread it out with the light, and it became water, and I spread it out over the darkness,

below the light, and then I made firm the waters, that is to say, the bottomless, and I made the foundation of light around the water, and created seven circles from inside, and imaged (the water) like crystal wet and dry, that is to say like glass, (and) the circumcision of the waters and the other elements, and I showed each one of them its road, and the seven stars each one of them in its heaven, that they go thus, and I saw that it was good.

2. And I separated between the light and between darkness, that is to say in the midst of the water hither and thither, and I said to the light, that it should be the day, and to the darkness, that it should be the night, and there was evening and there was morning the first day.

## Chapter 28.

1. And then I made firm the heavenly circle, and (made) that the lower water which is under heaven collect itself together, into one whole, and that the chaos become dry, and it became so. 2. Out of the waves I created rock hard and big, and from the rock, I piled up the dry, and the dry I called earth, and the midst of the earth I called abyss, that is to say the bottomless, I collected the sea in one place and bound it together with a yoke. 3. And I said to the sea, 'Behold I give you (your) eternal limits, and you shalt not break loose from your component parts.

4. Thus I made fast the firmament. This day I called the first-created [Sunday].

## Chapter 29.

1. And for all the heavenly troops I imaged the image and essence of fire, and My eye looked at the very hard, firm rock, and from the gleam of my eye the lightning received its wonderful nature, (which) is both fire in water and water in fire, and one does not put out the other, nor does the one dry up the other, therefore the lightning is brighter than the sun, softer than water and firmer than hard rock. 2. And from the rock I cut off a great fire, and from the fire, I created the orders of the incorporeal ten troops of angels, and their weapons are fiery and their raiment a burning flame, and I commanded that

each one should stand in his order. 3. And one from out the order of angels, having turned away with the order that was under him, conceived an impossible thought, to place his throne higher than the clouds above the earth, that he might become equal in rank to my power. 4. And I threw him out from the height with his angels, and he was flying in the air continuously above the bottomless.

## Chapter 30.

1. On the third day I commanded the earth to make grow great and fruitful trees, and hills, and seed to sow, and I planted Paradise, and enclosed it, and placed as armed (guardians) flaming angels, and thus I created renewal.

2. Then came evening, and came morning the fourth day.

3. [Wednesday]. On the fourth day, I commanded that there should be great lights on the heavenly circles. 4. On the first uppermost circle I placed the stars, Kruno, and on the second Aphrodit, on the third Aris, on the fifth Zoues, on the sixth Ermis, on the seventh lesser the moon, and adorned it with the lesser stars. 5. And on the lower, I placed the sun for the illumination of day, and the moon and stars for the illumination of night. 6. The sun that it should go according to each constellation, twelve, and I appointed the succession of the months and their names and lives, their thunderings, and their hour markings, how they should succeed.

7. Then evening came and morning came the fifth day.

8. [Thursday]. On the fifth day, I commanded the sea, that it should bring forth fishes, and feathered birds of many varieties, and all animals creeping over the earth, going forth over the earth on four legs, and soaring in the air, male sex and female, and every soul breathing the spirit of life.

9. And there came evening, and there came morning the sixth day.

10. [Friday]. On the sixth day, I commanded my wisdom to create man from seven consistencies: one, his flesh from the earth; two, his blood from the dew; three, his eyes from the sun; four, his bones

from stone; five, his intelligence from the swiftness of the angels and from cloud; six, his veins and his hair from the grass of the earth; seven, his soul from my breath and from the wind. 11. And I gave him seven natures: to the flesh hearing, the eyes for sight, to the soul smell, the veins for touch, the blood for taste, the bones for endurance, to the intelligence sweetness [enjoyment].

12. I conceived a cunning saying to say, I created man from invisible (spiritual) and from visible (physical) nature, of both are his death and life and image, he knows speech like some created thing, small in greatness and again great in smallness, and I placed him on earth, a second angel, honorable, great and glorious, and I appointed him as ruler to rule on earth and to have my wisdom, and there was none like him of earth of all my existing creatures. 13. And I appointed him a name, from the four component parts, from east, from west, from south, from north, and I appointed for him four special stars, and I called his name Adam, and showed him the two ways, the light, and the darkness, and I told him, 14. 'This is good, and that bad,' that I should learn whether he has love towards me or hatred, that it be clear which in his race love me. 15. For I have seen his nature, but he has not seen his own nature, therefore (through) not seeing he will sin worse, and I said, 'After sin (what is there) but death?'

16. And I put sleep into him and he fell asleep. And I took from him a rib and created him a wife, that death should come to him by his wife, and I took his last word and called her name mother, that is to say, Eva (Eve).

## Chapter 31.

1. Adam has life on earth, and I created a garden in Eden in the east, that he should observe the testament and keep the command. 2. I made the heavens open to him, that he should see the angels singing the song of victory and the gloomless light. 3. And he was continuously in paradise, and the devil understood that I wanted to create another world, because Adam was lord on earth, to rule and control it.

4. The devil is the evil spirit of the lower places, as a fugitive he made Sotona from the heavens as his name was Satanail (Satan), thus he became different from the angels, (but his nature) did not change (his) intelligence as far as (his) understanding of righteous and sinful (things). 5. And he understood his condemnation and the sin which he had sinned before, therefore he conceived thought against Adam, in such form, he entered and seduced Eva (Eve), but did not touch Adam.

6. But I cursed ignorance, but what I had blessed previously, those I did not curse, I cursed not man, nor the earth, nor other creatures, but man's evil fruit, and his works.

## Chapter 32.

1. I said to him, 'Earth you are, and into the earth whence I took you, you shalt go, and I will not ruin you, but send you whence I took you. 2. Then I can again receive you at My second presence.'

3. And I blessed all my creatures visible (physical) and invisible (spiritual). And Adam was five and a half hours in paradise. 4. And I blessed the seventh day, which is the Sabbath, on which he rested from all his works.

## Chapter 33.

1. And I appointed the eighth day also, that the eighth day should be the first created after My work, and that (the first seven) revolve in the form of the seventh thousand, and that at the beginning of the eighth thousand, there should be a time of not-counting, endless, with neither years nor months nor weeks nor days nor hours.

2. And now, Enoch, all that I have told you, all that you have understood, all that you have seen of heavenly things, all that you have seen on earth, and all that I have written in books by My great wisdom, all these things I have devised and created from the uppermost foundation to the lower and to the end, and there is no counselor nor inheritor to My creations. 3. I am self-eternal, not made with hands, and without change. 4. My thought is My counselor, My wisdom,

and My word are made, and My eyes observe all things how they stand here and tremble with terror. 5. If I turn away My face, then all things will be destroyed. 6. And apply your mind, Enoch, and know Him who is speaking to you, and take thence the books which you yourself have written.

7. And I give you Samuil and Raguil, who led you up, and the books, and go down to earth, and tell your sons all that I have told you, and all that you have seen, from the lower heaven up to my throne, and all the troops. 8. For I created all forces, and there is none that resists Me or that does not subject himself to Me. For all subject themselves to My monarchy, and labor for My sole rule. 9. Give them the books of the handwriting, and they will read (them) and will know Me for the creator of all things, and will understand how there is no other God but Me. 10. And let them distribute the books of your hand-writing–children to children, generation to generation, nations to nations. 11. And I will give you, Enoch, My intercessor, the archangel Michael, for the handwritings of your fathers Adam, Seth, Enos, Cainan, Mahaleleel, and Jared your father.

## Chapter 34.

1. They have rejected My commandments and My yoke, a worthless seed has come up, not fearing God, and they would not bow down to Me, but have begun to bow down to vain gods, and denied My unity, and have laden the whole earth with untruths, offenses, abominable lecheries, namely one with another, and all manner of other unclean wickedness, which are disgusting to relate. 2. And therefore I will bring down a deluge upon the earth and will destroy all men, and the whole earth will crumble together into great darkness.

## Chapter 35.

1. Behold from their seed shall arise another generation, much afterward, but of them, many will be very insatiate. 2. He who raises that generation, (shall) reveal to them the books of your handwriting, of your fathers, (to them) to whom he must point out the guardianship of the world, to the faithful men and workers of My pleasure, who

do not acknowledge My name in vain. 3. And they shall tell another generation and those (others) having read shall be glorified thereafter, more than the first.

## Chapter 36.

1. Now, Enoch, I give you the term of thirty days to spend in your house and tell your sons and all your household, that all may hear from My face what is told them by you, that they may read and understand, how there is no other God but Me. 2. And that they may always keep My commandments, and begin to read and take in the books of your handwriting. 3. And after thirty days I shall send My angel for you, and he will take you from earth and from your sons to Me."

## Chapter 37.

1. And the Lord called upon one of the older angels, terrible and menacing, and placed him by me, in appearance white as snow, and his hands like ice, having the appearance of great frost, and he froze my face, because I could not endure the terror of the Lord, just as it is not possible to endure a stove's fire and the sun's heat, and the frost of the air.

2. And the Lord said to me, "Enoch if your face be not frozen here, no man will be able to behold your face."

## Chapter 38.

1. And the Lord said to those men who first led me up, "Let Enoch go down on to earth with you and await him till the determined day." 2. And they placed me by night on my bed.

3. And Mathusal (Methuselah) expecting my coming, keeping watch by day and by night at my bed, was filled with awe when he heard my coming, and I told him, 'Let all my household come together, that I tell them everything.'

## Chapter 39.

1. Oh my children, my beloved ones, hear the admonition of your father, as much as is according to the Lord's will. 2. I have been let

come to you today, and announce to you, not from my lips, but from the Lord's lips, all that is and was and all that is now, and all that will be till judgment day. 3. For the Lord has let me come to you, you hear therefore the words of my lips, of a man made big for you, but I am one who has seen the Lord's face like iron made to glow from fire it sends forth sparks and burns.

4. You look now upon my eyes, (the eyes) of a man big with meaning for you, but I have seen the Lord's eyes, shining like the sun's rays and filling the eyes of man with awe. 5. You see now, my children, the right hand of a man that helps you, but I have seen the Lord's right hand filling heaven as he helped me. 6. You see the compass of my work like your own, but I have seen the Lord's limitless and perfect compass, which has no end. 7. You hear the words of my lips, as I heard the words of the Lord, like great thunder incessantly with hurling of clouds.

8. And now, my children, hear the discourses of the father of the earth, how fearful and awful it is to come before the face of the ruler of the earth, how much more terrible and awful it is to come before the face of the ruler of heaven, the controller (judge) of quick and dead, and of the heavenly troops. Who can endure that endless pain?

## Chapter 40.

1. And now, my children, I know all things, for this (is) from the Lord's lips, and this my eyes have seen, from beginning to end. 2. I know all things, and have written all things into books, the heavens and their end, and their plenitude, and all the armies and their marchings. 3. I have measured and described the stars, the great countless multitude (of them). 4. What man has seen their revolutions, and their entrances? For not even the angels see their number, while I have written all their names.

5. And I measured the sun's circle and measured its rays, counted the hours, I wrote down too all things that go over the earth, I have written the things that are nourished, and all seed sown and unsown, which the earth produces and all plants, and every grass and every

flower, and their sweet smells, and their names, and the dwelling places of the clouds, and their composition, and their wings, and how they bear rain and raindrops.

6. And I investigated all things and wrote the road of the thunder and of the lightning, and they showed me the keys and their guardians, their rise, the way they go; it is let out (gently) in measure by a chain, lest by A heavy chain and violence, it hurls down the angry clouds and destroys all things on earth.

7. I wrote the treasure houses of the snow and the store-houses of the cold and the frosty airs, and I observed their season's key-holder, he fills the clouds with them, and does not exhaust the treasure houses.

8. And I wrote the resting places of the winds and observed and saw how their key holders bear weighing scales and measures; first, they put them in (one) weighing scale, then in the other the weights and let them out according to measure cunningly over the whole earth, lest by heavy breathing they make the earth to rock.

9. And I measured out the whole earth, its mountains, and all hills, fields, trees, stones, rivers, all existing things I wrote down, the height from earth to the seventh heaven, and downwards to the very lowest hell, and the judgment-place, and the very great, open and weeping hell.

10. And I saw how the prisoners are in pain, expecting the limitless judgment. 11. And I wrote down all those being judged by the judge, and all their judgment (and sentences) and all their works.

## Chapter 41.

1. And I saw all forefathers from (all) time with Adam and Eva (Eve), and I sighed and broke into tears and said of the ruin of their dishonor, 2. 'Woe is me for my infirmity and (for that) of my forefathers,' and thought in my heart and said, 3. 'Blessed (is) the man who has not been born or who has been born and shall not sin before the Lord's face, that he come not into this place, nor bring the yoke of this place.'

## Chapter 42.

I saw the key-holders and guards of the gates of hell standing, like great serpents, and their faces like extinguishing lamps, and their eyes of fire, their sharp teeth, and I saw all the Lord's works, how they are right, while the works of man are some (good), and others bad, and in their works are known those who lie evilly.

## Chapter 43.

1. I, my children, measured and wrote out every work and every measure and every righteous judgment. 2. As (one) year is more honorable than another, so is (one) man more honorable than another, some for great possessions, some for wisdom of heart, some for particular intellect, some for cunning, one for silence of lip, another for cleanliness, one for strength, another for comeliness, one for youth, another for sharp wit, one for shape of body, another for sensibility, let it be heard everywhere, but there is none better than he who fears God, he shall be more glorious in time to come.

## Chapter 44.

1. The Lord with his hands having created man, in the likeness of his own face, the Lord made him small and great. 2. Whoever reviles the ruler's face, and abhors the Lord's face, has despised the Lord's face, and he who vents anger on any man without injury, the Lord's great anger will cut him down, he who spits on the face of man reproachfully, will be cut down at the Lord's great judgment.

3. Blessed is the man who does not direct his heart with malice against any man, and helps the injured and condemned, and raises the broken down, and shall do charity to the needy, because on the day of the great judgment every weight, every measure, and every makeweight (will be) as in the market, that is to say (they are) hung on scales and stand in the market, (and everyone) shall learn his own measure, and according to his measure shall take his reward.

## Chapter 45.

1. Whoever hastens to make offerings before the Lord's face, the

Lord for His part will hasten that offering by granting of his work. 2. But whoever increases his lamp before the Lord's face and makes not true judgment, the Lord will (not) increase his treasure in the realm of the highest.

3. When the Lord demands bread, or candles, or (the) flesh (of beasts), or any other sacrifice, then that is nothing; but God demands pure hearts, and with all that (only) tests the heart of man.

## Chapter 46.

1. Hear, my people, and take in the words of my lips.

2. If anyone brings any gifts to an earthly ruler and has disloyal thoughts in his heart, and the ruler knows this, will he not be angry with him, and not refuse his gifts, and not give him over to judgment? 3. Or (if) one man make himself appear good to another by deceit of tongue, but (have) evil in his heart, then will not (the other) understand the treachery of his heart, and himself be condemned since his untruth was plain to all? 4. And when the Lord shall send a great light, then there will be judgment for the just and the unjust, and there no one shall escape notice.

## Chapter 47.

1. And now, my children, lay thought on your hearts, mark well the words of your father, which are all (come) to you from the Lord's lips. 2. Take these books of your father's handwriting and read them. 3. For the books are many, and in them, you will learn all the Lord's works, all that has been from the beginning of creation and will be till the end of time. 4. And if you will observe my handwriting, you will not sin against the Lord; because there is no other except the Lord, neither in heaven, nor in the earth, nor in the very lowest (places), nor in the (one) foundation.

5. The Lord has placed the foundations in the unknown, and has spread forth heavens visible (physical) and invisible (spiritual); He fixed the earth on the waters, and created countless creatures, and who has counted the water and the foundation of the unfixed, or

the dust of the earth, or the sand of the sea, or the drops of the rain, or the morning dew, or the wind's breathing? Who has filled earth and sea, and the indissoluble winter? 6. Who cut the stars out of fire, and decorated heaven, and put it in their midst?

## Chapter 48.

1. That the sun go along the seven heavenly circles, which are the appointment of one hundred and eighty-two thrones, that it go down on a short day, and again one hundred and eighty-two, that it go down on a big day, and he has two thrones on which he rests, revolving hither and thither above the thrones of the months, from the seventeenth day of the month Tsivan it goes down to the month Thevan, from the seventeenth of Thevan it goes up. 2. And thus it goes close to the earth, then the earth is glad and makes grow its fruits, and when it goes away, then the earth is sad, and trees and all fruits have no florescence.

3. All this He measured, with good measurement of hours, and fixed a measure by His wisdom, of the visible (physical) and the invisible (spiritual). 4. From the invisible (spiritual) He made all things visible (physical), Himself being invisible (spiritual).

5. Thus I make known to you, my children, and distribute the books to your children, into all your generations, and amongst the nations who shall have the sense to fear God, let them receive them, and may they come to love them more than any food or earthly sweets, and read them and apply themselves to them. 6. And those who understand not the Lord, who fear not God, who accept not, but reject, who do not receive the (books), a terrible judgment awaits these.

7. Blessed is the man who shall bear their yoke and shall drag them along, for he shall be released on the day of the great judgment.

## Chapter 49.

1. I swear to you, my children, but I swear not by any oath, neither by heaven nor by earth, nor by any other creature which God created. 2. The Lord said, "There is no oath in me, nor injustice, but truth."

3. If there is no truth in men, let them swear by the words, 'Yea, yea,' or else, 'Nay, nay.'

4. And I swear to you, yea, yea, that there has been no man in his mother's womb, (but that) already before, even to each one there is a place prepared for the repose of that soul, and a measure fixed how much it is intended that a man be tried in this world. 5. Yea, children, deceive not yourselves, for there has been previously prepared a place for every soul of man.

## Chapter 50.

1. I have put every man's work in writing, and none born on earth can remain hidden nor his works remain concealed. 2. I see all things. 3. Now therefore, my children, in patience and meekness spend the number of your days, that you inherit endless life. 4. Endure for the sake of the Lord every wound, every injury, every evil word and attack. 5. If ill-requitals befall you, return (them) not either to neighbor or enemy, because the Lord will return (them) for you and be your avenger on the day of great judgment, that there be no avenging here among men. 6. Whoever of you spends gold or silver for his brother's sake, he will receive ample treasure in the world to come. 7. Injure not widows nor orphans nor strangers, lest God's wrath come upon you.

## Chapter 51.

1. Stretch out your hands to the poor according to your strength. 2. Hide not your silver in the earth. 3. Help the faithful man in affliction, and affliction will not find you in the time of your trouble. 4. And every grievous and cruel yoke that come upon you bear all for the sake of the Lord, and thus you will find your reward in the day of judgment.

5. It is good to go morning, midday, and evening into the Lord's dwelling, for the glory of your creator. 6. Because every breathing (thing) glorifies him, and every creature visible (physical) and invisible (spiritual) returns him praise.

## Chapter 52.

1. Blessed is the man who opens his lips in praise of the God of Sabaoth and praises the Lord with his heart. 2. Cursed every man who opens his lips for the bringing into contempt and calumny of his neighbor, because he brings God into contempt.

3. Blessed is he who opens his lips blessing and praising God. 4. Cursed is he before the Lord all the days of his life, who opens his lips to curse and abuse.

5. Blessed is he who blesses all the Lord's works. 6. Cursed is he who brings the Lord's creation into contempt.

7. Blessed is he who looks down and raises the fallen. 8. Cursed is he who looks to and is eager for the destruction of what is not his.

9. Blessed is he who keeps the foundations of his fathers made firm from the beginning. 10. Cursed is he who perverts the decrees of his forefathers.

11. Blessed is he who imparts peace and love. 12. Cursed is he who disturbs those who love their neighbors.

13. Blessed is he who speaks with humble tongue and heart to all. 14. Cursed is he who speaks peace with his tongue, while in his heart there is no peace but a sword.

15. For all these things will be laid bare in the weighing scales and in the books, on the day of the great judgment.

## Chapter 53.

1. And now, my children, do not say, "Our father is standing before God, and is praying for our sins, for there is there no helper of any man who has sinned." 2. You see how I wrote all works of every man, before his creation, (all) that is done amongst all men for all time, and none can tell or relate my handwriting, because the Lord see all imaginings of man, how they are vain, where they lie in the treasure houses of the heart. 3. And now, my children, mark well all the words of your father, that I tell you, lest you regret, saying, "Why did our father not tell us?"

## Chapter 54.

1. At that time, not understanding this let these books which I have given you be for an inheritance of your peace. 2. Hand them to all who want them, and instruct them, that they may see the Lord's very great and marvelous works.

## Chapter 55.

1. My children, behold, the day of my term and time have approached. 2. For the angels who shall go with me are standing before me and urge me to my departure from you; they are standing here on earth, awaiting what has been told them. 3. For tomorrow I shall go up on to heaven, to the uppermost Jerusalem to my eternal inheritance. 4. Therefore I bid you do before the Lord's face all (his) good pleasure.

## Chapter 56.

1. Mathosalam having answered his father Enoch, said, "What is agreeable to your eyes, father, that I may make before your face, that you may bless our dwellings, and your sons, and that your people may be made glorious through you, and then (that) you may depart thus, as the Lord said?"

2. Enoch answered to his son Mathosalam (and) said, 'Hear, child, from the time when the Lord anointed me with the ointment of his glory, (there has been no) food in me, and my soul remembers not earthly enjoyment, neither do I want anything earthly.'

## Chapter 57.

1. My child Methosalam, summon all your brethren and all your household and the elders of the people, that I may talk to them and depart, as is planned for me. 2. And Methosalam made haste, and summoned his brethren, Regim, Riman, Uchan, Chermion, Gaidad, and all the elders of the people before the face of his father Enoch; and he blessed them, (and) said to them,

## Chapter 58.

1. 'Listen to me, my children, today. 2. In those days when the Lord came down onto earth for Adam's sake, and visited all His creatures,

which He created himself, after all these He created Adam, and the Lord called all the beasts of the earth, all the reptiles, and all the birds that soar in the air, and brought them all before the face of our father Adam. 3. And Adam gave the names to all things living on earth. 4. And the Lord appointed him ruler over all, and subjected to him all things under his hands, and made them dumb and made them dull that they be commanded of man, and be in subjection and obedience to him. 5. Thus also the Lord created every man lord over all his possessions.

6. The Lord will not judge a single soul of beast for man's sake but adjudges the souls of men to their beasts in this world; for men have a special place. 7. And as every soul of man is according to number, similarly beasts will not perish, nor all souls of beasts which the Lord created, till the great judgment, and they will accuse man, if he feed them ill.

## Chapter 59.

1. Whoever defiles the soul of beasts, defiles his own soul. 2. For man brings clean animals to make a sacrifice for sin, that he may have a cure of his soul. 3. And if they bring for sacrifice clean animals, and birds, man has a cure, he cures his soul.

4. All is given you for food, bind it by the four feet, that is to make good the cure, he cures his soul. 5. But whoever kills the beast without wounds, kills his own soul and defiles his own flesh. 6. And he who does any beast any injury whatsoever, in secret, it is an evil practice, and he defiles his own soul.

## Chapter 60.

1. He who works the killing of a man's soul, kills his own soul, and kills his own body, and there is no cure for him for all time. 2. He who puts a man in any snare, shall stick in it himself, and there is no cure for him for all time. 3. He who puts a man in any vessel, his retribution will not be wanting at the great judgment for all time. 4. He who works crookedly or speaks evil against any soul, will not make justice for himself for all time.

## Chapter 61.

1. And now, my children, keep your hearts from every injustice which the Lord hates. Just as a man asks something for his own soul from God, so let him do to every living soul, because I know all things, how in the great time to come there is much inheritance prepared for men, good for the good, and bad for the bad, without number many. 2. Blessed are those who enter the good houses, for in the bad houses there is no peace nor return from them.

3. Hear, my children, small and great! When man puts a good thought in his heart, brings gifts from his labors before the Lord's face and his hands made them not, then the Lord will turn away His face from the labor of his hand, and (that) man cannot find the labor of his hands. 4. And if his hands made it, but his heart murmur and his heart cease not making murmur incessantly, he has not any advantage.

## Chapter 62.

1. Blessed is the man who in his patience brings his gifts with faith before the Lord's face, because he will find forgiveness of sins. 2. But if he takes back his words before the time, there is no repentance for him; and if the time passes and he does not of his own will what is promised, there is no repentance after death. 3. Because every work which man does before the time, is all deceit before men, and sin before God.

## Chapter 63.

1. When man clothes the naked and fills the hungry, he will find reward from God. 2. But if his heart murmurs, he commits a double evil; ruin of himself and of that which he gives; and for him there will be no finding of reward on account of that. 3. And if his own heart is filled with his food and his own flesh, clothed with his own clothing, he commits contempt, and will forfeit all his endurance of poverty, and will not find reward of his good deeds. 4. Every proud and magniloquent man is hateful to the Lord, and every false speech, clothed in untruth; it will be cut with the blade of the sword of death,

and thrown into the fire, and shall burn for all time.'

## Chapter 64.

1. When Enoch had spoken these words to his sons, all people far and near heard how the Lord was calling Enoch. They took counsel together: 2. "Let us go and kiss Enoch," and two thousand men came together and came to the place Achuzan where Enoch was, and his sons.

3. And the elders of the people, the whole assembly, came and bowed down and began to kiss Enoch and said to him, 4. "Our father Enoch, (may) you (be) blessed of the Lord, the eternal ruler, and now bless your sons and all the people, that we may be glorified today before your face. 5. For you shalt be glorified before the Lord's face for all time, since the Lord chose you, rather than all men on earth, and designated you writer of all His creation, visible (physical) and invisible (spiritual), and redeemed of the sins of man, and helper of your household."

## Chapter 65.

1. And Enoch answered all his people saying, 'Hear, my children, before that all creatures were created, the Lord created the visible (physical) and invisible (spiritual) things. 2. And as much time as there was and went past, understand that after all that he created man in the likeness of His own form, and put into him eyes to see, and ears to hear, and heart to reflect, and intellect wherewith to deliberate. 3. And the Lord saw all man's works, and created all his creatures, and divided time, from time he fixed the years, and from the years He appointed the months, and from the months He appointed the days, and of days He appointed seven. 4. And in those He appointed the hours, measured them out exactly, that man might reflect on time and count years, months, and hours, (their) alternation, beginning, and end, and that he might count his own life, from the beginning until death, and reflect on his sin and write his work bad and good; because no work is hidden before the Lord, that every man might know His works and never transgress all His commandments, and

keep my handwriting from generation to generation.

5. When all creation visible (physical) and invisible (spiritual), as the Lord created it, shall end, then every man goes to the great judgment, and then all time shall perish, and the years, and thenceforward there will be neither months nor days nor hours, they will be adhered together and will not be counted. 6. There will be one eon, and all the righteous who shall escape the Lord's great judgment, shall be collected in the great eon, for the righteous the great eon will begin, and they will live eternally, and then too there will be amongst them neither labor, nor sickness, nor humiliation, nor anxiety, nor need, nor brutality, nor night, nor darkness, but great light. 7. And they shall have a great indestructible wall, and a paradise bright and incorruptible (eternal), for all corruptible (mortal) things shall pass away, and there will be eternal life.

## Chapter 66.

1. And now, my children, keep your souls from all injustice, such as the Lord hates. 2. Walk before his face with terror and trembling and serve him alone. 3. Bow down to the true God, not to dumb idols, but bow down to his similitude, and bring all just offerings before the Lord's face. The Lord hates what is unjust. 4. For the Lord sees all things; when man takes thought in his heart, then he counsels the intellects, and every thought is always before the Lord, who made firm the earth and put all creatures on it.

5. If you look to heaven, the Lord is there; if you take thought of the sea's depth and all the under-earth, the Lord is there. 6. For the Lord created all things. Bow not down to things made by man, leaving the Lord of all creation, because no work can remain hidden before the Lord's face.

7. Walk, my children, in long-suffering, in meekness, honesty, in provocation, in grief, in faith, and in truth, in (reliance on) promises, in illness, in abuse, in wounds, in temptation, in nakedness, in privation, loving one another, till you go out from this age of ills, that you become inheritors of endless time.

8. Blessed are the just who shall escape the great judgment, for they shall shine forth more than the sun sevenfold, for in this world the seventh part is taken off from all, light, darkness, food, enjoyment, sorrow, paradise, torture, fire, frost, and other things; he put all down in writing, that you might read and understand.'

## Chapter 67.

1. When Enoch had talked to the people, the Lord sent out darkness onto the earth, and there was darkness, and it covered those men standing with Enoch, and they took Enoch up on to the highest heaven, where the Lord (is); and He received him and placed him before His face, and the darkness went off from the earth, and light came again. 2. And the people saw and understood not how Enoch had been taken, and glorified God, and found a roll in which was traced the Invisible (spiritual) God; and all went to their dwelling places.

## Chapter 68.

1. Enoch was born on the sixth day of the month Tsivan and lived three hundred and sixty-five years. 2. He was taken up to heaven on the first day of the month Tsivan and remained in heaven sixty days.

3. He wrote all these signs of all creation, which the Lord created, and wrote three hundred and sixty-six books, and handed them over to his sons and remained on earth thirty days and was again taken up to heaven on the sixth day of the month Tsivan, on the very day and hour when he was born.

4. As every man's nature in this life is dark, so are also his conception, birth, and departure from this life. 5. At what hour he was conceived, at that hour he was born, and at that hour too he died.

6. Methosalam and his brethren, all the sons of Enoch, made haste, and erected an altar at that place called Achuzan, whence and where Enoch had been taken up to heaven. 7. And they took sacrificial oxen and summoned all people and sacrificed the sacrifice before the Lord's face. 8. All people, the elders of the people, and the whole

assembly came to the feast and brought gifts to the sons of Enoch. 9. And they made a great feast, rejoicing and making merry three days, praising God, who had given them such a sign through Enoch, who had found favor with Him, and that they should hand it on to their sons from generation to generation, from age to age.

10. Amen.

# 3
# ENOCH

ALSO KNOWN AS THE HEBREW ENOCH
& THE REVELATION OF METATRON
TRANSLATION BY HUGO ODEBERG, 1928

# REVELATION OF METATRON

## Chapter 1.

Rabbi Ishmael said:

1. When I ascended on high to behold the vision of the Merkaba and had entered the six Halls, one within the other; 2. as soon as I reached the door of the seventh Hall I stood still in prayer before the Holy One, blessed be He, and, lifting up my eyes on high (i.e. towards the Divine Majesty), I said, 3. "Lord of the Universe, I pray thee, that the merit of Aaron, the son of Amram, the lover of peace and pursuer of peace, who received the crown of priesthood from Thy Glory on the mount of Sinai, be valid for me in this hour, so that Qafsiel, the prince, and the angels with him may not get power over me nor throw me down from the heavens."

4. Forthwith the Holy One, blessed be He, sent to me Metatron, his Servant ('Ebed) the angel, the Prince of the Presence, and he, spreading his wings, with great joy came to meet me so as to save me from their hand. 5. And he took me by his hand in their sight, saying to me, "Enter in peace before the high and exalted King and behold the picture of the Merkaba."

6. Then I entered the seventh Hall, and he led me to the camp(s) of Shekina and placed me before the Holy One, blessed be He, to behold the Merkaba. 7. As soon as the princes of the Merkaba and the flaming Seraphim perceived me, they fixed their eyes upon me. Instantly trembling and shuddering seized me, and I fell down and was benumbed by the radiant image of their eyes and the splendid appearance of their faces; until the Holy One, blessed be He, rebuked

them, saying, 8. "My servants, my Seraphim, my Kerubim, and my 'Ophanniml, cover ye your eyes before Ishmael, my son, my friend, my beloved one and my glory, that he tremble not nor shudder!"

9. Forthwith Metatron the Prince of the Presence, came and restored my spirit and put me upon my feet. 10. After that (moment) there was not in me strength enough to say a song before the Throne of Glory of the glorious King, the mightiest of all kings, the most excellent of all princes, until after the hour had passed.

11. After one hour (had passed) the Holy One, blessed be He, opened to me the gates of Shekina, the gates of Peace, the gates of Wisdom, the gates of Strength, the gates of Power, the gates of Speech (Dibbur), the gates of Song, the gates of Qedushsha, the gates of Chant.

12. And he enlightened my eyes and my heart by words of psalm, song, praise, exaltation, thanksgiving, extolment, glorification, hymn, and eulogy. And as I opened my mouth, uttering a song before the Holy One, blessed be He, the Holy Chayyoth beneath and above the Throne of Glory answered and said, "Holy and blessed be the glory of YHWH from his place!" (i.e. chanted the Qedushsha).

## Chapter 2.

R. Ishmael said:

1. In that hour the eagles of the Merkaba, the flaming 'Ophannim, and the Seraphim of consuming fire asked Metatron, saying to him, 2. "Youth! Why sufferest thou one born of woman to enter and behold the Merkaba? From which nation, from which tribe is this one? What is his character?"

3. Metatron answered and said to them, "From the nation of Israel whom the Holy One, blessed be He, chose for his people from among seventy tongues (nations), from the tribe of Levi, whom he set aside as a contribution to his name and from the seed of Aaron whom the Holy One, blessed be He, did choose for his servant and put upon him the crown of priesthood on Sinai."

4. Forthwith they spake and said, "Indeed, this one is worthy to

behold the Merkaba." And they said, "Happy is the people that is in such a case!"

## Chapter 3.

R. Ishmael said:

1. In that hour I asked Metatron, the angel, the Prince of the Presence: "What is thy name?" 2. He answered me, "I have seventy names, corresponding to the seventy tongues of the world and all of them are based upon the name Metatron, angel of the Presence; but my King calls me 'Youth' (Na'ar)."

## Chapter 4.

R. Ishmael said:

1. I asked Metatron and said to him, "Why art thou called by the name of thy Creator, by seventy names? Thou art greater than all the princes, higher than all the angels, beloved more than all the servants, honored above all the mighty ones in kingship, greatness, and glory; why do they call thee 'Youth' in the high heavens?" 2. He answered and said to me, "Because I am Enoch, the son of Jared. 3. For when the generation of the flood sinned and were confounded in their deeds, saying unto God, 'Depart from us, for we desire not the knowledge of thy ways' (Job xxi. 14), then the Holy One, blessed be He, removed me from their midst to be a witness against them in the high heavens to all the inhabitants of the world, that they may not say, 'The Merciful One is cruel.'"

4. What sinned all those multitudes, their wives, their sons and their daughters, their horses, their mules and their cattle and their property, and all the birds of the world, all of which the Holy One, blessed be He, destroyed from the world together with them in the waters of the flood?

5. Hence the Holy One, blessed be He, lifted me up in their lifetime before their eyes to be a witness against them to the future world. And the Holy One, blessed be He, assigned me as a prince and a ruler among the ministering angels.

6. In that hour three of the ministering angels, 'Uzza, 'Azza, and 'Azzael came forth and brought charges against me in the high heavens, saying before the Holy One, blessed be He, "Did not the Ancient Ones (First Ones) rightly say before Thee, 'Do not create man!'" The Holy One, blessed be He, answered and said unto them, "I have made, and I will bear, yea, I will carry and will deliver." (Is. xlvi. 4.)

7. As soon as they saw me, they said before Him, "Lord of the Universe! What is this one that he should ascend to the height of heights? Is not he one from among the sons of [the sons of] those who perished in the days of the Flood? What doeth he in the Raqia?"

8. Again, the Holy One, blessed be He, answered and said to them, "What are ye, that ye enter and speak in my presence? I delight in this one more than in all of you, and hence he shall be a prince and a ruler over you in the high heavens."

9. Forthwith all stood up and went out to meet me, prostrated themselves before me, and said: "Happy art thou and happy is thy father for thy Creator doth favor thee." 10. And because I am small and a youth among them in days, months, and years, therefore they call me 'Youth' (Na'ar).

## Chapter 5.

R. Ishmael said: Metatron, the Prince of the Presence, said to me:

1. "From the day when the Holy One, blessed be He, expelled the first Adam from the Garden of Eden (and onwards), Shekina was dwelling upon a Kerub under the Tree of Life. 2. And the ministering angels were gathering together and going down from heaven in parties, from the Raqia in companies, and from the heavens in camps to do His will in the whole world. 3. And the first man and his generation were sitting outside the gate of the Garden to behold the radiant appearance of the Shekina. 4. For the splendor of the Shekina traversed the world from one end to the other (with a splendor) 365,000 times (that) of the globe of the sun. And everyone who made use of the splendor of the Shekina, on him no flies and no gnats did rest, neither was he ill nor suffered he any pain. No demons got power over him,

neither were they able to injure him.

5. When the Holy One, blessed be He, went out and went in from the Garden to Eden, from Eden to the Garden, from the Garden to Raqia, and from Raqia to the Garden of Eden, then all and everyone beheld the splendor of His Shekina and they were not injured; 6. until the time of the generation of Enosh who was the head of all idol worshippers of the world.

7. And what did the generation of Enosh do? They went from one end of the world to the other, and each one brought silver, gold, precious stones, and pearls in heaps like unto mountains and hills making idols out of them throughout all the world. And they erected the idols in every quarter of the world: the size of each idol was 1000 parasangs. 8. And they brought down the sun, the moon, planets, and constellations, and placed them before the idols on their right hand and on their left, to attend them even as they attend the Holy One, blessed be He, as it is written (1 Kgs. xxii. 19): 'And all the host of heaven was standing by him on his right hand and his left.'

9. What power was in them that they were able to bring them down? They would not have been able to bring them down but for 'Uzza, 'Azza, and 'Azzael who taught them sorceries whereby they brought them down and made use of them.

10. In that time the ministering angels brought charges (against them) before the Holy One, blessed be He, saying before Him, 'Master of the World! What hast thou to do with the children of men? As it is written (Ps. viii. 4): 'What is man (Enosh) that thou art mindful of him?' 'Mah Adam' is not written here, but 'Mah Enosh', for he (Enosh) is the head of the idol worshippers. 11. Why hast Thou left the highest of the high heavens, the abode of Thy glorious Name, and the high and exalted Throne in 'Araboth Raqia' in the highest and art gone and dwellest with the children of men who worship idols and equal thee to the idols? 12. Now Thou art on earth and the idols likewise. What hast Thou to do with the inhabitants of the earth who worship idols?'

13. Forthwith the Holy One, blessed be He, lifted up His Shekina from the earth, from their midst. 14. In that moment came the ministering angels, the troops of hosts, and the armies of 'Araboth in thousand camps and ten thousand hosts; they fetched trumpets and took the horns in their hands and surrounded the Shekina with all kinds of songs. And He ascended to the high heavens, as it is written (Ps. xlvii. 5): 'God is gone up with a shout, the Lord with the sound of a trumpet.'"

## Chapter 6.

R. Ishmael said: Metatron, the Angel, the Prince of the Presence, said to me:

1. "When the Holy One, blessed be He, desired to lift me up on high, He first sent 'Anaphiel H (H = Tetragrammaton) the prince, and he took me from their midst in their sight and carried me in great glory upon a fiery chariot with fiery horses, servants of glory. And he lifted me up to the high heavens together with the Shekina. 2. As soon as I reached the high heavens, the Holy Chayyoth, the 'Ophannim, the Seraphim, the Kerubim, the Wheels of the Merkaba (the Galgallim), and the ministers of the consuming fire, perceiving my smell from a distance of 365,000 myriads of parasangs, said, 'What smell of one born of woman and what taste of a white drop (is this) that ascends on high, and (lo, he is merely) a gnat among those who divide flames (of fire)?'

3. The Holy One, blessed be He, answered and spake unto them, 'My servants, my hosts, my Kerubim, my 'Ophannim, my Seraphim! Be ye not displeased on account of this! Since all the children of men have denied me and my great Kingdom and are gone worshipping idols, I have removed my Shekina from among them and have lifted it up on high. But this one whom I have taken from among them is an Elect One among (the inhabitants of) the world and he is equal to all of them in faith, righteousness, and perfection of deed and I have taken him for (as) a tribute from my world under all the heavens.'"

## Chapter 7.

R. Ishmael said: Metatron, the Angel, the Prince of the Presence, said to me:

"When the Holy One, blessed be He, took me away from the generation of the Flood, he lifted me on the wings of the wind of Shekina to the highest heaven and brought me into the great palaces of the 'Araboth Raqia' on high, where are the glorious Throne of Shekina, the Merkaba, the troops of anger, the armies of vehemence, the fiery Shin'anim', the flaming Kerubim, and the burning 'Ophannim, the flaming servants, the flashing Chashmattim, and the lightening Seraphim. And he placed me (there) to attend the Throne of Glory day after day."

## Chapter 8.

R. Ishmael said: Metatron, the Prince of the Presence, said to me:

1. "Before He appointed me to attend the Throne of Glory, the Holy One, blessed be He, opened to me three hundred thousand gates of Understanding, three hundred thousand gates of Subtlety, three hundred thousand gates of Life, three hundred thousand gates of Grace and Loving-kindness, three hundred thousand gates of Love, three hundred thousand gates of Torah, three hundred thousand gates of Meekness, three hundred thousand gates of Maintenance, three hundred thousand gates of Mercy, three hundred thousand gates of Fear of Heaven.

2. In that hour the Holy One, blessed be He, added in me wisdom unto wisdom, understanding unto understanding, subtlety unto subtlety, knowledge unto knowledge, mercy unto mercy, instruction unto instruction, love unto love, loving-kindness unto loving-kindness, goodness unto goodness, meekness unto meekness, power unto power, strength unto strength, might unto might, brilliance unto brilliance, beauty unto beauty, splendor unto splendor, and I was honored and adorned with all these good and praiseworthy things more than all the children of heaven."

## Chapter 9.

R. Ishmael said: Metatron, the Prince of the Presence, said to me:

1. "After all these things the Holy One, blessed be He, put His hand upon me and blessed me with 5360 blessings. 2. And I was raised and enlarged to the size of the length and width of the world. 3. And He caused 72 wings to grow on me, 36 on each side. And each wing was as the whole world. 4. And He fixed on me 365 eyes; each eye was as the great luminary. 5. And He left no kind of splendor, brilliance, radiance, beauty in (of) all the lights of the universe that He did not fix on me."

## Chapter 10.

R. Ishmael said: Metatron, the Prince of the Presence, said to me:

1. "All these things the Holy One, blessed be He, made for me; He made me a Throne, similar to the Throne of Glory. And He spread over me a curtain of splendor and brilliant appearance, of beauty, grace, and mercy, similar to the curtain of the Throne of Glory; and on it were fixed all kinds of lights in the universe. 2. And He placed it at the door of the Seventh Hall and seated me on it.

3. And the herald went forth into every heaven, saying, 'This is Metatron, my servant. I have made him into a prince and a ruler over all the princes of my kingdoms and over all the children of heaven, except the eight great princes, the honored and revered ones who are called YHWH, by the name of their King. 4. And every angel and every prince who has a word to speak in my presence (before me) shall go into his presence (before him) and shall speak to him (instead). 5. And every command that he utters to you in my name do ye observe and fulfill. For the Prince of Wisdom and the Prince of Understanding have I committed to him to instruct him in the wisdom of heavenly things and of earthly things, in the wisdom of this world and of the world to come. 6. Moreover, I have set him over all the treasuries of the palaces of Araboth and over all the stores of life that I have in the high heavens.'"

## Chapter 11.

R. Ishmael said: Metatron, the angel, the Prince of the Presence, said to me:

1. "Henceforth the Holy One, blessed be He, revealed to me all the mysteries of Torah and all the secrets of wisdom and all the depths of the Perfect Law; and all living beings' thoughts of heart and all the secrets of the universe and all the secrets of Creation were revealed unto me even as they are revealed unto the Maker of Creation.

2. And I watched intently to behold the secrets of the depth and the wonderful mystery. Before a man did think in secret, I saw (it), and before a man made a thing I beheld it.

3. And there was nothing on high nor in the deep hidden from me."

## Chapter 12.

R. Ishmael said: Metatron, the Prince of the Presence, said to me:

1. "By reason of the love with which the Holy One, blessed be He, loved me more than all the children of heaven, He made me a garment of glory on which were fixed all kinds of lights, and He clad me in it.

2. And He made me a robe of honor on which were fixed all kinds of beauty, splendor, brilliance, and majesty. 3. And he made me a royal crown in which were fixed forty-nine costly stones like unto the light of the globe of the sun. 4. For its splendor went forth in the four quarters of the 'Araboth Raqia, and in (through) the seven heavens, and in the four quarters of the world. And he put it on my head.

5. And He called me The Lesser YHWH in the presence of all His heavenly household, as it is written (Ex. xxiii. 21): 'For my name is in him.'"

## Chapter 13.

R. Ishmael said: Metatron, the angel, the Prince of the Presence, the Glory of all heavens, said to me:

1. "Because of the great love and mercy with which the Holy One, blessed be He, loved and cherished me more than all the children of

heaven, He wrote with his finger with a flaming style upon the crown on my head the letters by which were created heaven and earth, the seas and rivers, the mountains and hills, the planets and constellations, the lightnings, winds, earthquakes and voices (thunders), the snow and hail, the storm wind and the tempest; the letters by which were created all the needs of the world and all the orders of Creation.

2. And every single letter sent forth time after time as it were lightning, time after time as it were torches, time after time as it were flames of fire, time after time (rays) like [as] the rising of the sun and the moon and the planets."

## Chapter 14.

R. Ishmael said: Metatron, the Angel, the Prince of the Presence, said to me:

1. "When the Holy One, blessed be He, put this crown on my head, (then) trembled before me all the Princes of Kingdoms who are in the height of 'Araboth Raqiaf' and all the hosts of every heaven; and even the princes (of) the 'Elim, the princes (of) the 'Er'ellim and the princes (of) the Tafsarim, who are greater than all the ministering angels who minister before the Throne of Glory, shook, feared and trembled before me when they beheld me. 2. Even Sammael, the Prince of the Accusers, who is greater than all the princes of kingdoms on high; feared and trembled before me. 3. And even the angel of fire, and the angel of hail, and the angel of the wind, and the angel of the lightning, and the angel of anger, and the angel of the thunder, and the angel of the snow, and the angel of the rain; and the angel of the day, and the angel of the night, and the angel of the sun and the angel of the moon, and the angel of the planets and the angel of the constellations who rule the world under their hands, feared and trembled and were affrighted before me when they beheld me.

4. These are the names of the rulers of the world: Gabriel, the angel of the fire, Baradiel, the angel of the hail, Ruchiel who is appointed over the wind, Baraqiel who is appointed over the lightning, Za'amiel who is appointed over the vehemence, Ziqiel who is appointed over

the sparks, Zi'iel who is appointed over the commotion, Zdaphiel who is appointed over the storm wind, Ra'amiel who is appointed over the thunders, Rctashiel who is appointed over the earthquake, Shalgiel who is appointed over the snow, Matariel who is appointed over the rain, Shimshiel who is appointed over the day, Lailiel who is appointed over the night, Galgalliel who is appointed over the globe of the sun, 'Ophanniel who is appointed over the globe of the moon, Kokbiel who is appointed over the planets, Rahatiel who is appointed over the constellations.

5. And they all fell prostrate when they saw me. And they were not able to behold me because of the majestic glory and beauty of the appearance of the shining light of the crown of glory upon my head."

## Chapter 15.

R. Ishmael said: Metatron, the angel, the Prince of the Presence, the Glory of all heavens, said to me:

1. "As soon as the Holy One, blessed be He, took me in (His) service to attend the Throne of Glory and the Wheels (Galgallim) of the Merkaba and the needs of Shekina, forthwith my flesh was changed into flames, my sinews into the flaming fire, my bones into coals of burning juniper, the light of my eyelids into the splendor of lightning, my eyeballs into fire-brands, the hair of my head into dot flames, all my limbs into wings of burning fire and the whole of my body into glowing fire.

2. And on my right were divisions of fiery flames, on my left fire-brands were burning, round about me storm wind and tempest were blowing and in front of me and behind me was roaring of thunder with an earthquake."

### Fragment of Ascension of Moses

R. Ishmael said:

1. Said to me Metatron, the Prince of the Presence and the prince over all the princes, and he stands before Him who is greater than all the Elohim. And he goes in under the Throne of Glory. And he

has a great tabernacle of light on high. And he brings forth the fire of deafness and puts (it) into the ears of the Holy Chayyoth, that they may not hear the voice of the Word (Dibbur) that goes forth from the mouth of the Divine Majesty.

2. "And when Moses ascended on high, he fasted 121 fasts, till the habitations of the chasmal were opened to him; and he saw the heart within the heart of the Lion and he saw the innumerable companies of the hosts around about him. And they desired to burn him. But Moses prayed for mercy, first for Israel and after that for himself; and He who sitteth on the Merkaba opened the windows that are above the heads of the Kerubim. And a host of 1800 advocates and the Prince of the Presence, Metatron, with them went forth to meet Moses. And they took the prayers of Israel and put them as a crown on the head of the Holy One, blessed be He.

3. And they said (Deut. vi. 4), 'Hear, O Israel; the Lord our God is one Lord.' And their face shone and rejoiced over Shekina and they said to Metatron: 'What are these? And to whom do they give all this honor and glory?' And they answered: 'To the Glorious Lord of Israel.' And they spake, 'Hear, O Israel; the Lord, our God, is one Lord. To whom shall be given the abundance of honor and majesty but to Thee YHWH, the Divine Majesty, the King, living and eternal.'

4. In that moment spake Akatriel Yah Yehod Sebaoth and said to Metatron, the Prince of the Presence: 'Let no prayer that he prayeth before me return (to him) void. Hear thou his prayer and fulfill his desire whether (it be) great or small.'

5. Forthwith Metatron, the Prince of the Presence, said to Moses: 'Son of Amram! Fear not, for now, God delights in thee. And ask thou u thy desire of the Glory and Majesty. For thy face shines from one end of the world to the other.' But Moses answered him, '(I fear) lest I bring guiltiness upon myself.' Metatron said to him: 'Receive the letters of the oath, in (by) which there is no breaking the covenant,' (which precludes any breach of the covenant)."

## Chapter 16.

R. Ishmael said: Metatron, the Angel, the Prince of the Presence, the Glory of all heaven, said to me:

1. "At first, I was sitting upon a great Throne at the door of the Seventh Hall, and I was judging the children of heaven, the household on high by authority of the Holy One, blessed be He. And I divided Greatness, Kingship, Dignity, Rulership, Honor and Praise, and Diadem and Crown of Glory unto all the princes of kingdoms, while I was presiding (lit. sitting) in the Celestial Court (Yeshiba), and the princes of kingdoms were standing before me, on my right and on my left by authority of the Holy One, blessed be He.

2. But when Acher came to behold the vision of the Merkaba and fixed his eyes on me, he feared and trembled before me, and his soul was affrighted even unto departing from him, because of fear, horror, and dread of me, when he beheld me sitting upon a throne like a king with all the ministering angels standing by me as my servants and all the princes of kingdoms adorned with crowns surrounding me. 3. In that moment he opened his mouth and said, 'Indeed, there are two Divine Powers in heaven!'

4. Forthwith Bath Qol (the Divine Voice) went forth from heaven from before the Shekina and said, 'Return, ye backsliding children (Jer. iii. 22), except Acher!'

5. Then came 'Aniyel, the Prince, the honored, glorified, beloved, wonderful, revered and fearful one, in commission from the Holy One, blessed be He and gave me sixty strokes with lashes of fire and made me stand on my feet."

## Chapter 17.

R. Ishmael said: Metatron, the angel, the Prince of the Presence, the glory of all heavens, said to me:

1. "Seven (are the) princes, the great, beautiful, revered, wonderful, and honored ones who are appointed over the seven heavens. And these are they: Mikael, Gabriel, Shatqiel, Shachaqiel, Bakariel,

Badariel, Pachriel. 2. And every one of them is the prince of the host of (one) heaven. And each one of them is accompanied by 496,000 myriads of ministering angels.

3. Mikael, the great prince, is appointed over the seventh heaven, the highest one, which is in the 'Araboth. Gabriel, the prince of the host, is appointed over the sixth heaven which is in Makon. Shataqiel, prince of the host, is appointed over the fifth heaven which is in Ma'on. Shahaqi'el, prince of the host, is appointed over the fourth heaven which is in Zebul. Badariel, prince of the host, is appointed over the third heaven which is in Shehaqim. Barakiel, prince of the host, is appointed over the second heaven which is at the height of (Merom) Raqia. Pazriel, prince of the host, is appointed over the first heaven which is in Wilon, which is in Shamayim.

4. Under them is Galgalliel, the prince who is appointed over the globe (galgal) of the sun, and with him are 96 great and honored angels who move the sun in Raqia.

5. Under them is 'Ophanniel, the prince who is set over the globe ('ophari) of the moon. And with him are 88 angels who move the globe of the moon 354,000 parasangs every night at the time when the moon stands in the East at its turning point. And when is the moon sitting in the East at its turning point? Answer: on the fifteenth day of every month.

6. Under them is Rahatiel, the prince who is appointed over the constellations. And he is accompanied by 72 great and honored angels. And why is he called Rahatiel? Because he makes the stars run (marhit) in their orbits and courses 339 thousand parasangs every night from the East to the West, and from the West to the East. For the Holy One, blessed be He, has made a tent for all of them, for the sun, the moon, the planets, and the stars in which they travel at night from the West to the East.

7. Under them is Kokbiel, the prince who is appointed over all the planets. And with him are 365,000 myriads of ministering angels, great and honored ones who move the planets from city to city and

from province to province in the Raqia of heavens.

8. And over them are seventy-two princes of kingdoms on high corresponding to the 72 tongues of the world. And all of them are crowned with royal crowns clad in royal garments and wrapped in royal cloaks. And all of them are riding on royal horses and they are holding royal scepters in their hands. And before each one of them when he is traveling in Raqia, royal servants are running with great glory and majesty even as on earth they (princes) are traveling in chariot(s) with horsemen and great armies and in glory and greatness with praise, song, and honor."

## Chapter 18.

R. Ishmael said: Metatron, the Angel, the Prince of the Presence, the glory of all heaven, said to me:

1. "The angels of the first heaven, when(ever) they see their prince, they dismount from their horses and fall on their faces. And the prince of the first heaven, when he sees the prince of the second heaven, he dismounts, removes the crown of glory from his head, and falls on his face. And the prince of the second heaven, when he sees the prince of the third heaven, he removes the crown of glory from his head and falls on his face. And the prince of the third heaven, when he sees the prince of the fourth heaven, he removes the crown of glory from his head and falls on his face. And the prince of the fourth heaven, when he sees the prince of the fifth heaven, he removes the crown of glory from his head and falls on his face. And the prince of the fifth heaven, when he sees the prince of the sixth heaven, he removes the crown of glory from his head and falls on his face. And the prince of the sixth heaven, when he sees the prince of the seventh heaven, he removes the crown of glory from his head and falls on his face.

2. And the prince of the seventh heaven, when he sees the seventy-two princes of kingdoms, he removes the crown of glory from his head and falls on his face. 3. And the seventy-two princes of kingdoms, when they see the door keepers of the first Hall in the

Araboth Raqia in the highest, they remove the royal crown from their head and fall on their faces. 3 And the door keepers of the first Hall, when they see the doorkeepers of the second Hall, remove the crown of glory from their heads and fall on their faces. And the door keepers of the second Hall, when they see the doorkeepers of the third Hall, remove the crown of glory from their heads and fall on their faces. And the door keepers of the third Hall, when they see the doorkeepers of the fourth Hall, remove the crown of glory from their heads and fall on their faces. And the door keepers of the fourth Hall, when they see the doorkeepers of the fifth Hall, they remove the crown of glory from their head and fall on their faces. And the door keepers of the fifth Hall, when they see the doorkeepers of the sixth Hall, they remove the crown of glory from their head and fall on their faces. And the door keepers of the sixth Hall, when they see the door keepers of the seventh Hall, they remove the crown of glory from their head and fall on their faces. 4. And the doorkeepers of the seventh Hall, when they see the four great princes, the honored ones, who are appointed over the four camps of Shekina, they remove the crown(s) of glory from their head and fall on their faces.

5. And the four great princes, when they see Tag'as, the prince, great and honored with song (and) praise, at the head of all the children of heaven, they remove the crown of glory from their head and fall on their faces. 6. And Tag'as, the great and honored prince, when he sees Barattiel, the great prince of three fingers in the height of 'Araboth, the highest heaven, he removes the crown of glory from his head and falls on his face.

7. And Barattiel, the great prince, when he sees Hamon, the great prince, the fearful and honored, pleasant and terrible one who maketh all the children of heaven to tremble when the time draweth nigh (that is set) for the saying of the '(Thrice) Holy', as it is written (Isa. xxxiii. 3): "At the noise of the tumult (hamon) the peoples are fled; at the lifting up of thyself the nations are scattered," he removes the crown of glory from his head and falls on his face.

8. And Hamon, the great prince, when he sees Tutresiel H', the great prince, he removes the crown of glory from his head and falls on his face.

9. And Tutresiel H', the great prince, when he sees Atrugiel, the great prince, he removes the crown of glory from his head and falls on his face.

10. And Atrugiel the great prince, when he sees Na'aririel H', the great prince, he removes the crown of glory from his head and falls on his face.

11. And Na'aririel H', the great prince, when he sees Sasnigiel H', the great prince, he removes the crown of glory from his head and falls on his face.

12. And Sasnigiel H', when he sees Zazriel H', the great prince, he removes the crown of glory from his head and falls on his face.

13. And Zazriel H', the prince, when he sees Geburatiel H', the prince, he removes the crown of glory from his head and falls on his face.

14. And Geburatiel H', the prince, when he sees 'Araphiel H', the prince, he removes the crown of glory from his head and falls on his face.

15. And 'Araphiel H', the prince, when he sees 'Ashruylu, the prince, who presides in all the sessions of the children of heaven, he removes the crown of glory from his head and falls on his face.

16. And 'Ashruylu H', the prince, when he sees Gallisur H', the prince, who reveals all the secrets of the Law (Torah), he removes the crown of glory from his head and falls on his face.

17. And Gallisur H', the prince, when he sees Zakzakiel H', the prince who is appointed to write down the merits of Israel on the Throne of Glory, he removes the crown of glory from his head and falls on his face.

18. And Zakzakiel H', the great prince, when he sees 'Anaphiel H', the prince who keeps the keys of the heavenly Halls, he removes the

crown of glory from his head and falls on his face. Why is he called by the name of 'Anaphiel? Because the bough of his honor and majesty and his crown and his splendor and his brilliance covers (overshadows) all the chambers of 'Araboth Raqia on high even as the Maker of the World (doth overshadow them). Just as it is written with regard to the Maker of the World (Hab. iii. 3): 'His glory covered the heavens, and the earth was full of his praise,' even so, do the honor and majesty of 'Anaphiel cover all the glories of 'Araboth the highest.

19. And when he sees Sother 'Ashiel H', the prince, the great, fearful, and honored one, he removes the crown of glory from his head and falls on his face. Why is he called Sother 'Ashiel? Because he is appointed over the four heads of the fiery river over against the Throne of Glory; and every single prince who goes out or enters before the Shekina, goes out or enters only by his permission. For the seals of the fiery river are entrusted to him. And furthermore, his height is 7000 myriads of parasangs. And he stirs up the fire of the river; and he goes out and enters before the Shekina to expound what is written (recorded) concerning the inhabitants of the world. According as it is written (Dan. vii. 10): 'the judgment was set, and the books were opened.'

20. And Sother 'Ashiel the prince, when he sees Shoqed Chozi, the great prince, the mighty, terrible and honored one, he removes the crown of glory from his head and falls upon his face. And why is he called Shoqed Chozi? Because he weighs all the merits (of man) in a balance in the presence of the Holy One, blessed be He.

21. And when he sees Zehanpuryu H', the great prince, the mighty and terrible one, honored, glorified, and feared in all the heavenly household, he removes the crown of glory from his head and falls on his face. Why is he called Zehanpuryu? Because he rebukes the fiery river and pushes it back to its place.

22. And when he sees 'Azbuga H', the great prince, glorified, revered, honored, adored, wonderful, exalted, beloved, and feared among all the great princes who know the mystery of the Throne of Glory, he

removes the crown of glory from his head and falls on his face. Why is he called 'Azbuga? Because in the future he will gird (clothe) the righteous and pious of the world with the garments of life and wrap them in the cloak of life, that they may live in them an eternal life.

23. And when he sees the two great princes, the strong and glorified ones who are standing above him, he removes the crown of glory from his head and falls on his face. And these are the names of the two princes: Sopheriel H' (who) Killeth, (Sopheriel H' the Killer), the great prince, the honored, glorified, blameless, venerable, ancient and mighty one; (and) Sopheriel H' (who) Maketh Alive (Sopheriel H' the Lifegiver), the great prince, the honored, glorified, blameless, ancient and mighty one. 24. Why is he called Sopheriel H' who Killeth (Sopheriel H' the Killer)? Because he is appointed over the books of the dead; [so that] everyone, when the day of his death draws nigh, he writes him in the books of the dead. Why is he called Sopheriel H' who Maketh Alive (Sopheriel H' the Lifegiver)? Because he is appointed over the books of the living (of life), so that everyone whom the Holy One, blessed be He, will bring into life, he writes him in the book of the living (of life), by authority of Maqom. Thou might perhaps say, 'Since the Holy One, blessed be He, is sitting on a throne, they also are sitting when writing.' (Answer): The Scripture teaches us (1 Kgs. xxii. 19, 2 Chron. xviii. 18): 'And all the host of heaven are standing by him.' 'The host of heaven' (it is said) in order to show us, that even the Great Princes, none like whom there is in the high heavens, do not fulfill the requests of the Shekina otherwise than standing. But how is it (possible that) they (are able to) write, when they are standing? It is like this:

25. One is standing on the wheels of the tempest and the other is standing on the wheels of the storm wind. The one is clad in kingly garments; the other is clad in kingly garments. The one is wrapped in a mantle of majesty and the other is wrapped in a mantle of majesty. The one is crowned with a royal crown, and the other is crowned with a royal crown. The one's body is full of eyes, and the other's body

is full of eyes. The appearance of one is like unto the appearance of lightning, and the appearance of the other is like unto the appearance of lightning. The eyes of the one are like the sun in its might, and the eyes of the other are like the sun in its might. The one's height is like the height of the seven heavens, and the other's height is like the height of the seven heavens. The wings of the one are as (many as) the days of the year, and the wings of the other are as (many as) the days of the year. The wings of the one extend over the breadth of Raqia, and the wings of the other extend over the breadth of Raqia. The lips of the one, are as the gates of the East, and the lips of the other are as the gates of the East. The tongue of the one is as high as the waves of the sea, and the tongue of the other is as high as the waves of the sea. From the mouth of the one a flame goes forth, and from the mouth of the other a flame goes forth. From the mouth of the one, there go forth lightning and from the mouth of the other, there go forth lightning. From the sweat of the one fire is kindled, and from the perspiration of the other fire is kindled. From the one's tongue, a torch is burning, and from the tongue of the other, a torch is burning. On the head of the one, there is a sapphire stone, and upon the head of the other, there is a sapphire stone. On the shoulders of the one, there is a wheel of a swift cherub, and on the shoulders of the other, there is a wheel of a swift cherub. One has in his hand a burning scroll, the other has in his hand a burning scroll. The one has in his hand a flaming style, the other has in his hand a flaming style. The length of the scroll is 3000 myriads of parasangs; the size of the style is 3000 myriads of parasangs; the size of every single letter that they write is 365 parasangs."

## Chapter 19.

R. Ishmael said: Metatron, the Angel, the Prince of the Presence, said to me:

1. "Above 2 these three angels, these great princes there is one Prince, distinguished, honored, noble, glorified, adorned, fearful, valiant, strong, great, magnified, glorious, crowned, wonderful, exalted,

blameless, beloved, lordly, high and lofty, ancient and mighty, like unto whom there is none among the princes. His name is Rikbiel H', the great and revered Prince who is standing by the Merkaba. 2. And why is he called Rikbiel? Because he is appointed over the wheels of the Merkaba, and they are given in his charge. 3. And how many are the wheels? Eight; two in each direction. And there are four winds compassing them roundabout. And these are their names: 'the Storm Wind', 'the Tempest', 'the Strong Wind', and 'the Wind of Earthquake'. 4. And under them four fiery rivers are continually running, one fiery river on each side. And round about them, between the rivers, four clouds are planted (placed), and these they are: 'clouds of fire', 'clouds of lamps', 'clouds of coal', 'clouds of brimstone' and they are standing over against [their] wheels. 5. And the feet of the Chayyoth are resting upon the wheels. And between one wheel and the other earthquake is roaring and thunder is thundering.

6. And when the time draws nigh for the recital of the Song, (then) the multitudes of wheels are moved, the multitude of clouds tremble, all the chieftains (shallishim) are made afraid, all the horsemen (parashim) do rage, all the mighty ones (gibborim) are excited, all the hosts (seba'im) are afrighted, all the troops (gedudim) are in fear, all the appointed ones (memunnim) haste away, all the princes (sarim) and armies (chayyelim) are dismayed, all the servants (mesharetim) do faint and all the angels (mal'akim) and divisions (degalim) travail with pain.

7. And one wheel makes a sound to be heard to the other and one Kerub to another, one Chayya. to another, one Seraph to another (saying) (Ps. ixviii. 5), 'Extol to him that rideth in 'Araboth, by his name Jah and rejoice before him!'"

## Chapter 20.

R. Ishmael said: Metatron, the angel, the Prince of the Presence, said to me:

1. "Above these there is one great and mighty prince. His name is Chayyliel H', a noble and revered prince, a glorious and mighty

prince, a great and revered prince, a prince before whom all the children of heaven do tremble, a prince who is able to swallow up the whole earth in one moment (at a mouthful). 2. And why is he called Chayyliel H'? Because he is appointed over the Holy Chayyoth and smites the Chayyoth with lashes of fire, and glorifies them, when they give praise and glory and rejoicing, and he causes them to make haste to say, 'Holy and blessed be the Glory of H' from his place!' (i.e. the Qedushshd)."

### Chapter 21.

R. Ishmael said: Metatron, the angel, the Prince of the Presence, said to me:

1. "Four (are) the Chayyoth corresponding to the four winds. Each Chayya is as the space of the whole world. And each one has four faces; and each face is as the face of the East. 2. Each one has four wings and each wing is like the cover (roof) of the universe. 3. And each one has faces in the middle of faces and wings in the middle of wings. The size of the faces is (as the size of) 248 faces, and the size of the wings is (as the size of) 365 wings. 4. And everyone is crowned with 2000 crowns on his head. And each crown is like unto the bow in the cloud. And its splendor is like unto the splendor of the globe of the sun. And the sparks that go forth from everyone are like the splendor of the morning star (planet Venus) in the East."

### Chapter 22.

R. Ishmael said: Metatron, the angel, the Prince of the Presence, said to me:

1. "Above these there is one prince, noble, wonderful, strong, and praised with all kinds of praise. His name is Kerubiel H', a mighty prince, full of power and strength a prince of highness, and Highness (is) with him, a righteous prince, and righteousness (is) with him, a holy prince, and holiness (is) with him, a prince glorified in (by) thousand hosts, exalted by ten thousand armies. 2. At his wrath the earth trembles, at his anger the camps are moved, from fear of him the foundations are shaken, at his rebuke the 'Araboth do tremble.

3. His stature is full of (burning) coals. The height of his stature is as the height of the seven heavens the breadth of his stature is as the wideness of the seven heavens and the thickness of his stature is as the seven heavens. 4. The opening of his mouth is like a lamp of fire. His tongue is a consuming fire. His eyebrows are like unto the splendor of the lightning. His eyes are like sparks of brilliance. His countenance is like a burning fire.

5. And there is a crown of holiness upon his head on which (crown) the Explicit Name is graven, and lightning go forth from it. And the bow of Shekina is between his shoulders. 6. And his sword is like unto a lightning; and upon his loins, there are arrows like unto a flame, and upon his armor and shield there is a consuming fire, and upon his neck, there are coals of burning juniper and (also) round about him (there are coals of burning juniper).

7. And the splendor of Shekina is on his face; and the horns of majesty on his wheels; and a royal diadem upon his skull. 8. And his body is full of eyes. And wings are covering the whole of his high stature (lit. the height of his stature is all wings). 9. On his right hand a flame is burning, and on his left, a fire is glowing; and coals are burning from it. And firebrands go forth from his body. And lightnings are cast forth from his face. With him there is always thunder upon (in) thunder, by his side, there is ever earthquake upon (in) earthquake.

10. And the two princes of the Merkaba are together with him.

11. Why is he called Kerubiel H', the Prince? Because he is appointed over the chariot of the Kerubim. And the mighty Kerubim are given in his charge. And he adorns the crowns on their heads and polishes the diadem upon their skull. 12. He magnifies the glory of their appearance. And he glorifies the beauty of their majesty. And he increases the greatness of their honor. He causes the song of their praise to be sung. He intensifies their beautiful strength. He causes the brilliance of their glory to shine forth. He beautifies their goodly mercy and lovingkindness. He frames the fairness of their radiance. He makes their merciful beauty even more beautiful. He glorifies

their upright majesty. He extols the order of their praise, to establish the dwelling place of him 'who dwelleth on the Kerubim.'

13. And the Kerubim are standing by the Holy Chayyoth, and their wings are raised up to their heads (lit. are as the height of their heads) and Shekina is (resting) upon them and the brilliance of the Glory is upon their faces and song and praise in their mouth and their hands are under their wings and their feet are covered by their wings and horns of glory are upon their heads and the splendor of Shekina on their face and Shekina is (resting) upon them and sapphire stones are round about them and columns of fire on their four sides and columns of firebrands beside them. 14. There is one sapphire on one side and another sapphire on another side and under the sapphires, there are coals of burning juniper.

15. And one Kerub is standing in each direction but the wings of the Kerubim compass each other above their skulls in glory; and they spread them to sing with them a song to him that inhabiteth the clouds and to praise with them the fearful majesty of the king of kings.

16. And Kerubiel H', the prince who is appointed over them, he arrays them in comely, beautiful, and pleasant orders and he exalts them in all manner of exaltation, dignity, and glory. And he hastens them in glory and might to do the will of their Creator every moment. For above their lofty heads abides continually the glory of the high king 'who dwelleth on the Kerubim.'"

### Chapter 22*b*.

1. "And there is a court before the Throne of Glory, 2. which no seraph nor angel can enter, and it is 36,000 myriads of parasangs, as it is written: 'and the Seraphim are standing above him,' (the last word of the scriptural passage being 'Lamech-Vav' [numerical value: 36]). 3. As the numerical value Lamech-Vav (36) the number of the bridges there.

4. And there are 24 myriads of wheels of fire. And the ministering angels are 12,000 myriads. And there are 12,000 rivers of hail and

12,000 treasuries of snow. And in the seven Halls are chariots of fire and flames, without reckoning, or end or searching."

R. Ishmael said to me: Metatron, the angel, the Prince of the Presence, said to me:

1. "How are the angels standing on high? Pie said: Like a bridge that is placed over a river so that everyone can pass over it, likewise a bridge is placed from the beginning of the entry to the end. 2. And three ministering angels surround it and utter a song before YHWH, the God of Israel. And there are standing before it lords of dread and captains of fear, thousand times thousand and ten thousand times ten thousand in number and they sing praise and hymns before YHWH, the God of Israel.

3. Numerous bridges are there: bridges of fire and numerous bridges of hail. Also, numerous rivers of hail, numerous treasuries of snow and numerous wheels of fire. 4. And how many are the ministering angels? 12,000 myriads: six (thousand myriads) above and six (thousand myriads] below. And 12,000 are the treasuries of snow, six above and six below. And 24 myriads of wheels of fire, 12 (myriads) above and 12 (myriads) below. And they surround the bridges and the rivers of fire and the rivers of hail. And there are numerous ministering angels, forming entries, for all the creatures that are standing in the midst thereof, corresponding to (over against) the paths of Raqia Shamayim.

5. What doeth YHWH, the God of Israel, the King of Glory? The Great and Fearful God, mighty in strength, doth cover his face.

6. In 'Araboth are 660,000 myriads of angels of glory standing over against the Throne of Glory and the divisions of flaming fire. And the King of Glory doth cover His face; for else the 'Araboth Raqia would be rent asunder in its midst because of the majesty, splendor, beauty, radiance, loveliness, brilliancy, brightness, and excellency of the appearance of the Holy One, blessed be He.

7. There are numerous ministering angels performing his will, numerous kings, numerous princes in the 'Araboth of his delight,

angels who are revered among the rulers in heaven, distinguished, adorned with song and bringing love to remembrance: (who) are affrighted by the splendor of the Shekina, and their eyes are dazzled by the shining beauty of their King, their faces grow black and their strength doth fail.

8. There go forth rivers of joy, streams of gladness, rivers of rejoicing, streams of triumph, rivers of love, streams of friendship (another reading) of commotion and they flow over and go forth before the Throne of Glory and wax great and go through the gates of the paths of 'Araboth Raqia at the voice of the shouting and music of the Chayyoth, at the voice of the rejoicing of the timbrels of his 'Ophannim and at the melody of the cymbals of His Kerubim. And they wax great and go forth with commotion with the sound of the hymn: 'Holy, holy, holy, is the Lord of Hosts; the whole earth is full of His glory!'"

## Chapter 22c.

R. Ishmael said: Metatron, the Prince of the Presence said to me:

1. "What is the distance between one bridge and another? 12 myriads of parasangs. Their ascent is 12 myriads of parasangs, and their descent is 12 myriads of parasangs.

2. (The distance) between the rivers of dread and the rivers of fear is 22 myriads of parasangs; between the rivers of hail and the rivers of darkness 36 myriads of parasangs; between the chambers of lightning and the clouds of compassion 42 myriads of parasangs; between the clouds of compassion and the Merkaba 84 myriads of parasangs; between the Merkaba and the Kerubim 148 myriads of parasangs; between the Kerubim and the 'Ophannim 24 myriads of parasangs; between the Ophannim and the chambers of chambers 24 myriads of parasangs; between the chambers of chambers and the Holy Chayyoth 40,000 myriads of parasangs; between one wing (of the Chayyoth) and another 12 myriads of parasangs; and the breadth of each one wing is of that same measure; and the distance between the Holy Chayyoth and the Throne of Glory is 30,000

myriads of parasangs.

3. And from the foot of the Throne to the seat there are 40,000 myriads of parasangs. And the name of Him that sitteth on it: let the name be sanctified!

4. And the arches of the Bow are set above the 'Araboth, and they are 1000 thousand and 10,000 times ten thousand (of parasangs) high. Their measure is after the measure of the 'Irin and Qaddishin (Watchers and Holy Ones). As it is written (Gen. ix. 13): 'My bow I have set in the cloud.' It is not written here: 'I will set' but 'I have set', (*i.e.*) already; clouds that surround the Throne of Glory. As His clouds pass by, the angels of hail (turn into) burning coal.

5. And a fire of the voice goes down from by the Holy Chayyoth. And because of the breath of that voice they 'run' (Ezek. i. 14) to another place, fearing lest it command them to go; and they 'return' lest it injure them from the other side. Therefore 'they run and return' (Ezek. i. 14).

6. And these arches of the Bow are more beautiful and radiant than the radiance of the sun during the summer solstice. And they are whiter than a flaming fire and they are great and beautiful. 7. Above the arches of the Bow are the wheels of the 'Ophannim. Their height is 1000 thousand and 10,000 times 10,000 units of measure after the measure of the Seraphim and the Troops (Gedudim)."

## Chapter 23.

R. Ishmael said: Metatron, the Angel, the Prince of the Presence, said to me:

1. "There are numerous winds blowing under the wings of the Kerubim. There blows 'the Brooding Wind', as it is written (Gen. i. 2): 'and the wind of God was brooding upon the face of the waters.'

2. There blows 'the Strong Wind', as it is said (Ex. xiv. 21): 'and the Lord caused the sea to go back by a strong east wind all that night.'

3. There blows 'the East Wind', as it is written (Ex. x. 13): 'the east wind brought the locusts.'

4. There blows 'the Wind of Quails', as it is written (Num. xi. 31): 'And there went forth a wind from the Lord and brought quails.'

5. There blows 'the Wind of Jealousy', as it is written (Num. v. 14): 'And the wind of jealousy came upon him.'

6. There blows the 'Wind of Earthquake', as it is written (1 Kgs. xix. 11): 'and after that the wind of the earthquake; but the Lord was not in the earthquake.'

7. There blows the 'Wind of H'', as it is written (Ezek. xxxvii. 1): 'and he carried me out by the wind of H' and set me down.'

8. There blows the 'Evil Wind' as it is written (1 Sam. xvi. 23): 'and the evil wind departed from him.'

9. There blow the 'Wind of Wisdom' and the 'Wind of Understanding' and the 'Wind of Knowledge' and the 'Wind of the Fear of H'', as it is written (Is. xi. 2): 'And the wind of H' shall rest upon him; the wind of wisdom and understanding, the wind of counsel and might, the wind of knowledge and of the fear.'

10. There blows the 'Wind of Rain', as it is written (Prov. xxv. 23): 'the north wind bringeth forth rain.'

11. There blows the 'Wind of Lightnings', as it is written (Jer. x. 13, li. 16): 'He maketh lightnings for the rain and bringeth forth the wind out of his treasuries.'

12. There blows the 'Wind, Breaking the Rocks', as it is written (1 Kings xix. 11): 'the Lord passed by and a great and strong wind (rent the mountains and break in pieces the rocks before the Lord).'

13. There blows the 'Wind of Assuagement of the Sea', as it is written (Gen. viii. 1): 'and God made a wind to pass over the earth, and the waters assuaged.'

14. There blows the 'Wind of Wrath', as it is written (Job i. 19): 'and behold there came a great wind from the wilderness and smote the four corners of the house and it fell.'

15. There blows the 'Storm Wind', as it is written (Ps. cxlviii. 8): 'Storm wind, fulfilling his word.'

16. And Satan is standing among these winds, for 'storm wind' is nothing else but 'Satan', and all these winds do not blow but under the wings of the Kerubim, as it is written (Ps. xviii. 10): 'And He rode upon a cherub and did fly, yea, and He flew swiftly upon the wings of the wind.'

17. And whither go all these winds? The Scripture teaches us, that they go out from under the wings of the Kerubim and descend on the globe of the sun, as it is written (Eccl. i. 6): 'The wind goeth toward the south and turneth about unto the north; it turneth about continually in its course and the wind returneth again to its circuits.' And from the globe of the sun they return and descend upon the rivers and the seas, upon the mountains and upon the hills, as it is written (Am. iv. 13): 'For lo, he that formeth the mountains and createth the wind.'

18. And from the mountains and the hills they return and descend to the seas and the rivers; and from the seas and the rivers they return and descend upon (the) cities and provinces; and from the cities and provinces they return and descend into the Garden, and from the Garden they return and descend to Eden, as it is written (Gen. iii. 8): 'walking in the Garden in the wind of day.' And in the midst of the Garden they join together and blow from one side to the other and are perfumed with the spices of the Garden even from its remotest parts, until they separate from each other, and, filled with the scent of the pure spices, they bring the odor from the remotest parts of Eden and the spices of the Garden to the righteous and godly who in the time to come shall inherit the Garden of Eden and the Tree of Life, as it is written (Cant. iv. 16): 'Awake, O north wind; and come thou south; blow upon my garden, that the spices thereof may flow out. Let my beloved come into his garden and eat his precious fruits.'"

## Chapter 24.

R. Ishmael said: Metatron, the Angel, the Prince of the Presence, the glory of all heaven, said to me:

1. "Numerous chariots has the Holy One, blessed be He; He has the

'Chariots of (the) Kerubim', as it is written (Ps. xviii. 11, 2 Sam. xxii. 11): 'And he rode upon a cherub and did fly.'

2. He has the 'Chariots of Wind', as it is written (ib.): 'and he flew swiftly upon the wings of the wind.'

3. He has the 'Chariots of (the) Swift Cloud', as it is written (Is. xix. 1): 'Behold, the Lord rideth upon a swift cloud.'

4. He has 'the Chariots of Clouds', as it is written (Ex. xix. 9): 'Lo, I come unto thee in a cloud.'

5. He has the 'Chariots of the Altar', as it is written (Am. ix. 1): 'I saw the Lord standing upon the Altar.'

6. He has the 'Chariots of Ribbotaim', as it is written (Ps. ixviii. 18): 'The chariots of God are Ribbotaim; thousands of angels.'

7. He has the 'Chariots of the Tent', as it is written (Deut. xxxi. 15): 'And the Lord appeared in the Tent in a pillar of cloud.'

8. He has the 'Chariots of the Tabernacle', as it is written (Lev. i. 1): 'And the Lord spake unto him out of the tabernacle.'

9. He has the 'Chariots of the Mercy Seat', as it is written (Num. vii. 89): 'Then he heard the Voice speaking unto him from upon the mercy seat.'

10. He has the 'Chariots of Sapphire Stone', as it is written (Ex. xxiv. 10): 'and there was under his feet as it were a paved work of sapphire stone.'

11. He has the 'Chariots of Eagles', as it is written (Ex. xix. 4): 'I bare you on eagles' wings.' Eagles literally are not meant here but 'they that fly swiftly as eagles.'

12. He has the 'Chariots of Shout', as it is written (Ps. xlvii. 6): 'God is gone up with a shout.'

13. He has the 'Chariots of 'Araboth', as it is written (Ps. ixviii. 5): 'Extol Him that rideth upon the 'Araboth.'

14. He has the 'Chariots of Thick Clouds', as it is written (Ps. civ. 3): 'who maketh the thick clouds His chariot.'

15. He has the 'Chariots of the Chayyoth', as it is written (Ezek. i. 14): 'and the Chayyoth ran and returned.' They run by permission and return by permission, for Shekina is above their heads.

16. He has the 'Chariots of Wheels' (Galgallim), as it is written (Ezek. x. 2): 'And he said: Go in between the whirling wheels.'

17. He has the 'Chariots of a Swift Kerub', as it is written (Ps. xviii. 10, Is. xix. 1): 'riding on a swift cherub.' And at the time when He rides on a swift kerub, as He sets one of His feet upon him before He sets the other foot upon his back, He looks through eighteen thousand worlds at one glance. And He discerns and sees into them all and knows what is in all of them and then He sets down the other foot upon him, according as it is written (Ezek. xlviii. 35): 'Roundabout eighteen thousand.' Whence do we know that He looks through every one of them every day? It is written (Ps. xiv. 2): 'He looked down from heaven upon the children of men to see if there were any that did understand, that did seek after God.'

18. He has the 'Chariots of the 'Ophannim', as it is written (Ezek. x. 12): 'and the 'Ophannim were full of eyes round about.'

19. He has the 'Chariots of His Holy Throne', as it is written (Ps. xlvii. 8): 'God sitteth upon his holy throne.'

20. He has the 'Chariots of the Throne of Yah', as it is written (Ex. xvii. 16): 'Because a hand is lifted up upon the Throne of Jah.'

21. He has the 'Chariots of the Throne of Judgement', as it is written (Is. v. 16): 'but the Lord of hosts shall be exalted in judgment.'

22. He has the 'Chariots of the Throne of Glory', as it is written (Jer. xvii. 12): 'The Throne of Glory, set on high from the beginning, is the place of our sanctuary.'

23. He has the 'Chariots of the High and Exalted Throne', as it is written (Is. vi. 1): 'I saw the Lord sitting upon the high and exalted throne.'"

## Chapter 25.

R. Ishmael said: Metatron, the Angel, the Prince of the Presence, said to me:

1. "Above these there is one great prince, revered, high, lordly, fearful, ancient, and strong. 'Ophanniel H' is his name. 2. He has sixteen faces, four faces on each side, and (also) a hundred wings on each side. And he has 8466 eyes, corresponding to the days of the year (2190, and some say, 2116 on each side). (2191, 2196, and sixteen on each side.) 3. And those two eyes of his face, in each one of them lightning are flashing, and from each one of them firebrands are burning, and no creature is able to behold them; for anyone who looks at them is burnt instantly. 4. His height is (as) the distance of 2500 years' journey. No eye can behold, and no mouth can tell the mighty power of his strength save the King of kings, the Holy One, blessed be He, alone.

5. Why is he called 'Ophanniel? Because he is appointed over the 'Ophannim and the 'Ophannimare given in his charge. He stands every day and attends and beautifies them. And he exalts and orders their apartment and polishes their standing place and makes bright their dwellings, makes their corners even, and cleanses their seats. And he waits upon them early and late, by day and by night, to increase their beauty, to make great their dignity and to make them diligent in praise of their Creator.

6. And all the 'Ophannim are full of eyes, and they are all full of brightness; seventy-two sapphire stones are fixed on their garments on their right side and seventy-two sapphire stones are fixed on their garments on their left side. 7. And four carbuncle stones are fixed on the crown of every single one, the splendor of which proceeds in the four directions of 'Araboth even as the splendor of the globe of the sun proceeds in all the directions of the universe. And why is it called Carbuncle (Bareqet)? Because its splendor is like the appearance of lightning (Baraq). And tents of splendor, tents of brilliance, tents of brightness as of sapphire and carbuncle enclose them because of

the shining appearance of their eyes."

## Chapter 26.

R. Ishmael said: Metatron, the Angel, the Prince of the Presence, said to me:

1. Above these there is one prince, wonderful, noble, great, honorable, mighty, terrible, a chief and leader, and a swift scribe, glorified, honored, and beloved. 2. He is altogether filled with splendor, full of praise and shining; and he is wholly full of brilliance, of light and of beauty; and the whole of him is filled with goodliness and greatness. 3. His countenance is altogether like (that of) angels, but his body is like an eagle's body. 4. His splendor is like unto lightning, his appearance like firebrands, his beauty like unto sparks, his honor like fiery coals, his majesty like chasmal, his radiance like the light of the planet Venus. The image of him is like unto the Greater Light. His height is as the seven heavens. The light from his eyebrows is like the sevenfold light. 5. The sapphire stone upon his head is as great as the whole universe and like unto the splendor of the very heavens in radiance. 6. His body is full of eyes like the stars of the sky, innumerable and unsearchable. Every eye is like the planet Venus. Yet, there are some of them like the Lesser Light and some of them like unto the Greater Light. From his ankles to his knees (they are) like unto stars of lightning, from his knees to his thighs like unto the planet Venus, from his thighs to his loins like unto the moon, from his loins to his neck like the sun, from his neck to his skull like unto the Light Imperishable. (Cf. Zeph. iii. 5.) 7. The crown on his head is like unto the splendor of the Throne of Glory. The measure of the crown is the distance of 502 years' journey. There is no kind of splendor, no kind of brilliance, no kind of radiance, no kind of light in the universe but is fixed on that crown.

8. The name of that prince is Seraphiel H'. And the crown on his head, its name is the 'Prince of Peace'. And why is he called by the name of Seraphiel? Because he is appointed over the Seraphim. And the flaming Seraphim are given in his charge. And he presides over

them by day and by night and teaches them song, praise, proclamation of beauty, might and majesty; that they may proclaim the beauty of their King in all manner of Praise and Sanctification (Qedushsha).

9. How many are the Seraphim? Four, corresponding to the four winds of the world. And how many wings have they each one of them? Six, corresponding to the six days of Creation. And how many faces have they? Each one of them four faces. 10. The measure of the Seraphim and the height of each one of them correspond to the height of the seven heavens. The size of each wing is like the measure of all Raqia. The size of each face is like that of the face of the East. 11. And each one of them gives forth light like unto the splendor of the Throne of Glory; so that not even the Holy Chayyoth, the honored 'Ophannim, nor the majestic Kerubim are able to behold it. For everyone who beholds it, his eyes are darkened because of its great splendor.

12. Why are they called Seraphim? Because they burn (seraph) the writing tables of Satan. Every day Satan is sitting, together with Sammael, the Prince of Rome, and with Dubbiel, the Prince of Persia, and they write the iniquities of Israel on writing tables which they hand over to the Seraphim, in order that they may present them before the Holy One, blessed be He, so that He may destroy Israel from the world. But the Seraphim know from the secrets of the Holy One, blessed be He, that he desires not, that this people Israel should perish. What do the Seraphim do? Every day do they receive (accept) them from the hand of Satan and burn them in the burning fire over against the high and exalted Throne in order that they may not come before the Holy One, blessed be He, at the time when He is sitting upon the Throne of Judgement, judging the whole world in truth."

## Chapter 27.

R. Ishmael said: Metatron, the Angel of H', the Prince of the Presence, said to me:

1. "Above the Seraphim there is one prince, exalted above all the princes, more wondrous than all the servants. His name is Radweriel

H' who is appointed over the treasuries of the books. 2. He fetches forth the Case of Writings (with) the Book of Records in it, and brings it before the Holy One, blessed be He. And he breaks the seals of the case, opens it, takes out the books, and delivers them before the Holy One, blessed be He. And the Holy One, blessed be He, receives them of his hand and gives them in his sight to the Scribes, that they may read them in the Great Beth Din (The court of justice) in the height of 'Araboth Raqia, before the heavenly household.

3. And why is he called Radweriel? Because out of every word that goes forth from his mouth an angel is created; and he stands in the songs (in the singing company) of the ministering angels and utters a song before the Holy One, blessed be He when the time draws nigh for the recitation of the (Thrice) Holy."

## Chapter 28.

R. Ishmael said: Metatron, the Angel, the Prince of the Presence, said to me:

1. "Above all these there are four great princes, Irin and Qaddishin by name; high, honored, revered, beloved, wonderful, and glorious ones, greater than all the children of heaven. There is none like unto them among all the celestial princes and none their equal among all the servants. For each one of them is equal to all the rest together. 2. And their dwelling is over against the Throne of Glory, and their standing place over against the Holy One, blessed be He, so that the brilliance of their dwelling is a reflection of the brilliance of the Throne of Glory. And the splendor of their countenance is a reflection of the splendor of Shekina. 3. And they are glorified by the glory of the Divine Majesty (Gebura) and praised by (through) the praise of Shekina. 4. And not only that, but the Holy One, blessed be He, does nothing in his world without first consulting them, but after that He doeth it. As it is written (Dan. iv. 17): 'The sentence is by the decree of the 'Irin and the demand by the word of the Qaddishin.'

5. The Irin are two and the Qaddishin are two. And how are they standing before the Holy One, blessed be He? It is to be understood,

that one 'Ir is standing on one side and the other 'Ir on the other side, and one Qaddish is standing on one side and the other on the other side. 6. And ever do they exalt the humble, and they abase to the ground those that are proud, and they exalt to the height those that are humble.

7. And every day, as the Holy One, blessed be He, is sitting upon the Throne of Judgement and judges the whole world, and the Books of the Living and the Books of the Dead are opened before Him, then all the children of heaven are standing before Him in fear, dread, awe and trembling. At that time, (when) the Holy One, blessed be He, is sitting upon the Throne of Judgement to execute judgment, His garment is white as snow, the hair on his head as pure wool, and the whole of his cloak is like the shining light. And He is covered with righteousness all over as with a coat of mail.

8. And those 'Irin and Qaddishin are standing before Him like court officers before the judge. And they raise and argue every case and close the case that comes before the Holy One, blessed be He, in judgment, according as it is written (Dan. iv. 17): 'The sentence is by the decree of the 'Irin and the demand by the word of the Qaddishin.' 9. Some of them argue and others pass the sentence in the Great Beth Din in 'Araboth. Some of them make the requests from before the Divine Majesty and some close the cases before the Most High. Others finish by going down and (confirming) executing the sentences on earth below. According as it is written (Dan. iv. 13, 14): 'Behold an 'Ir and a Qaddish came down from heaven and cried aloud and said thus, 'Hew down the tree, and cut off his branches, shake off his leaves, and scatter his fruit; let the beasts get away from under it, and the fowls from his branches.'

10. Why are they called 'Irin and Qaddishin? By reason that they sanctify the body and the spirit with lashes of fire on the third day of the judgment, as it is written (Hos. vi. 2): 'After two days will he revive us; on the third, he will raise us up, and we shall live before him.'"

## Chapter 29.

R. Ishmael said: Metatron, the Angel, the Prince of the Presence, said to me:

1. "Each one of them has seventy names corresponding to the seventy tongues of the world. And all of them are (based) upon the name of the Holy One, blessed be He. And every name is written with a flaming style upon the Fearful Crown (Keiher Nora) which is on the head of the high and exalted King. 2. And from each one of them there go forth sparks and lightnings. And each one of them is beset with horns of splendor round about. From each one lights are shining forth, and each one is surrounded by tents of brilliance so that not even the Seraphim and the Chayyoth who are greater than all the children of heaven are able to behold them."

## Chapter 30.

R. Ishmael said: Metatron, the Angel, the Prince of the Presence, said to me:

1. "Whenever the Great Beth Din is seated in the 'Araboth Raqia on high there is no opening of the mouth for anyone in the world save those great princes who are called H' by the name of the Holy One, blessed be He.

2. How many are those princes? Seventy-two princes of the kingdoms of the world besides the Prince of the World who speaks (pleads) in favor of the world before the Holy One, blessed be He, every day, at the hour when the book is opened in which are recorded all the doings of the world, according as it is written (Dan. vii. 10): 'The judgment was set and the books were opened.'"

## Chapter 31.

R. Ishmael said: Metatron, the Angel, the Prince of the Presence, said to me:

1. "At the time when the Holy One, blessed be He, is sitting on the Throne of Judgement, (then) Justice is standing on His right, Mercy on His left, and Truth before His face. 2. And when man enters

before Him to judgment, (then) there comes forth from the splendor of the Mercy towards him as (it were) a staff and stands in front of him. Forthwith man falls upon his face, (and) all the angels of destruction fear and tremble before Him, according as it is written (Is. xvi. 5): 'And with mercy shall the throne be established, and He shall sit upon it in truth.'"

### Chapter 32.

R. Ishmael said: Metatron, the Angel, the Prince of the Presence, said to me:

1. "When the Holy One, blessed be He, opens the Book, half of which is fire and half flame, (then) they go out from before Him in every moment to execute the judgment on the wicked by His sword (that is) drawn forth out of its sheath and the splendor of which shines like a lightning and pervades the world from one end to the other, as it is written (Is. ixvi. 16): 'For by fire will the Lord plead (and by His sword with all flesh).' 2. And all the inhabitants of the world (lit. those who come into the world) fear and tremble before Him, when they behold His sharpened sword like unto lightning from one end of the world to the other, and sparks and flashes of the size of the stars of Raqia going out from it; according as it is written (Deut. xxxii. 41): 'If I whet the lightning of my sword.'"

### Chapter 33.

R. Ishmael said: Metatron, the Angel, the Prince of the Presence, said to me:

1. "At the time that the Holy One, blessed be He, is sitting on the Throne of Judgement, (then) the angels of Mercy are standing on His right, the angels of Peace are standing on His left and the angels of Destruction are standing in front of Him. 2. And one scribe is standing beneath Him, and another scribe above Him. 3. And the glorious Seraphim surround the Throne on its four sides with walls of lightning, and the 'Ophannim surround them with firebrands round about the Throne of Glory. And clouds of fire and clouds of flames compass them to the right and to the left, and the Holy

Chayyoth carry the Throne of Glory from below; each one with three fingers. The measure of the fingers of each one is 800,000 and 700 times hundred, (and) 66,000 parasangs. 4. And underneath the feet of the Chayyoth seven fiery rivers are running and flowing. And the breadth of each river is 365 thousand parasangs and its depth is 248 thousand myriads of parasangs. Its length is unsearchable and immeasurable. 5. And each river turns round in a bow in the four directions of 'Araboth Raqia, and (from there) it falls down to Ma'on and is stayed, and from Ma'on on to Zebul, from Zebul to Shechaqim, from Shechaqim to Raqia, from Raqia to Shamayim, and from Shamayim upon the heads of the wicked who are in Gehenna, as it is written (Jer. xxiii. 19): 'Behold a whirlwind of the Lord, even his fury, is gone, yea, a whirling tempest; it shall burst upon the head of the wicked.'"

## Chapter 34.

R. Ishmael said: Metatron; the Angel, the Prince of the Presence, said to me:

1. "The hoofs of the Chayyoth are surrounded by seven clouds of burning coals. The clouds of burning coals are surrounded on the outside by seven walls of flame(s). The seven walls of flame(s) are surrounded on the outside by seven walls of hailstones (stones of 'Et-gabish, Ezek. xiii. 11, 13, xxviii. 22). The hailstones are surrounded on the outside by stones of hail (stone of Barad). The stones of hail are surrounded on the outside by stones of 'the wings of the tempest'. The stones of 'the wings of the tempest' are surrounded on the outside by flames of fire. The flames of fire are surrounded by the chambers of the whirlwind. The chambers of the whirlwind are surrounded on the outside by the fire and the water.

2. Round about the fire and the water are those who utter the 'Holy'. Round about those who utter the 'Holy' are those who utter the 'Blessed'. Round about those who utter the 'Blessed' are the bright clouds. The bright clouds are surrounded on the outside by coals of burning jumper, and on the outside surrounding the coals of

burning juniper there are a thousand camps of fire and ten thousand hosts of flame(s). And between every several camp and every several host, there is a cloud, so that they may not be burnt by the fire."

## Chapter 35.

R. Ishmael said: Metatron, the Angel, the Prince of the Presence, said to me:

1. "506 thousand myriads of camps has the Holy One, blessed be He, in the height of 'Araboth Raqia. And each camp is (composed of) 496 thousand angels. 2. And every single angel, the height of his stature is as the great sea; and the appearance of their countenance as the appearance of the lightning, and their eyes as lamps of fire, and their arms and their feet like in color to polished brass and the roaring voice of their words like the voice of a multitude. 3. And they are all standing before the Throne of Glory in four rows. And the princes of the army are standing at the head of each row. 4. And some of them utter the 'Holy' and others utter the 'Blessed', some of them run as messengers, others are standing in attendance, according as it is written (Dan. vii. 10): 'Thousand thousands ministered unto him, and ten thousand times ten thousand stood before him: the judgment was set and the books were opened.'

5. And in the hour, when the time draws nigh for to say the 'Holy', (then) first there goes forth a whirlwind from before the Holy One, blessed be He, and bursts upon the camp of Shekina and there arises a great commotion among them, as it is written (Jer. xxx. 23): 'Behold, the whirlwind of the Lord goeth forth with fury, a continuing commotion.'

6. At that moment four thousand thousands of them are changed into sparks, thousand thousands of them into firebrands, thousand thousands into flashes, thousand thousands into flames, thousand thousands into males, thousand thousands into females, thousand thousands into winds, thousand thousands into burning fires, thousand thousands into flames, thousand thousands into sparks, thousand thousands into chashmals of light; until they take upon

themselves the yoke of the kingdom of heaven, the high and lifted up, of the Creator of them all with fear, dread, awe and trembling, with commotion, anguish, terror and trepidation. Then they are changed again into their former shape to have the fear of their King before them always, as they have set their hearts on saying the Song continually, as it is written (Is. vi. 3): 'And one cried unto another and said holy, holy, holy.'"

## Chapter 36.

R. Ishmael said: Metatron, the Angel, the Prince of the Presence, said to me:

1. "At the time when the ministering angels desire to say (the) Song, (then) Nehar di-Nur (the fiery stream) rises with many thousand thousands and myriads of myriads (of angels) of power and strength of fire and it runs and passes under the Throne of Glory, between the camps of the ministering angels and the troops of 'Araboth.

2. And all the ministering angels first go down into Nehar di-Nur, and they dip themselves in the fire and dip their tongue and their mouth seven times; and after that, they go up and put on the garment of 'Machaqe Samal' and cover themselves with cloaks of chashmal and stand in four rows over against the Throne of Glory, in all the heavens."

## Chapter 37.

R. Ishmael said: Metatron, the Angel, the Prince of the Presence, said to me:

1. "In the seven Halls there are standing four chariots of Shekina, and before each one are standing the four camps of Shekina. Between each camp, a river of fire is continually flowing. 2. Between each river there are bright clouds [surrounding them], and between each cloud, there are put up pillars of brimstone. Between one pillar and another, there are standing flaming wheels, surrounding them. And between one wheel and another, there are flames of fire roundabout. Between one flame and another there are treasuries of lightning; behind the

treasuries of lightning are the wings of the storm wind. Behind the wings of the storm wind are the chambers of the tempest; behind the chambers of the tempest there are winds, voices, thunders, sparks [upon] sparks, and earthquakes [upon] earthquakes."

## Chapter 38.

R. Ishmael said: Metatron, the Angel, the Prince of the Presence, said to me:

1. "At the time, when the ministering angels utter (the Thrice) Holy, then all the pillars of the heavens and their sockets do tremble, and the gates of the Halls of 'Araboth Raqia are shaken and the foundations of Shechaqim and the Universe (Tebel) are moved, and the orders of Ma'on and the chambers of Makon quiver, and all the orders of Raqia and the constellations and the planets are dismayed, and the globes of the sun and the moon haste away and flee out of their courses and run 12,000 parasangs and seek to throw themselves down from heaven, 2. by reason of the roaring voice of their chant, and the noise of their praise and the sparks and lightning that go forth from their faces; as it is written (Ps. lxxvii. 18): 'The voice of thy thunder was in the heaven (the lightning lightened the world, the earth trembled and shook).' 3. Until the prince of the world calls them, saying: 'Be ye quiet in your place! Fear not because of the ministering angels who sing the Song before the Holy One, blessed be He.' As it is written (Job. xxxviii. 7): 'When the morning stars sang together and all the children of heaven shouted for joy.'"

## Chapter 39.

R. Ishmael said: Metatron, the Angel, the Prince of the Presence, said to me:

1. "When the ministering angels utter the 'Holy' then all the explicit names that are graven with a flaming style on the Throne of Glory fly off like eagles, with sixteen wings. And they surround and compass the Holy One, blessed be He, on the four sides of the place of His Shekina.

2. And the angels of the host, and the flaming Servants, and the mighty 'Ophannim, and the Kerubim of the Shekina, and the Holy Chayyoth, and the Seraphim, and the 'Er'ellim, and the Taphsarim and the troops of consuming fire, and the fiery armies, and the flaming hosts, and the holy princes, adorned with crowns, clad in kingly majesty, wrapped in glory, girt with loftiness, fall upon their faces three times, saying, 'Blessed be the name of His glorious kingdom forever and ever.'"

## Chapter 40.

R. Ishmael said: Metatron, the Angel, the Prince of the Presence, said to me:

1. "When the ministering angels say 'Holy' before the Holy One, blessed be He, in the proper way, then the servants of His Throne, the attendants of His Glory, go forth with great mirth from under the Throne of Glory. 2. And they all carry in their hands, each one of them thousand and ten thousand times ten thousand crowns of stars, similar in appearance to the planet Venus, and put them on the ministering angels and the great princes who utter the 'Holy'. Three crowns they put on each one of them; one crown because they say 'Holy', another crown because they say 'Holy, Holy', and a third crown because they say 'Holy, Holy, Holy, is the Lord of Hosts.'

3. And in the moment that they do not utter the 'Holy' in the right order, a consuming fire goes forth from the little finger of the Holy One, blessed be He, and falls down in the midst of their ranks and is divided into 496 thousand parts corresponding to the four camps of the ministering angels, and consumes them in one moment, as it is written (Ps. xcvii. 3): 'A fire goeth before Him and burneth up His adversaries round about.'

4. After that the Holy One, blessed be He, opens His mouth and speaks one word and creates others in their stead, new ones like them. And each one stands before His Throne of Glory, uttering the 'Holy', as it is written (Lam. iii. 23): 'They are new every morning; great is thy faithfulness.'"

## Chapter 41.

R. Ishmael said: Metatron, the Angel, the Prince of the Presence, said to me:

1. "Come and behold the letters by which the heaven and the earth were created, the letters by which were created the mountains and hills, the letters by which were created the seas and rivers, the letters by which were created the trees and herbs, the letters by which were created the planets and the constellations, the letters by which were created the globe of the moon and the globe of the sun, Orion, the Pleiades and all the different luminaries of Raqia. 2. The letters by which were created the Throne of Glory and the Wheels of the Merkaba, the letters by which were created the necessities of the worlds, 3. the letters by which were created wisdom, understanding, knowledge, prudence, meekness and righteousness by which the whole world is sustained.

4. And I walked by his side and he took me by his hand and raised me upon his wings and showed me those letters, all of them, that are graven with a flaming style on the Throne of Glory; and sparks go forth from them and cover all the chambers of 'Araboth."

## Chapter 42.

R. Ishmael said: Metatron, the Angel, the Prince of the Presence, said to me:

1. "Come and I will show thee, where the waters are suspended in the highest, where fire is burning in the midst of hail, where lightnings lighten out of the midst of snowy mountains, where thunders are roaring in the celestial heights, where a flame is burning in the midst of the burning fire and where voices make themselves heard in the midst of thunder and earthquake.

2. Then I went by his side and he took me by his hand and lifted me up on his wings and showed me all those things. I beheld the waters suspended on high in 'Araboth Raqia by (force of) the name Yah 'Ehye 'Asher 'Ehye (Jah, I am that I am), and their fruits going down

from heaven and watering the face of the world, as it is written (Ps. civ. 13): 'He watereth the mountains from his chambers; the earth is satisfied with the fruit of thy work.'

3. And I saw fire and snow and hailstone that were mingled together within each other and yet were undamaged, by (force of) the name 'Esh 'Okela (consuming fire), as it is written (Deut. iv. 24): 'For the Lord, thy God, is a consuming fire.'

4. And I saw lightnings that were lightening out of mountains of snow and yet were not damaged (quenched), by (force of) the name Yah Sur 'Olamim (Jah, the everlasting rock), as it is written (Is. xxvi. 4): 'For in Jah, YHWH, the everlasting rock.'

5. And I saw thunders and voices that were roaring in the midst of fiery flames and were not damaged (silenced), by (force of) the name 'El-Shaddai Rabba (the Great God Almighty) as it is written (Gen. xvii. 1): 'I am God Almighty.'

6. And I beheld a flame (and) a glow (glowing flames) that were flaming and glowing in the midst of burning fire, and yet were not damaged (devoured), by (force of) the name Yad 'Al Kes Yah (the hand upon the Throne of the Lord) as it is written (Ex. xvii. 16): 'And he said, for the hand is upon the Throne of the Lord.'

7. And I beheld rivers of fire in the midst of rivers of water and they were not damaged (quenched) by (force of) the name 'Ose Shalom (Maker of Peace) as it is written (Job xxv. 2): 'He maketh peace in his high places.' For He makes peace between the fire and the water, between the hail and the fire, between the wind and the cloud, between the earthquake and the sparks."

## Chapter 43.

R. Ishmael said: Metatron said to me:

1. "Come and I will show thee where are the spirits of the righteous that have been created and have returned, and the spirits of the righteous that have not yet been created. 2. And he lifted me up to his side, took me by his hand and lifted me up near the Throne of Glory by

the place of the Shekina; and he revealed the Throne of Glory to me, and he showed me the spirits that have been created and had returned: and they were flying above the Throne of Glory before the Holy One, blessed be He.

3. After that I went to interpret the following verse of Scripture and I found in what is written (Isa. ivii. 16): 'for the spirit clothed itself before me, and the souls I have made.' That ('for the spirit was clothed before me') means the spirits that have been created in the chamber of creation of the righteous and that have returned before the Holy One, blessed be He; (and the words,) 'and the souls I have made' refer to the spirits of the righteous that have not yet been created in the chamber (GUPH)."

## Chapter 44.

R. Ishmael said: Metatron, the Angel, the Prince of the Presence, said to me:

1. "Come and I will show thee the spirits of the wicked and the spirits of the intermediate where they are standing, and the spirits of the intermediate, whither they go down, and the spirits of the wicked, where they go down."

2. And he said to me, "The spirits of the wicked go down to She'ol by the hands of two angels of destruction; Za'phiel and Simkiel are their names.

3. Simkiel is appointed over the intermediate to support them and purify them because of the great mercy of the Prince of the Place (Maqom). Za'phiel is appointed over the spirits of the wicked in order to cast them down from the presence of the Holy One, blessed be He, and from the splendor of the Shekina to She'ol, to be punished in the fire of Gehenna with staves of burning coal."

4. And I went by his side, and he took me by his hand and showed me all of them with his fingers. 5. And I beheld the appearance of their faces (and, lo, it was) as the appearance of children of men, and their bodies like eagles. And not only that but (furthermore)

the color of the countenance of the intermediate was like pale grey on account of their deeds, for there are stains upon them until they have become cleaned from their iniquity in the fire. 6. And the color of the wicked was like the bottom of a pot on account of the wickedness of their doings.

7. And I saw the spirits of the Patriarchs Abraham Isaac and Jacob and the rest of the righteous whom they have brought up out of their graves and who have ascended to the Heaven (Raqia). And they were praying before the Holy One, blessed be He, saying in their prayer: "Lord of the Universe! How long wilt thou sit upon (thy) Throne like a mourner in the days of his mourning with thy right hand behind thee and not deliver thy children and reveal thy Kingdom in the world? And for how long wilt thou have no pity upon thy children who are made slaves among the nations of the world? Nor upon thy right hand that is behind thee wherewith, thou didst stretch out the heavens and the earth and the heavens of heavens? When wilt thou have compassion?"

8. Then the Holy One, blessed be He, answered every one of them, saying: "Since these wicked do sin so and so, and transgress with such and such transgressions against Me, how could I deliver My great Right Hand in the downfall by their hands (caused by them)?"

9. In that moment Metatron called me and spoke to me: "My servant! Take the books and read their evil doings!" Forthwith I took the books and read their doings and there were to be found 36 transgressions (written down) with regard to each wicked one and besides, that they have transgressed all the letters in the Torah, as it is written (Dan. ix. 11): 'Yea, all Israel have transgressed thy Law.' It is not written 'al torateka but 'et (JIN) torateka, for they have transgressed from 'Aleph to Taw, 40 statutes have they transgressed for each letter.

10. Forthwith Abraham, Isaac, and Jacob wept. Then said to them the Holy One, blessed be He, "Abraham, My beloved, Isaac, My Elect one, Jacob, My firstborn! How can I now deliver them from among the nations of the world?" And forthwith Mikael, the Prince of Israel,

cried and wept with a loud voice and said (Ps. x. 1), "Why standest thou afar off, O Lord?"

## Chapter 45.

R. Ishmael said: Metatron said to me:

1. "Come, and I will show thee the Curtain of Maqom (the Divine Majesty) which is spread before the Holy One, blessed be He, (and) whereon are graven all the generations of the world and all their doings, both what they have done and what they will do until the end of all generations."

2. And I went, and he showed it to me pointing it out with his fingers like a father who teaches his children the letters of Torah. And I saw each generation, the rulers of each generation, and the heads of each generation, the shepherds of each generation, the oppressors (drivers) of each generation, the keepers of each generation, the scourgers of each generation, the overseers of each generation, the judges of each generation, the court officers of each generation, the teachers of each generation, the supporters of each generation, the chiefs of each generation, the presidents of academies of each generation, the magistrates of each generation, the princes of each generation, the counselors of each generation, the nobles of each generation, and the men of might of each generation, the elders of each generation, and the guides of each generation.

3. And I saw Adam, his generation, their doings and their thoughts; Noah and his generation, their doings and their thoughts; and the generation of the flood, their doings and their thoughts; Shem and his generation, their doings and their thoughts; Nimrod and the generation of the confusion of tongues, and his generation, their doings and their thoughts; Abraham and his generation, their doings and their thoughts; Isaac and his generation, their doings and their thoughts; Ishmael and his generation, their doings and their thoughts; Jacob and his generation, their doings and their thoughts; Joseph and his generation, their doings and their thoughts; the tribes and their generation, their doings and their thoughts; Amram and

his generation, their doings and their thoughts; Moses and his generation, their doings and their thoughts. 4. Aaron and Mirjam their works and their doings; the princes and the elders, their works and doings; Joshua and his generation, their works and doings; the judges and their generation, their works and doings; Eli and his generation, their works and doings; Phinehas and his generation, their works and doings; Elkanah and his generation, their works and their doings; Samuel and his generation, their works and doings; the kings of Judah with their generations, their works and their doings; the kings of Israel and their generations, their works and their doings; the princes of Israel, their works and their doings; the princes of the nations of the world, their works and their doings; the heads of the councils of Israel, their works and their doings; the heads of (the councils in) the nations of the world, their generations, their works and their doings; the rulers of Israel and their generation, their works and their doings; the nobles of Israel and their generation, their works and their doings; the nobles of the nations of the world and their generation(s), their works and their doings; the men of reputation in Israel, their generation, their works and their doings; the judges of Israel, their generation, their works and their doings; the judges of the nations of the world and their generation, their works and their doings; the teachers of children in Israel, their generations, their works and their doings; the teachers of children in the nations of the world, their generations, their works and their doings; the counsellors (interpreters) of Israel, their generation, their works and their doings; the counsellors (interpreters) of the nations of the world, their generation, their works and their doings; all the prophets of Israel, their generation, their works and their doings; all the prophets of the nations of the world, their generation, their works and their doings. 5. And all the fights and wars that the nations of the world wrought against the people of Israel in the time of their kingdom. And I saw Messiah, son of Joseph, and his generation and their works and their doings that they will do against the nations of the world. And I saw Messiah, son of David, and his generation, and all the fights and wars, and their works and their doings that they will do with Israel both for good and evil. And I saw all the fights and wars that Gog and Magog will fight in the days of Messiah, and all that the Holy One, blessed be He, will do with them in the time to come.

6. And all the rest of all the leaders of the generations and all the works of the generations both in Israel and in the nations of the world, both what is done and what will be done hereafter to all generations until the end of time, (all) were graven on the Curtain of Maqom. And I saw all these things with my eyes; and after I had seen it, I opened my mouth in praise of Maqom (the Divine Majesty) saying thus (Eccl. viii. 4, 5), "For the King's word hath power and who may say unto Him, 'What doest thou?' Whoso keepeth the commandments shall know no evil thing." And I said (Ps. civ. 24), "O Lord, how manifold are thy works!"

## Chapter 46.

R. Ishmael said: Metatron said to me:

1. "Come and I will show thee the space of the stars that are standing in Raqia night by night in fear of the Almighty (Maqom) and (I will show thee) where they go and where they stand."

2. I walked by his side, and he took me by his hand and pointed out all to me with his fingers. And they were standing on sparks of flames round the Merkaba of the Almighty (Maqom). What did Metatron do? At that moment he clapped his hands and chased them off from their place. Forthwith they flew off on flaming wings, rose and fled from the four sides of the Throne of the Merkaba, and (as they flew) he told me the names of every single one. As it is written (Ps. cxlvii. 4): "He telleth the number of the stars; he giveth them all their names," teaching, that the Holy One, blessed be He, has given a name to each one of them. 3. And they all enter in counted order under the guidance of (lit. through, by the hands of) Rahatiel to Raqia ha-shamayim to serve the world. And they go out in counted order to praise the Holy One, blessed be He, with songs and hymns, according as it is written (Ps. xix. 1): "The heavens declare the glory of God."

4. But in the time to come the Holy One, blessed be He, will create them anew, as it is written (Lam. iii. 23): "They are new every morning." And they open their mouth and utter a song. Which is the song that they utter? (Ps. viii. 3): "When I consider thy heavens."

## Chapter 47.

R. Ishmael said: Metatron said to me:

1. "Come and I will show thee the souls of the angels and the spirits of the ministering servants whose bodies have been burnt in the fire of Maqom (the Almighty) that goes forth from his little finger. And they have been made into fiery coals in the midst of the fiery river (Nehar di-Nur). But their spirits and their souls are standing behind the Shekina. 2. Whenever the ministering angels utter a song at a wrong time or as not appointed to be sung they are burnt and consumed by the fire of their Creator and by a flame from their Maker, in the places (chambers) of the whirlwind, for it blows upon them and drives them into the Nehar di-Nur; and there they are made into numerous mountains of burning coal. But their spirit and their soul return to their Creator, and all are standing behind their Master."

3. And I went by his side, and he took me by his hand, and he showed me all the souls of the angels and the spirits of the ministering servants who were standing behind the Shekina upon wings of the whirlwind and walls of fire surrounding them.

4. At that moment Metatron opened to me the gates of the walls within which they were standing behind the Shekina, And I lifted up my eyes and saw them, and behold, the likeness of everyone was as (that of) angels and their wings like birds' (wings), made out of flames, the work of burning fire. In that moment I opened my mouth in praise of Maqom and said (Ps. xcii. 5): "How great are thy works, O Lord."

## Chapter 48.

R. Ishmael said: Metatron said to me:

1. "Come, and I will show thee the Right Hand of Maqom, laid behind (Him) because of the destruction of the Holy Temple; from which all kinds of splendor and light shine forth and by which the 955 heavens were created; and whom not even the Seraphim and the 'Ophannim are permitted (to behold) until the day of salvation shall arrive."

2. And I went by his side, and he took me by his hand and showed me (the Right Hand of Maqom), with all manner of praise, rejoicing and song; and no mouth can tell its praise, and no eye can behold it, because of its greatness, dignity, majesty, glory, and beauty. 3. And not only that, but all the souls of the righteous who are counted worthy to behold the joy of Jerusalem, they are standing by it, praising, and praying before it three times every day, saying (Is. li. 9), "Awake, awake, put on strength, O arm of the Lord," according as it is written (Is. ixiii. 12): "He caused his glorious arm to go at the right hand of Moses."

4. In that moment the Right Hand of Maqom was weeping. And there went forth from its five fingers five rivers of tears and fell down into the great sea and shook the whole world, according as it is written (Is. xxiv. 19, 20): "The earth is utterly broken (1), the earth is clean dissolved (2), the earth is moved exceedingly (3), the earth shall stagger like a drunken man (4) and shall be moved to and fro like a hut (5)," five times corresponding to the fingers of his Great Right Hand.

5. But when the Holy One, blessed be He, sees, that there is no righteous man in the generation, and no pious man (Chasid) on earth, and no justice in the hands of men; and (that there is) no man like unto Moses, and no intercessor as Samuel who could pray before Maqom for the salvation and for the deliverance, and for His Kingdom, that it be revealed in the whole world; and for His great Right Hand that He put it before Himself again to work great salvation by it for Israel, 6. then forthwith will the Holy One, blessed be He, remember His

own justice, favor, mercy, and grace; and He will deliver His great Arm by himself, and His righteousness will support Him. According as it is written (Is. lix. 16): "And he saw, that there was no man," (that is) like unto Moses who prayed countless times for Israel in the desert and averted the (Divine) decrees from them; and He wondered, that there was no intercessor like unto Samuel who intreated the Holy One, blessed be He, and called unto Him and He answered him and fulfilled his desire, even if it was not fit (in accordance with the Divine plan), according as it is written (1 Sam. xii. 17): "Is it not wheat harvest today? I will call unto the Lord." 7. And not only that, but He joined fellowship with Moses in every place, as it is written (Ps. xcix. 6): "Moses and Aaron among His priests." And again, it is written (Jer. xv. 1): "Though Moses and Samuel stood before Me," (Is. ixiii. 5): "Mine own arm brought salvation unto Me."

8. Said the Holy One, blessed be He in that hour, "How long shall I wait for the children of men to work salvation according to their righteousness for My arm? For My own sake and for the sake of My merit and righteousness will I deliver My arm and by it redeem my children from among the nations of the world." As it is written (Is. xlviii. 11): "For my own sake will I do it. For how should my name be profaned."

9. In that moment will the Holy One, blessed be He, reveal His Great Arm and show it to the nations of the world, for its length is as the length of the world and its breadth is as the width of the world. And the appearance of its splendor is like unto the splendor of the sunshine in its might, in the summer solstice. 10. Forthwith Israel will be saved from among the nations of the world. And Messiah will appear unto them, and he will bring them up to Jerusalem with great joy. And not only that but Israel will come from the four quarters of the world and eat with Messiah. But the nations of the world shall not eat with them, as it is written (Is. lii. 10): "The Lord hath made bare his holy arm in the eyes of all the nations, and all the ends of the earth shall see the salvation of our God." And again (Deut. xxxii.

12): "The Lord alone did lead him, and there was no strange god with him." (Zech. xiv. 9): "And the Lord shall be king over all the earth."

VOLUME 1
IN THE NEPHILIM SERIES

The Nephilim Series by Relic Press is devoted to the reproduction of critical ancient texts pertaining to the biblical narrative, especially as they relate to the subject of Nephilim.

To purchase the other volumes in the series, or for more information, visit **NephilimSeries.com**

Made in United States
Orlando, FL
14 December 2024

55653580R00143